'This book is the perfect starting point to understand how language professions are changing and what the implications of these changes are.'

Claudio Fantinuoli, *University of Mainz, Germany*

'This is a useful resource for trainers of subtitlers and interpreters. Using data gathered via methods such as situated learning, action-research, self-reported evidence or quantitative surveys, it offers results from interpreting and respeaking training scenarios, particularly in the context of the COVID-19 pandemic and the continuous technologisation of the profession and its related practices.'

Alina Secară, *University of Vienna, Austria*

'As the unique skills of simultaneous interpreters are increasingly recognised as key components of human speech-to-text services, this timely volume represents a significant step towards an integrated approach to interpreter education.'

Franz Pöchhacker, *University of Vienna, Austria*

'This volume sets out to explore how technological advancements and the COVID-19 pandemic have reshaped interpreting and live subtitling, highlighting their converging skill sets and shared challenges in the era of generative AI. The chapters offer a comprehensive roadmap for trainers, practitioners and researchers, reflecting on the future of training in these dynamic fields. A valuable contribution for anyone committed to advancing the pedagogy of these disciplines in our rapidly evolving world.'

Elena Davitti, *University of Surrey, UK*

'Despite the overlaps between interpreting and live subtitling, academia has been somewhat slow at bringing these two areas together. This volume makes a valuable contribution to fill this gap in a way that should be relevant to researchers, trainers and professionals, while also providing the much-needed empirical data and posing key questions about the role of cutting-edge technology in interpreting and live subtitling.'

Pablo Romero Fresco, *University of Vigo, Spain*

TEACHING INTERPRETING AND LIVE SUBTITLING

Teaching Interpreting and Live Subtitling: Contexts, Modes and Technologies provides a cross section of multinational perspectives on teaching various dimensions of interpreting and live subtitling, both within dedicated programmes and as part of individual modules on interpreting and/or live subtitling-adjacent programmes.

Interpreting training and live subtitling training have been undergoing rapid and far-reaching transformations in recent years because of technological advances and the sweeping shifts in the contexts within which they seek to mediate, ultimately bringing about new modes. This volume covers the broad spectrum of interpreting and live subtitling trainings and discusses the possibility of how a more unified approach to training for live subtitlers and interpreters could lead to a future where the topics merge to become a single, complementary specialised stream of training that brings live subtitling equally into the forefront of the translation teaching field.

This book provides an overview of the role played by technology in interpreting in general and uses up-to-date perspectives and research to ensure that interpreting and live subtitling training remains robust and resilient far into the 21st century. It will be of particular interest to professionals, scholars and teachers of translation studies and interpreting studies.

Carlo Eugeni is an Associate Professor of Audiovisual Translation at the University of Leeds, where he teaches subtitling for the deaf and the hard-of-hearing, audio description, voice-over and dubbing, live subtitling and reporting through respeaking, and simultaneous and consecutive interpreting. He is editor of Tiro, CoMe and SPECIALinguaggi.

Martin Ward is an Associate Professor of Chinese and Japanese Translation at the University of Leeds and is the founder of the East Asian Translation Pedagogy Advance (EATPA) network. He chaired the organising committee of the APTIS 2022 conference, and his research has been published in *The Translator*.

Callum Walker is an Associate Professor of Translation Technology and Director of the Centre for Translation Studies at the University of Leeds, where he teaches computer-assisted translation technology, project management, translation theory and specialised translation. He is the author of *Translation Project Management*.

TEACHING INTERPRETING AND LIVE SUBTITLING

Contexts, Modes and Technologies

Edited by Carlo Eugeni, Martin Ward and Callum Walker

LONDON AND NEW YORK

Designed cover image: Getty Images | Dedraw Studio

First published 2025
by Routledge
4 Park Square, Milton Park, Abingdon, Oxon, OX14 4RN

and by Routledge
605 Third Avenue, New York, NY 10158

Routledge is an imprint of the Taylor & Francis Group, an informa business

© 2025 selection and editorial matter, Carlo Eugeni, Martin Ward and Callum Walker; individual chapters, the contributors

The right of Carlo Eugeni, Martin Ward and Callum Walker to be identified as the authors of the editorial material, and of the authors for their individual chapters, has been asserted in accordance with sections 77 and 78 of the Copyright, Designs and Patents Act 1988.

All rights reserved. No part of this book may be reprinted or reproduced or utilised in any form or by any electronic, mechanical, or other means, now known or hereafter invented, including photocopying and recording, or in any information storage or retrieval system, without permission in writing from the publishers.

Trademark notice: Product or corporate names may be trademarks or registered trademarks, and are used only for identification and explanation without intent to infringe.

British Library Cataloguing-in-Publication Data
A catalogue record for this book is available from the British Library

Library of Congress Cataloging-in-Publication Data
Names: Eugeni, Carlo, editor. | Ward, Martin (Translator), editor. | Walker, Callum, editor.
Title: Teaching interpreting and live subtitling: contexts, modes and technologies / edited by Carlo Eugeni, Martin Ward, and Callum Walker.
Description: Abingdon, Oxon; New York, NY: Routledge, 2025. | Includes bibliographical references and index.
Identifiers: LCCN 2024029483 (print) | LCCN 2024029484 (ebook) | ISBN 9781032577883 (hardback) | ISBN 9781032571867 (paperback) | ISBN 9781003440994 (ebook)
Subjects: LCSH: Simultaneous interpreting—Study and teaching. | Real-time closed captioning—Study and teaching. | Translating and interpreting—Study and teaching. | Translators—Training of. | LCGFT: Essays.
Classification: LCC P306.95 .T43 2025 (print) | LCC P306.95 (ebook) | DDC 418/.02071—dc23/eng/20240925
LC record available at https://lccn.loc.gov/2024029483
LC ebook record available at https://lccn.loc.gov/2024029484

ISBN: 978-1-032-57788-3 (hbk)
ISBN: 978-1-032-57186-7 (pbk)
ISBN: 978-1-003-44099-4 (ebk)

DOI: 10.4324/9781003440994

Typeset in Sabon
by codeMantra

CONTENTS

List of Contributors — ix

1 Introduction — 1
  Carlo Eugeni

PART I
Interpreting Training and the Classroom — 7

2 Challenges in Conference Interpreting Training: How to Bridge the Gap Between Academia and Professional Practice? — 9
  Fanny Chouc

3 The Importance of Vision in Interpreter Training — 26
  Jenny Wong

4 Towards Effective Interpreter Training: The Impact of Learning Environment Types and Students' Procedural Learning Abilities — 38
  Yinghua Wang

PART II
Interpreting Training and the Profession   53

5 An Experimental Study on Interpreters' Experience of RSI: Implications for Post-Pandemic Research and Practice   55
Clarissa Guarini

6 Interpreting for Minors in Legal Encounters in Ireland during the COVID-19 Pandemic: A Case Study of Patterns of Practice and Implications   69
Eddie López-Pelén

7 Implementing Higher Education Training for Intercultural Mediators in Schools   86
Letizia Leonardi

PART III
Live Subtitling Training, the Classroom and the Profession   101

8 Redefining Respeakers' Training: A Practical Approach to Diamesic Translation Tactics and Respeaking Skills   103
Martina A. Bruno

9 Reaching MARS: How to Increase Speed and Accuracy in Formal and Informal Training in Live Subtitling   121
Carlo Eugeni and Alessio Popoli

10 Intralingual and Interlingual Respeaking Didactics: Redefining Human-Machine Interaction Challenges into Opportunities   137
Alice Pagano

11 Teaching Live Subtitling Through Mock Conferences   152
Faruk Mardan

12 Professional Training in Valencian Live Subtitling: Navigating Diglossia and Language Variation   169
Luz Belenguer Cortés

Index   *182*

CONTRIBUTORS

Luz Belenguer Cortés holds a degree in Translation and Interpreting and a Master's in Translation and Interpreting Research from Universitat Jaume I (UJI). She also has a Master's in Conference Interpreting (UEV). She is a PhD candidate in the Translation Doctoral Programme (UJI), in which her thesis won the 2nd UJI Social Commitment Research Projects Banco Santander 2022 award. She is a member of the TRAMA research group. Since 2018, she has worked as a linguist, live and SDH subtitler and audio descriptor, which she has combined with that of associate lecturer at Universitat Jaume I since 2020.

Martina A. Bruno is a PhD candidate at the University of Bologna with a research proposal on museum accessibility through Easy-to-Read Language and Machine Translation. She is also part of the third cohort of the Una Europa Doctoral programme on Cultural Heritage jointly with University Paris 1 Panthéon-Sorbonne. She collaborated with FIADDA ROMA APS, the Italian association of deaf people and their families, on the Erasmus+ project "Capito! Compris! Understood! Verstanden!" in 2023 and 2024. She is a professional respeaker and trained conference interpreter. She graduated from the University of Bologna with a thesis on the quality assessment of live subtitles produced through respeaking for French deaf and hard-of-hearing audiences. Her research interests cover cultural heritage, comparative linguistics, diamesic translation, accessibility studies and live subtitling.

Fanny Chouc is an Assistant Professor in the Languages and Intercultural Studies Department, Heriot-Watt University. She teaches at UG and PG levels and coordinates the Undergraduate Conference Interpreting programme and the annual Multilingual Debate. She is also a Career Liaison Advisor for the department. Her research interests lie in pedagogical strategies, employability, ICT tools and interpreting training. Recent publications include "Enhancing the learning experience of interpreting students outside the classroom. A study of the benefits of situated learning at the Scottish Parliament" (*The Interpreter and Translator Trainer Journal*, 2016), and "Relay Interpreting as a tool for Conference Interpreting training" (*International Journal of Interpreter Education*, 2018), both co-written with José María Conde (Heriot-Watt University).

Clarissa Guarini is a PhD student at the University of Leeds and her thesis focuses on the strategies professional interpreters use when working simultaneously from German to English. Following an MA in Conference Interpreting, Clarissa worked as an interpreter and gathered some experience in different sectors (such as diplomacy and economy). Working as an interpreter allowed her to have a practical approach to the profession, which served as the basis for developing her research interests in interpreting. Due to the Covid-19 pandemic, Clarissa was able to experience Remote Simultaneous Interpreting (RSI) both as a practitioner and as a researcher, which contributed to her interest in analysing RSI under different aspects and to adapt it to the interpreters' needs and exploit its full potential.

Letizia Leonardi has been recently awarded her PhD in Translation Studies from the University of Aberdeen. Currently, she is Teaching Assistant in French and Honorary Research Assistant at the University of Aberdeen. Her PhD research project focused on the translation of poetry and investigated how translation shapes the reception of poetic texts by using the English-language renderings of the poems by the 19th-century Italian poet G. Leopardi as a case study. She received a Master's degree in Translation Studies from the University of Aberdeen and a bachelor's degree in Linguistic and Intercultural Mediation from the University of Catania (Italy). She speaks English, Italian, French and Spanish proficiently.

Eddie López-Pelén is a senior lecturer in Translation and Interpreting at Universidad Nacional Autónoma de Honduras (UNAH). He holds a Master's degree in Translation and Interpreting Studies from the University of Manchester (UK), funded by UNAH. Additionally, Dr. López-Pelén holds a Master's degree in the Management and Administration of Educational Centres from Universidad de Barcelona (Spain) and a Master's degree in Online Learning from Universidad de Sevilla (Spain). He also earned a PhD in Interpreting Studies from Dublin City University (DCU) (Ireland) funded by the School of Applied Language and Intercultural Studies (SALIS) at the same university. Dr. López-Pelén's research interests focus on legal translation and interpreting for minors in legal settings.

Faruk Mardan is a lecturer in Translation and Technologies and a PhD student in machine translation at the University of Leeds. In his teaching capacities, his areas of expertise include Computer-Assisted Translation, localisation, specialised English-Chinese translation and Machine Translation. His PhD research explores ways in which a lack of language and translation data can be compensated to build machine translation models for Uyghur. Faruk is also a professional translator and interpreter working with English, Chinese and Uyghur, specialising in diplomatic and medical interpreting, and medical, legal, sports and marketing translation.

Alice Pagano is adjunct lecturer in Spanish Language and Translation at the Department of Modern Languages and Cultures and the Department of Education of the University of Genoa (Italy). She also taught Language and Culture of Spanish Speaking Countries and Intercultural Communication and Spanish Language Variation at the Department of Linguistic and Cultural Studies of the University of Modena and Reggio Emilia (Italy). She holds a PhD in Digital Languages, Cultures and Technologies, and a Master's degree in Conference Interpreting from the University of Strasbourg (France). She recently won a post-doctoral research contract at the University of Trieste (Italy). She has worked as an interpreter, translator and post-editor. Her research areas include interpreting studies, audiovisual translation, media accessibility and machine translation.

Alessio Popoli holds a BA in Computer Science from the University of Modena and Reggio Emilia (Italy). He is a senior software engineer at the Italian branch of the French software house Doctolib, specialising in healthcare, and a member of the International Association of Respeaking on AIR. Among other software programmes, Alessio has developed Emendo for Intersteno, used to mark their world speech-to-text championships, and MARS, one of the outcomes of the Erasmus+ LTA project, used for the ECQA certification of live subtitlers, and as an open access tool by an increasing number of practitioners and trainers. Alessio won the bronze medal at the Intersteno World Contest of Audio Transcription in 2015, and the silver medal at the Intersteno World Contests of Speech Capturing in 2015 and 2022.

Yinghua Wang is a PhD candidate at Swansea University (UK), specialising in interpreter training. She has been an accredited English-Mandarin interpreter since 2015, providing language services to international organisations and institutions. She holds a Master's degree in Interpreting from Wuhan

University of Technology in China and a Master's degree in translation and interpreting studies from the University of Manchester (UK). During her PhD studies at Swansea University, Yinghua has also participated in delivering lectures on interpreting modules, such as conference interpreting and dialogue interpreting. This unique experience of engaging with various interpreting classrooms in both China and the UK provides Yinghua with valuable insights into interpreter training.

Jenny Wong is an Assistant Professor in Modern Languages (Chinese Interpreting) and programme leader of the MA in Interpreting with Translation programme in the Department of Modern Languages, University of Birmingham (UK). Prior to joining the University of Birmingham, she taught translation at Hang Seng University of Hong Kong, Beijing Normal University, Hong Kong Baptist University, United International College and the Chinese University of Hong Kong, amongst others. A published translator, she has translated over ten books on religion, health and finance. Her current research focuses on the translatability of religious dimensions in English literature, including Shakespeare.

1
INTRODUCTION

Carlo Eugeni

In the last three centuries, the world has undergone significant technical, scientific, and technological revolutions. And during each of these, humans have traditionally adopted two different and conflicting stands towards technology and its role in the labour market: a pessimistic one and an optimistic one. The former would stress the inevitable economic and human disruption such changes entail for global industry, the sector concerned, the people involved, and the quality their expertise could guarantee; the latter would concentrate on exactly the same aspects from an opposite perspective, that is, one of opportunity, not disruption. For instance, the Luddites who protested against the introduction of spinning frames and power looms in the nascent Industrial Revolution that threatened to leave them without jobs. Similarly, in 1986, the winner of the Nobel Prize for Economics Wassily Leontief and Computer Scientist Faye Duchin compared the future of humans in the labour market to that of horses to predict their end (see Leontief & Duchin 1986). In contrast, in 1930, John Maynard Keynes predicted that mankind was already solving its economic problems caused by widespread technological unemployment, or "the unemployment due to our discovery of means of economising the use of labour outrunning the pace at which we can find new uses for labour" (Keynes 1932). Similarly, the US National Academy of Sciences claimed, in 1987, that "technological change frequently leads to increases in output demand" (Cyert & Mowery 1987), meaning more job opportunities.

When it comes to what Professor Klaus Schwab – founder and executive chairman of the World Economic Forum – defined as the "fourth industrial

DOI: 10.4324/9781003440994-1

revolution" in his famous contribution to the 12 December 2015 issue of Foreign Affairs, he claimed that:

> we stand on the brink of a technological revolution that will fundamentally alter the way we live, work, and relate to one another. In its scale, scope, and complexity, the transformation will be unlike anything humankind has experienced before. We do not yet know just how it will unfold, but one thing is clear: the response to it must be integrated and comprehensive, involving all stakeholders of the global polity, from the public and private sectors to academia and civil society.
>
> *(Schwab 2015)*

Economist Daniel Susskind seems to adopt a more sophisticated approach in his 2020 *A World Without Work* (2020). Susskind sees technological unemployment as a symptom of success, capable of solving current problems. Machines can easily beat humans in many tasks – for instance, the IBM system Deep Blue defeated world chess champion Kasparov in 1997 – but this is arguably not true for creativity.

When it comes to professions, Susskind shows how only 5% of jobs can be fully automated because machines can only replace routine tasks. In his keynote speech given at the GALA conference in Valencia on 22 April 2024, interpreting scholar Claudio Fantinuoli asked Susskind a question related to training in the era of generative Artificial Intelligence (AI). Susskind's answer clearly articulated the future of training as based on what, in his view, machines still cannot do: develop skills. In particular, teaching students how to develop skills would depend, in Susskind's view, on the answers provided to three main aspects: which skills to train, how to train them, and when to train them. As a consequence, successful training would entail, he said, trainees learning how to deal with what the machine can do better than them and to make the most out of that; in a context where they receive as personalised a training as possible; and at any time of their life when those skills are needed, regardless of their profession and achievements.

In Translation and Interpreting Studies, this introduction of technology and its massive use in the profession have generated friends and foes of AI. To begin with, we cannot ignore that, in this fourth industrial revolution, translation disciplines have all been potentially fusing across the related professional fields, meaning that traditional notions of translation research and teaching have been increasingly challenged, with notions like Computer-Aided Interpreting and Post-Editing Machine Translation being taken for granted by all stakeholders. And if we take the interpreting and live subtitling contexts, a serious reflection on the future of training must start from the COVID-19 pandemic, which has significantly impacted the profession. Indeed, both interpreters and live subtitlers had to accept working from home as the new normal. This did not happen without problems. Notorious challenges this entailed for both live subtitlers and interpreters include, among others, connection issues, poor audio input, and lack of more physical interaction with colleagues, speakers, and audience. Coupled with the groundbreaking advent of generative AI, this has increased and diversified the amount of Human-Computer Interaction in interpreting and live subtitling to a point that today we can recognise the existence of four main categories of practices: human only, where the input of technologies is limited to a minimum; computer-aided, where machines help humans produce a more rapid and accurate output; human-aided, where humans help machines produce a more accurate output, though not more rapid; and computer-only, where the human input can be easily skipped. This changing scenario has important implications for training in both disciplines.

The reader of this volume may wonder why the editors decided to bring together two apparently different professions, interpreting and live subtitling, into one volume. This is based on a strong conviction stemming from the experience of numerous practitioners, trainers, and researchers. If in 2008 the two professions were associated from a sociolinguistic point of view based on speculation (see Eugeni 2008), professional evidence, and research (see Eugeni & Bernabé 2021)[1] show how two specific and distinctive practices, namely simultaneous interpreting and live interlingual subtitling, require very similar skills and fulfil a very similar function. The only aspects that differ are the nature, function, and target of the output, which are the main reasons why the two professions are still considered to be distinct, requiring two different professional figures, hence two different types of training.

The enduring inspiration of the Association of Programmes in Translation and Interpreting Studies (APTIS) 2022 Conference "Translation and interpreting pedagogy in a post-pandemic world: new opportunities and challenges", held at the University of Leeds (United Kingdom) on 18–19 November 2022 motivated the editors to bring together the present volume and its partner volume *Teaching Translation: Contexts, Modes and Technologies*. Discussions at the conference prompted debate around teaching, technology, and the interaction between conference and community interpreting as well as live subtitling, which eventually resulted in a collection of chapters from speakers and other colleagues. The focus being on how COVID-19 accelerated the development and widespread adoption of more technology in both practice and teaching, the similarities between the two disciplines are more and more evident. The eleven contributions you will find here are offered in a conceptually linear manner: the first three chapters deal with research on interpreting training; the next three deal with research on interpreting practice; the final five deal with research on live-subtitling training and practice.

Part I of this volume is titled *Interpreting Training and the Classroom*. It begins with Chapter 2 "Challenges in conference interpreting training: how to bridge the gap between academia and the professional booth?", by **Fanny Chouc (Heriot-Watt University)**, where the author aims at establishing a broader skills framework for interpreting training. To that effect, Chouc uses a quantitative survey, inviting practising professional interpreters to reflect on their transition to the professional booth and on challenges and new developments they observe in their practice, with a view to identifying elements such as technical skills, ancillary soft skills, or ethical strategies, which could enrich the curriculum. In Chapter 3 "The Importance of Vision in Interpreter Training", **Jenny Wong (University of Birmingham)** focuses on a sample of 10 interpreting students of Chinese origin at a British university and collects self-reported evidence as well as more objective measurements, using various learning style indicators. Wong aims to illuminate the relationship among learner characteristics related to sensory and mental imagery aspects and learning achievement, by investigating how the students with mental imagery and vision of mastering interpreting skills in future states compare with those who do not. In Chapter 4 "Does an Implicit Learning Environment Always Lead to Successful Interpreter Training? Students' Procedural Learning Abilities and Interpreting Skill Types Can Have the Con", **Yinghua Wang (Swansea University)** hypothesises that the implicit learning environment does not effectively facilitate the training of student interpreters to master all interpreting skills. To test this, Wang shows that after a semester of training in consecutive interpreting, an implicit learning environment benefit student interpreters listening comprehension and memory skills, but hinders their expression skills, regardless of their procedural learning ability levels.

Part II is titled *Interpreting Training and the Profession*. It starts with Chapter 5 "An Experimental Study on Interpreters' Experience of RSI: Implications for Post-pandemic Research and Practice", by **Clarissa Guarini (University of Leeds)**, where the author aims to use the experience of remote simultaneous interpreting (RSI) during the COVID-19 worldwide crisis to identify the disadvantages of this type of interpreting and amplify its advantages in the post-pandemic landscape. In particular, Guarini highlights the increasing necessity of including RSI, not just in the profession but also in training programmes and research activities, to let future researchers and practitioners make the most of this new working environment. In Chapter 6 "Interpreting for Minors in Legal Encounters in Ireland during the COVID-19 Pandemic: Patterns of practice and implications", **Eddie López-Pelén (Universidad Nacional Autónoma de Honduras)** reports on the patterns of practice and implications of interpreter-mediated legal encounters with minors during the COVID-19 pandemic. Based on a case study in Ireland, López-Pelén examines the feedback provided by two interpreters and four professionals working remotely with minors in legal encounters and shows how recurrent were the deployment of untrained interpreters, the lack of briefings with interpreters, and issues with rapport-building and non-verbal communication.

In Chapter 7 "The Importance of Implementing Higher Education Training Opportunities for Interpreters in Schools", **Letizia Leonardi (University of Aberdeen)**, seeks to offer a pedagogical model that could be used to implement university courses for intercultural mediators working in UK schools. Leonardi evidences that courses in intercultural mediation could be introduced in UK MA programmes, by adapting existing degree programmes in other countries to the social specificities of the UK, thus contributing to mediators' professional recognition which will have important repercussions on the promotion of migrant inclusion.

Part III is titled *Live Subtitling Training, the Classroom and the Profession*. It starts with Chapter 8 "Redefining Respeakers' Training: A Practical Approach to Diamesic Translation Tactics and Respeaking Skills", by **Martina A. Bruno (University of Bologna)**, where the author seeks to identify the essential skills to teach students in a respeaking course, thus contributing to the advancement of respeaking training and improving the accessibility of live events for a wider audience. Bruno proposes a comprehensive set of production strategies and exit strategies respeakers need in order to navigate the various cognitive, textual, and translating challenges of the intralingual live subtitling task. In Chapter 9 "Reaching MARS: how to increase speed and accuracy in live subtitling formal and informal training", **Carlo Eugeni (University of Leeds)** and **Alessio Popoli (Intersteno)** provide an overview of the skills a respeaker needs to produce live subtitles and introduce the Most Accurate and Rapid Speech-to-text subtitling rate (MARS), an online tool that allows for testing a trainee's capacity to produce accurate subtitles while guaranteeing a given accuracy, whatever the technology used to produce it. Eugeni and Popoli also discuss the importance of teaching MARS for formal and informal live subtitling education. In Chapter 10 "Intralingual and Interlingual Respeaking Didactics: Redefining Human-Machine Interaction Challenges into Opportunities", **Alice Pagano (University of Trieste)** focuses on intralingual and interlingual respeaking didactics, outlining the modules of a respeaking course, adapted over time according to an action-research observation process. In the trade-off between humans and machines, Pagano aims to outline a more comprehensive and personalised course in intralingual and interlingual respeaking and stresses the importance of training interpreting students in Media Accessibility to make the most out of their interpreting skills. In Chapter 11 "Respeaker training through mock conferences", **Faruk Mardan (University of Leeds)** discusses a case study on the training of respeakers through mock conferences. In particular, the chapter explores the effectiveness of training respeakers through situated learning, by drawing on established best practices in interpreter training. By analysing the performance of two respeakers – one producing intralingual subtitles, the other interlingual subtitles – Mardan bridges the gaps for research into training respeakers through mock conferences, and provides an insight into factors that impact a respeaker performance. In the last chapter, Chapter 12, **Luz Belenguer Cortés** (Universitat Jaume I) discusses the challenges, and implications of live subtitling training, faced by live subtitlers at the Valencian TV station À Punt. In particular, the chapter focuses on language variation in the region, where both Spanish and Valencian are spoken, and the effects of code-switching and code-mixing on the live subtitling workflow. Belenguer Cortés also provides insightful suggestions for effective training.

Note

1 See also outputs from the EU-funded ILSA project (http://ka2-ilsa.webs.uvigo.es) and those from the ESRC-funded SMART project (https://smartproject.surrey.ac.uk).

References

Cyert, R. M. and Mowery, D. C. (eds.) (1987) *Technology and Employment: Innovation and Growth in the US Economy*. Washington DC: National Academy Press.

Eugeni, C. (2008) "A Sociolinguistic Approach to Real-Time Subtitling: Respeaking vs. Shadowing and Simultaneous Interpreting". In Kellett Bidoli, C. J. and Ochse, E. (eds.) *English in International Deaf Communication*, Linguistic Insights series, vol. 72, Berne: Peter Lang, pp. 357–382.

Eugeni, C. and Bernabé, R. (2021) "Written Interpretation: When Simultaneous Interpreting Meets Real-Time Subtitling". In Seeber, K. (ed.) *100 Years of Conference Interpreting – A Legacy*, Newcastle upon Tyne: Cambridge Scholars Publishing, pp. 93–109.

Keynes, J. M. ([1930]/1931) "Economic Possibilities for our Grandchildren". In Keynes, J. M. (ed.) *Essays in Persuasion*. London: Macmillan and Co., pp. 358–373.

Leontief, W. and Duchin, F. (1986) *The Future Impact of Automation on Workers*. New York: Oxford University Press.

Schwab, K. (2015) "The Fourth Industrial Revolution – What It Means and How to Respond. In *Foreign Affairs*, 12 December 2015.

Susskind, D. (2020) *A World Without Work*. London: Penguin Books Limited.

PART I
Interpreting Training and the Classroom

2

CHALLENGES IN CONFERENCE INTERPRETING TRAINING

How to Bridge the Gap Between Academia and Professional Practice?

Fanny Chouc

Introduction

Interpreting training has been the object of significant literature over the years (Seleskovitch and Lederer, 1989; Jones, 1998; Gile, 1995, 2005, to name a few), and this field remains very relevant in a constantly changing professional environment, affected by the pandemic and the necessary shift towards online remote interpreting platforms (ORI) outlined by Buján and Collard (2022). New challenges emerge for professionals, for which they are not necessarily prepared (Braun, 2007). However, the introduction of ORI has not been the only phenomenon affecting the industry: globalisation has led to an increased need for multilingual exchanges, not only at an institutional level but also for businesses and civil society organisations. The need for professional linguists has risen significantly, and while international institutions remain a significant employer of translation and interpreting (T&I) professionals, the proportion of freelancers has increased (Olohan, 2007).

As a result, curricula need to be regularly adjusted to remain relevant to trainees, and trainers face this challenge: while interpreting training techniques have been studied at length, leading to solid training principles for the acquisition of techniques needed by practising professionals (Gile, 1995; Pöchhacker, 2001), and while collaboration with institutions (Mouzourakis, 1996; Moser-Mercer, 2003; Seeber et al., 2019) has led to valuable advances in understanding the cognitive processes at play when interpreting and the best ways to prepare conference interpreters to tackle the task they will have to perform, the changes in the profession call for a reflection to develop a broader grasp of what trainees need to be fully prepared to become conference interpreters. Considering the importance of freelance work in the profession, graduates "need to be equipped to approach their careers with an understanding of entrepreneurial and start up skills" (Rodríguez de Céspedes, 2017, p. 118).

To help graduates be better prepared to enter the field of conference interpreting, this study explores the perspective of practitioners on challenges encountered in their professional journey and activity, with a focus on freelancers, who now constitute the majority of professionals in this field. It dwells specifically on the range of skills deemed valuable to become a fully-fledged freelance professional in this industry, aside from the obvious need to master conference interpreting techniques, in a bid to inform curriculum design on possible gaps, and how and within which framework these may be addressed.

Literature Review

"Au début était la pratique" (Gile, 2005, p. 714): praxis was indeed instrumental in the early stages of interpreting training. The profession was born out of an immediate need for greater, cross-language cooperation in specific fields (Caminade, 1995, p. 252) and it was facilitated by technological developments. It was also, very significantly, born out of the needs of international institutions. Therefore, a number of seminal studies in interpreting training were produced by institutional interpreters-turned-trainers (Seleskovitch and Lederer, 1989; Jones, 1998). Further key work in the field was carried out by "practisearchers" who combine their praxis with an academic career (Gile, 1995, 2018; Pöchhacker, 2015 and 1999), and their work has shaped the pedagogical approaches adopted in the classroom, through the definition of learning models and skills-based curricula.

This unusual discipline history has led to a long-standing tension between two approaches in interpreter training: one more focused on ensuring that graduates are "better prepared for the real-world; in other words, (...) job-ready" (Schäffner, 2012, p. 42), and one emanating from the gradual placement of interpreting training under the aegis of university programmes, which meant, de facto, that the latter may resist the implicit vocational nature of T&I training (Kearns, 2012).[1] The advocates of a pedagogy anchored in practice seem to increasingly lead the way, as teaching based on "professional reality" (Bordes, 2014, p. 111) is fast becoming the norm. While analytical and theoretical skills are written into the curricula, a growing number of employers have deplored the "too academic" nature of the training provided (Olohan, 2007, p. 57) and a number of studies have established that T&I graduates tend to feel ill-equipped to set up as freelancers (Schnell and Rodriguez, 2017; Henter, 2016; Álvarez-Álvarez and Arnáiz-Uzquiza, 2017). High education fees in practice in the UK mean that students expect "value for their investment and more professional and career-enhancing activities in their degrees" (Rodríguez de Céspedes, 2017, p. 109).

Consequently, there has been an evolution towards a model in which curricula and teaching are delivered by "teacher-practitioners" (Bordes, 2014, p. 116). It has led to a pedagogy based not only on models designed to address specific cognitive processes and challenges encountered by interpreters but also drawing on the benefits of applied use of situated and experiential learning (Sawyer, 1994; Chouc and Conde, 2016). This evolution led to the design of teaching tasks based on authentic experiences, inspired by academic practitioners' professional experience or brought to the classroom by practitioners as guest contributors. It is a recruitment requirement for universities teaching interpreting in China (Bao, 2015, p. 403). Pedagogical strategies may also include taking the learning out of the classroom, for instance, through guided dummy-booth practice[2] (Chouc and Conde, 2016) or structured forms of shadowing or volunteering.[3] Experiential learning theory further backs the initial approach observed in interpreter training, highlighting the benefits of belonging to a "community of practice" (Lave and Wenger, 1991) for students and graduates.

While "having professional interpreters as trainers is desirable" (Bao, 2015, p. 414), practitioners are not necessarily de-facto good trainers. In other words, praxis may not be enough.

The focus on skills, practice and working environment may not be sufficient to fully equip trainees to become freelance conference interpreters, who make up a significant proportion of the profession based on professional bodies surveys such as the one carried out by the SFT (https://www.sft.fr/sites/default/files/pdf/webinaire-resultats-enquete-interpretes-2023_SFT-AIIC.pdf). The notion of Entrepreneurship Education (EE) has become key in European Education policies, which advocate for a "close cooperation between stakeholders, including them at all educational levels" (European Commission, 2020). A shift has been observed, from the Bologna Process launched in 1998, which treated employability and employment as fairly synonymous, to the Yerevan Communiqué in 2015, which focuses more on graduates' ability to develop new competencies and skills in order to adapt to rapidly evolving labour markets, and this shift underpins the new focus on EE.

Most of the existing literature has primarily focused on translation training and conference interpreting training in relation to institutional practice: the following study considers the matter of interpreting training from the perspective of freelance conference interpreters, who constitute a significant proportion of professionals working in this industry.

Methodology

To define a suitable framework for the study, a focus group of seven interpreters was held online; participants' experience levels ranged from new to the profession to over 25 years of experience. An open discussion was led to identify patterns and challenges to entering the profession, and skills needed for the current market based on newcomers' perspectives and the market knowledge of more experienced contributors. In line with the SFT (SFT, 2023) recent study findings, simultaneous interpreting seemed to be the most commonly used mode for this sample, and the mode that raised more comments in relation to remote work. Following this focus group, data collection was organised around two main aspects: preparedness for the professional world post-training and interpreters' experience. An online questionnaire was created using the survey tool Qualtrics, with a mix of demographic questions, multiple-choice questions, Likert scale questions and open-ended questions.

Demographic questions were used to ascertain whether a sample representative enough of the profession was featured, looking at years of experience and time elapsed since the completion of training.

The survey itself could be completed in about 10 minutes. Multiple-choice questions and Likert scale items were used to capture respondents' views and experiences in a quick and efficient way. Open-ended questions were also included to enable respondents to further elaborate on training needs, work settings, prospective challenges and the means to adequately prepare interpreting trainees for the job market.

The survey was distributed using the alumni mailing list of the author's institution and through the author's academic networks, as well as using the professional media platform, LinkedIn. Specific hashtags (#research, #interpreting, #conferenceinterpreting, #datacollection) were used to draw attention to the study and reach a wider range of professionals. It was also reposted on the social media platforms of the Centre for Translation and Interpreting Studies in Scotland.

The survey was completed by 24 professional interpreters, which constitutes a relatively small sample: an issue not inconsistent with challenges previously encountered by academics conducting research with conference interpreters (Gile, 2005, p. 721).

The sample, nonetheless, remains representative in that it features respondents from a range of age groups, representing different levels of experience and a diverse range of language combinations (see Figure 2.1).

As shown in Figure 2.2, this distribution is fairly consistent with the respondents' number of years of experience.

In terms of the languages used professionally, the sample is also very diverse: many spoken languages are represented (English, French, Spanish, German, Polish), as well as British and International Sign languages, so the study provides a wide range of perspectives.

The training profile of this sample is mixed: the majority have completed their postgraduation in interpreting (54.17%), while almost a third (29.17%) did a master's or undergraduate study in or featuring conference interpreting. A further 8.33% secured training in the profession through an intensive training course provided by a higher education institution. A small

Proportion of respondents

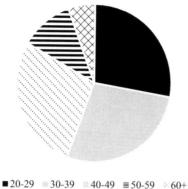

■ 20-29   30-39   40-49   ≡ 50-59   60+

FIGURE 2.1   Proportion of respondents by age groups.

No of years of experience

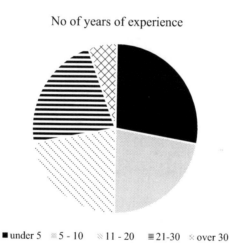

■ under 5   5 - 10   11 - 20   ≡ 21-30   over 30

FIGURE 2.2   Respondents' distribution by number of years' experience.

proportion (8.33%) did not do any specific training in conference interpreting, but fewer training programmes were available to interpreters falling into the longer experience age bracket at the time when they joined the profession.

A clear divide emerged in the number of semesters dedicated to simultaneous interpreting during training: it tended to be either two semesters (44.44%) or four semesters (38.89%). These patterns align with the most common MSc programme patterns in the UK and EU. It is worth noting that some respondents (11.11%) had a total of three semesters of academic training in simultaneous interpreting.

Findings and Analysis

Preparedness for the Professional World after Training

Respondents were asked a series of questions aimed at getting a clearer picture of what had been included in their initial training, what had not been featured and where gaps may have been problematic, to identify possible areas for curricular development.

Theoretical Training in Curricula

While 72.22% of respondents confirmed that their training had featured some interpreting theory, a component that would have been useful in the view of the 27.78% who did not cover the subject, shortcomings seem to remain in the ways interpreting theory is presented: only 20% considered it to have been "very useful", while the majority (60%) deemed the content as only "slightly useful".

It seems that remote interpreting was barely touched upon in these classes: only three out of the 24 respondents indicated that this specific practice had been considered, only "a little" or "not very much", and they are all recently qualified. A significant proportion of respondents trained pre-pandemic, which may account for the limited time dedicated to ORI in their initial training.

Learning One's Craft: Training Resources and Tools of the Trade

Respondents were asked what resources they had access to as part of their training; the question of confidence in usage was added for professional technical equipment such as booths, and online meeting environments like Zoom or ORI Platforms. It is worth remembering that some of the more experienced respondents trained before some of these technologies were in use.

Access to hard copies of training materials was available for 25%, but the proportion increases to 37.5% for access to digital copies.

Only 29.2% mentioned accessing the EU speech repository,[4] a low figure, even though a large part of this repository is publicly available.

On-site recording facilities for training purposes were available to 37.5% of respondents, but only 25% were given access to recording resources or guidance for recording, using devices and/or freeware at home.

While infoports[5] appear to have not been used or made available during training to any of the respondents, the technology was nonetheless mentioned (presumably simply demonstrated or shown) to 20.8% of respondents. The confidence levels for using this type of equipment were low at the end of the training, with 80% of respondents indicating "no confidence at all", and 20% feeling "slightly confident" about using such a device.

As for professional workspaces, specifically booths or sign language (SL) workstations, almost half (45.8%) of respondents used them during their training, and a significant proportion (41.7%) had access to such facilities for practice outside class. It still leaves over half of the respondents with no access to booths or SL workstations as part of their training or for practice. However, confidence levels were relatively high, with 66.7% of respondents feeling either "very confident" or "fully proficient" by the end of their training.

Online meeting platforms such as Zoom and simultaneous interpreting delivery platforms (SIDPs) were featured in the training of very few respondents (only 16.7%), mostly in the "new professionals" group, and confidence levels were low for most participants, with 57.14% of respondents declaring they felt "not confident at all" or just "slightly confident". However, over a quarter of respondents (28.57%) felt "fully proficient" using ORI technologies – a figure that relates to the proportion of recent practitioners in the study. Nevertheless, when it comes to practising on such platforms, none of the respondents were given access to either an online meeting software featuring interpreting or an SIDP outside of classes.

Collegial Training?

When looking at the linguistic organisation of the training provided, experiences are divided: 50% of respondents worked solely with their language combination, while the other 50% were able to work with their language combination and in conjunction with peers working with different language regimes.

The collaborative sessions used to bring together trainees with diverse language profiles took two different shapes: they were either joint sessions designed around one language common to all (an A or B language, depending on the student's language profile) or mock conferences with a range of languages used by speakers. The latter created an experience of relay interpreting for trainees, while the former did not.

Gaps in the Training

Respondents were invited to indicate whether some complementary skills which are part of professional conference interpreting practice, but not the practice of the discipline per se, were missing from the training. Then they rated their level of confidence with the proposed list, drawn from the focus group, to establish whether any gap in training was problematic.

While 21.43% did not cover stress management in training, the majority felt confident (42.86%) or very confident (7.14%) in dealing with interpreting-related stress, nonetheless.

Despite 21.43% not being taught booth or SL etiquette, the majority (50%) still felt confident handling this professional aspect, possibly thanks to practising in booths or with SL partners during their training. The lack of "proper (virtual) booth etiquette" training was deemed problematic, however, 21.43% noted that they had received no training on conference format and etiquette, but again, it did not translate into a complete lack of confidence, as 35.71% declared feeling "confident" and 14.29% "very confident" about handling this aspect.

Handling communication with clients or agencies is more of an issue: for 28.57%, it was not included in training and was a matter of concern. Confidence level was low, with 28.57% reporting "not confident at all" and 14.29% only "a little confident" in dealing with agencies or clients post-training. None of the respondents felt fully confident, in fact. When invited to elaborate on their answers, respondents mentioned entrepreneurship skills (European Commission, 2020) such as, "basic knowledge about building your clientele and your online presence". One person noted that "there was little mention of the market in my training. It was fully missing".

Information on fees and market rates were notably absent from training (42.86% indicated it had not been featured in curricula), with one person noting they "were not informed about the exact rates on the private market" for freelance work during their training, a situation echoed in several other comments. However, trainees seem to have secured the information nonetheless, as the impact on preparedness was not so clear cut: responses were evenly distributed, from "not confident at all" to "confident"; 92.84% did hear about professional bodies/organisations during their training, and subsequently, most respondents seem to have felt well-informed on that point.

Further gaps stand out nonetheless: 58.33% indicated they felt other necessary skills were missing from the curriculum. For instance, one respondent flagged the need for stamina-building, using "real-life speeches", as opposed to "short, structured EU-type speeches"; another mentioned "voice management and endurance", not developed enough because they were "not used to interpret for more than 15–20 min".

Additional Training Post-Academia?

Despite noting that there had been some gaps in their initial training, only 33.33% of respondents sought additional formal training, either directly or within four years of completing their initial course.

Most of the few respondents who sought additional training turned to academia (80%), while the remaining 20% targeted a form of focused training, on specific skills such as technical tools or platforms.

However, 91.67% noted that they needed further skills other than conference interpreting ones, for career purposes. Skills related to the professional development in interpreting were still mentioned, such as "more advanced technique on sim" and "booth and boothmate contact etiquette", along more generic skills like "language learning" and "voice management", or even "coworking", especially for online platforms (a recent development for which respondents may not have had any initial training), professional awareness specific to the industry, such as "rates, local agencies, knowing about what working conditions are considered 'normal' to be able to negotiate when a certain contract falls outside of them" and how to handle "ethical decision-making", generic business skills, which were by far the most frequently mentioned, with respondents talking about "taxes and accounting" (3 comments); "marketing" and "prospection" (4 comments); "administration, bureaucracy, and paperwork" (4 comments); negotiation skills and client relation management (3 comments); professional networking and interpersonal skills; and career management.

Professional Experience

Most Common and Preferred Working Conditions

Working remotely, from one's home, has become more widespread, yet only 18.18% of respondents deem themselves to be "very experienced" for that format, compared to 45.45% when it comes to working from a booth on-site; but if you factor in those who claimed to be "experienced" for ORI (54.55%), this format tops the list. There are however 9.09% of respondents who have never done any remote interpreting from home.

The next two types of work environments for which respondents are most experienced were contexts in which booths are used on-site. The most common format remains the booth-in-the-room (63.63% either "very experienced" or "experienced" for this set-up); however, working from booths at the same location but in another room has also been encountered by almost half of the respondents (45.45% either "very experienced" or "experienced" for that set-up). There was nonetheless a large proportion (27.27%) who never encountered the latter.

One of the newest and least experienced work environments is working from an interpreting hub[6]: 36.36% have never worked from such premises, and only 27.27% claim to be either experienced or very experienced in that set-up.

Respondents were also invited to rank the working environment by order of preference, leading to the following order (1 being the most popular and 5 the least popular):

1 working from a booth in a room
2 working from a booth in another room

3 working from hub
4 working from home

When asked to elaborate, respondents gave a nuanced picture of the situation: working from home is unpopular because of the added technical load and responsibility, and the need for a "separate room as an office", which isn't available to all, as well as due to the more challenging conditions, especially if speakers are also joining the event remotely. Issues related to remote speakers apply when working from home or a hub, so the latter remains less popular for some. One respondent noted that "working from a hub still [felt] alien to [them]". Nevertheless, for some, ORI "also has its perks": they welcomed the fact that it "saves a lot of time" on travel, and that "as long as you trust your equipment and connection, it is a very nice work setting too". But the "human contact aspect" remains important and connected to job satisfaction, as do working conditions.

Challenges Faced by Professionals

In order to encompass not only the transition from academia to the world of work but conference interpreters' career challenges as a whole, respondents were asked to rank and comment on the type of difficulties they encountered since completing their training, by order of importance.

Accessing the market and handling the business side, such as communication with the client, quoting, invoicing dealing with taxes etc. was rated as the number one difficulty encountered by 19.23% of respondents. On accessing the market, they mentioned the importance or issues with lack of connections, stating that "it's not easy to get people to know you", and that location and "serendipity" can play a key role in launching a career, because as a beginner, it can be tricky to know "which agency to trust and sign up with", for instance. Regarding the handling of the business side, such as communication with clients, quoting, etc., respondents noted that the lack of training was problematic. One person stated that "the quoting and negotiating would have been very difficult to handle on the sole basis of [their] training", and several respondents indicated relying on "support from colleagues", "helpful advice from peers and former trainers" or the "help of colleagues and friends" to face these specific challenges. This form of informal community support seems to have efficiently made up for training limitations, as two respondents stated it had altogether been a "relatively straight-forward" process, nonetheless.

Liaising with the client or an agency to secure adequate preparation materials was listed as the second most frequent professional challenge (15.38%): the process is described as a "constant struggle", as "quite often clients are reluctant to provide information". Personal stances on the need to chase agencies vary. One respondent stated: "I find it hard to insist on prep", while another recognised the need to "go round them or keep asking", but considered it was "not challenging in the sense that [they were] fully prepared to keep asking".

The actual conference interpreting and stress management were ranked a joint 3rd with 11.54% of responses for both: references to developing "stamina" and coping with the "speed of speakers and density of speeches" are seen as in "the nature of the profession", that "come with time". Similarly, issues with stress management tend to be associated primarily with early career: one respondent talked of "feelings of inadequacy" and "not knowing how you compare to people actually working in the field" as a challenge, but another put the matter into perspective, stating that "it comes with practice".

Preparing for an event adequately and handling the tech on-site were ranked a joint 4th: only 9.62% considered these to be a major challenge.

Only one other challenge was listed under "other": networking. But only 3.85% of respondents described it as the main challenge encountered.

Today's Training Needs and How to Address Them

The next part of the study explored the most suitable environment in which to acquire these crucial skills, or even whether, with experience, some skills become less essential.

Respondents were given a list of competencies identified by the preliminary focus group, and asked to indicate whether they considered that training on these aspects should be part of academic curricula or best addressed by continuous professional development (CPD) if needed at all.

Findings clearly show that the acquisition of technical knowledge of ORI, business management skills, marketing skills, stress management and awareness of professional organisations should be part of the initial training.

On the other hand, language consolidation and how best to design an adequate working space for ORI are seen as more of a CPD matter.

The acquisition of another language is deemed either not essential by professionals or as a matter of CPD. It is worth remembering that interpreters involved in this study work in the private market rather than in institutions.

To identify complementary, relevant learning experiences, respondents were asked to indicate any additional element that contributed to their transition from graduate to conference interpreter: About 30% mentioned the benefits of mentoring by an experienced colleague, 26.7% referred to volunteer conference interpreting, 20% indicated the relevance of additional, targeted training relating to conference interpreting and 16.7% mentioned non-interpreting specific business skills training. Further academic training and linguistic and/or cultural training were only cited by 3.3% of respondents.

In the interviews, participants reflected on the future of the profession and the most commonly cited aspect to consider was technologies: ORI and AI came up in a number of instances, with the threat these may represent for the profession and its quality standards, in that they are opening the market to untrained practitioners. One respondent also highlighted the risks presented by inadequate trainers, stating that "the fact that current trainers are not in touch with the current professional market will take a toll on students' training regarding remote interpreting".

Discussion

While there is a clear appreciation of the use of interpreting theory as part of an academic course, the way it is taught does not seem to relate sufficiently to authentic situations in which said theory could support professionals. Nor did it seem to feature enough reflection on ORI at the time of data collection.

It also appears that training does not yet systematically fully integrate the range of language combinations of students in the same cohort, thus leading to limited experience of relay and its benefits, not only as an insight into professional practice but also for skills and professional awareness development (Chouc and Conde, 2018).

Furthermore, access to training resources and materials during training seemed limited, with fewer than half the respondents given access to physical or e-copies of materials, the EU speech repository or recording facilities, either on campus or at home. None of the respondents had access to any of the more recent tools, such as interpreting-enabled SIDPs or Zoom, while according to the Nimdzi Interpreting Index, remote interpreting represented 49% of the market in 2023 (https://www.nimdzi.com/interpreting-index-top-interpreting-companies/#state-of-the-interpreting-market). A number of respondents trained at a time when ORI technologies were less widely accessible, but their experience of today's market enabled them to identify this as a key training need for newcomers. Similarly, access to professional equipment during training is currently not systematic: it leads to a lower level of awareness and confidence in using such tools at the time of graduation.

While some aspects of professional practice were not covered for a significant proportion of respondents, it did not necessarily impact the feeling of readiness for postgraduate study in the same proportion, possibly in part thanks to lessons derived from applied practice or thanks to connections established through professional bodies, which seems to be almost systematically featured in interpreting training.

The question of stamina and voice management or voice training was raised, highlighting the limits inherent to fixed academic timetables, and the subsequent need to find further training or learning experience to ensure that trainees are prepared to face lengthy conferences by the time they access professional booths.

What is more, two aspects seemed related: a lack of confidence or professional readiness in communications with clients and agencies, and the matter of fees and market rates. In both cases, there was a lack of training on these entrepreneurial aspects and the subsequent concerns expressed by respondents, as well as a clear call for featuring such components in the training to prepare trainees for the freelance market. This situation echoes shortcomings identified for the translation field (Galán-Mañas and Olalla-Soler, 2021; Rodríguez de Céspedes, 2017) and it is a significant gap if you consider, for instance, the French market where 47% of the SFT survey respondents worked through agencies (SFT, 2023). This lack of confidence led about a third of respondents to seek further training, mostly in the shape of additional academic training, but this complementary academic training did not necessarily fully address all their needs.

Consequently, there is clearly scope for curricular adjustments if academic programmes want to fully prepare future conference interpreters. Currently, it appears that the skills gap related to the diversity of tasks tied to self-employment are filled in an ad-hoc way by the interpreting community, through informal mentoring by tutors and peers. However, almost all respondents consider they would still have benefited from additional entrepreneurial training to better transition into the world of work, thus indicating that the move advocated by the European Commission (2020) and other higher education institutions towards more integration of entrepreneurial skills in curricula aligns with the needs identified by professionals.

Finally, while working from a booth still remains altogether the most commonly experienced type of set-up, ORI is fast catching up, as is the use of interpreting hubs, for which few have received training. Looking at interpreters' preferences, co-location remains paramount, at the conference venue or at least at a hub. Even if ORI is not favoured by practitioners, it is nonetheless becoming more widespread. Consequently, better or additional training could be valuable to enhance graduate readiness for these new types of working environments.

However, this study is based on a small sample of professional freelance conference interpreters and does not consider the specificities that may be attached to local markets. Furthermore, some of the shortcomings in the training encountered by some of the more experienced respondents don't represent the state of training available now, even though the current training needs highlighted by these respondents remain valid.

Conclusion

Based on this study, which turned to practicing professional freelance conference interpreters to identify shortcomings and training needs from their perspective, the curricula need to remain up to date with the evolution of the market, to better prepare graduates for the fast-evolving industry tools and environments. The rapid evolution was accelerated by COVID-19, and some of the emerging training needs could be addressed through CPD, to support practitioners whose training pre-dates some of the new ORI tools and did not necessarily feature as much applied interpreting studies theory compared with more recently trained professionals. There is a need to broaden the employability and entrepreneurial components featured in the initial training to better prepare graduates for a growing freelance market (Gerrard and Amoako, 2018).

Nevertheless, when it comes to the question: "whose responsibility is it to prepare budding professionals?" (Rodríguez de Céspedes, 2017), it seems that, in line with studies looking at translation training, the best strategies to address perceived gaps do not necessarily or entirely rest with the academia (Yorke and Knight, 2006; Yorke, 2006): there is scope to widen entrepreneurial enhancing experiences in curricula, through commonly used models like the ones described by Harvey (2005), but in the case of conference interpreting, it may also be worth considering volunteering experiences, supported or guided by academics and early enrolment in professional bodies.

Ultimately, curricula need to be widened to overcome the "negative connotations of entrepreneurship" (European Commission, 2020), to better address the needs of a profession for which freelancing is a significant route.

Creative ways to blur boundaries between higher education and the professional field need to be invented, to widen the range of skills covered in higher education institutions, and better integrate stakeholders in the process, though it need not be limited to in-class activities. Academics specialised in conference interpreting, who often have personal professional experience and industry contacts, are ideally placed to facilitate such an integration, and higher education institutions remain one of the most obvious places in which to create constructive training collaborations.

Notes

1 These conflicted perspectives can be related to the debate between Scarpa and Pym on translation studies (Kearns, 2012, pp. 23–25), and to the diverging views of Gouadec (2003) – who advocates for training models based on employability – in contrast with Mossop's perspective (2003).
2 This specific practice featured student preparation prior to the dummy or mute-booth experience, trainers were present with students during the session and regular breaks and feedback were provided, as well as a debriefing done post-practice.
3 This practice describes circumstances in which students will observe a practising professional at work in situ, or in the case of volunteering, when students or recent graduates work pro bono for recognised charities and NGOs, or specific events run in partnership with universities with interpreting training courses.
4 https://speech-repository.webcloud.ec.europa.eu/ speech repository developed by the Directorate General for Interpretation, initially for their interpreter's professional development, and now partly accessible to the wider public.

5 A device similar to tour-guide systems with a microphone for the interpreter and receivers for the users; this is often used for site visits and when whispered interpreting would not be adequate, for instance, if there is a quite large group of listeners.
6 Defined by the CBTI (Chambre Belge des traducteurs et interprètes) as locations used for remote interpreting, with « one or more separate rooms, equipped with fixed or mobile booths and large video screens".

References

AIIC. 2020. *Guidelines for Distance Interpreting (version 1.0)*. [Online]. [Accessed 30 September 2023]. Available from: https://aiic.org/document/4418/AIIC%20Guidelines%20for%20Distance%20Interpreting%20(Version%201.0)%20-%20ENG.pdf

Álvarez-Álvarez, S. and Arnáiz-Uzquiza, V. 2017. Translation Graduates under Construction: Do Spanish Translation and Interpreting Studies Curricula Answer the Challenge of Employability? In: Rodríguez de Céspedes, B., Sakamoto, A., and Berthand, S. *The Interpreter and Translator Trainer. Special Issue. Employability and the Translation Curriculum* 11 (2), pp. 139–159.

Bao, C. 2015. Pedagogy. In: Mikkelson, H. and Jourdenais, R. *The Routledge Handbook of Interpreting*. London and New York: Taylor and Francis, pp. 400–416.

Bordes, S. 2014. La pédagogie de l'interprétation à l'ISIT. *Le Bulletin du CRATIL* 12, pp. 111–127.

Braun, S. 2007. Interpreting in Small-Group Bilingual Videoconferences: Challenges and Adaptation Processes. *Interpreting* 9 (1), pp. 21–46.

Buján, M. and Collard, C. 2022. Remote Simultaneous Interpreting and COVID-19: Conference Interpreters' Perspective. In: Liu, K. and Cheung, A. K. F. Translation and Interpreting in the Age of COVID-19. Singapore: Springer, pp. 133–150.

Caminade, M. 1995. Les formations en traduction et interprétation: Perspectives en Europe de l'Ouest. *TTR* 8 (1), pp. 247–270.

Chambre belge des traducteurs et interprètes (CBDI). 2020. *Dossier ISD Interprétation Simultanée à Distance*. [Online]. [Accessed 30 September 2022]. Available from: https://www.cbti-bkvt.org/sdm_downloads/fr-cbti-csi-dossier-isd/

Chouc, F. and Conde, J. 2016. Enhancing the Learning Experience of Interpreting Students Outside the Classroom. A Study of the Benefits of Situated Learning at the Scottish Parliament. *The Interpreter and Translator Trainer* 10 (1), pp. 96–106.

Chouc, F. and Conde, J. 2018. Relay Interpreting as a Tool for Conference Interpreting Training. *International Journal of Interpreter Education* 10 (2), pp. 58–72.

European Commission. 2020. *A Guide to Fostering Entrepreneurship Education: Five Key Actions Towards a Digital, Green and Resilient Europe*. [Online]. [Accessed on 18 August 2023] Available from: https://eismea.ec.europa.eu/system/files/2022-01/A%20guide%20for%20fostering%20entrepreneurship%20education.pdf

Galán-Mañas, A. and Olalla-Soler, C. 2021. Perception of Entrepreneurship in Translation Training. *The Interpreter and Translator Trainer* 15 (4), pp 395–410.

Gerrard, A. and Amoako, I. O. 2018. Preparing Freelancers of the Future: A Teaching Case Study. [Online]. [Accessed 11 August 2023] Available from: https://researchonline.ljmu.ac.uk/id/eprint/9692/1/Gerrard%20and%20Amoako%20Preparing%20Freelancers%20of%20the%20Future%20ISBE%202018.pdf

Gile, D. 1995. *Basic Concepts and Models for Interpreter and Translator Training.* Amsterdam/Philadelphia: John Benjamins.

Gile, D. 2005. Research on the Translation Process and Training in Conference Interpretation. *Meta,* 50 (2), pp. 713–726.

Gile, D. 2018. Research into Translation as a Specialism: An Analysis and Recommendations. *Journal of Specialised Translation* 30, pp. 23–39.

Gouadec, D. 2003. Notes on Translator Training (Replies to a Questionnaire). In: Pym, A., Fallada, C., Biau, J. R. and Orenstein, J. *Innovation and E-Learning in Translator Training: Reports on Online Symposia.* Tarragona, Spain: Intercultural Studies Group, pp. 11–19.

Harvey, L. 2005. Embedding and Intergrating Employability. *New Directions for Institutional Research, Special Issue: Workforce Development and Higher Education: A Strategic Role for Institutional Research* 128, pp. 13–28.

Henter, S. 2016. How Happy Are Translators with Their Studies? *Current Trends in Translation and Learning E* 3, pp. 24–66.

Jones, R. 1998. *Conference Interpreting Explained.* Manchester: St Jerome.

Kearns, J. 2012. Global Trends in Translation and Interpreter Training. In: Hubscher-Davidson, S. and Borodo, M. *Global Trends in Translator and Interpreter Training. Mediation and Culture.* London and New York: Bloomsbury, pp. 30–44.

Lave, J. and Wenger, E. 1991. *Situated Learning: Legitimate Peripheral Participation.* Cambridge, England: Cambridge University Press.

Moser-Mercer, B. 2003. Remote Interpreting: Assessment of Human Factors and Performance Parameters. *Communicate!* Summer 2003 [Online]. [Accessed 30 September 22]. Available from: https://aiic.org/document/516/AIICWebzine_Summer2003_3_MOSER-MERCER_Remote_interpreting_Assessment_of_human_factors_and_performance_parameters_Original.pdf

Mossop, B. 2003. What Should Be Taught at Translation School? In: Pym, A., Fallada, C., Biau, J. R. and Orenstein, J. *Innovation and E-Learning in Translator Training: Reports on Online Symposia,* Tarragona, Spain: Intercultural Studies Group, pp. 20–22.

Mouzourakis, P. 1996. Videoconferencing: Techniques and Challenges. *Interpreting* 1 (1), pp. 21–38.

Nimdzi. The 2023 Nimdzi Interpreting Index. [Online] [Accessed 16 February 2024]. Available from: https://www.nimdzi.com/interpreting-index-top-interpreting-companies/#state-of-the-interpreting-market

Olohan, M. 2007. Economic Trends and Developments in the Translation Industry. *The Interpreter and Translator Trainer* 1 (1), pp. 37–63.

Pöchhacker, F. 1999. Teaching Practices in Simultaneous Interpreting. *The Interpreter's Newsletter* 9, pp. 157–176.

Pöchhacker, F. 2001. Quality Assessment in Conference and Community Interpreting. *Meta* 46 (2), pp. 410–425.

Pöchhacker, F. 2015. *Introducing Interpreting Studies.* London and New York: Routledge.

Rodríguez de Céspedes, B. 2017. Addressing Employability and Enterprise Responsibilities in the Translation Curriculum. *The Interpreter and Translator Trainer* 11 (2–3), pp. 107–122.

Sawyer, D. 1994. Monitoring Processes in Conference Interpreting: Towards a Model for Interpreter-Trainees. *Translators' Journal* 39 (3), pp. 433–438.

Schäffner, C. 2012. Translation Competence: Training for the Real World. In: Hubscher-Davidson, S. and Borodo, M. *Global Trends in Translator and Interpreter Training. Mediation and Culture.* London and New York: Bloomsbury, pp. 30–44.

Schnell, B. and Rodriguez, N. 2017. Ivory Tower versus Workplace Reality – Balancing Education and Vocational Requirements: A Study from the Employers' Perspective. In: Rodríguez de Céspedes, B., Sakamoto, A. and Berthand, S. *The Interpreter and Translator Trainer. Special Issue. Employability and the Translation Curriculum* 11 (2), pp. 160–186.

Seeber, K., Keller, L., Amos R. and Hengl, S. 2019. Expectations vs Experience: Attitudes Towards Video Remote Conference Interpreting. *Interpreting* 21 (2), pp. 270–304.

Seleskovitch, D. and Lederer, M. 1989. *Pédagogie raisonnée de l'interprétation.* Bruxelles: Didier Erudition.

SFT Résultats de l'enquête 2023 sur les pratiques professionnelles en interprétation [Online]. [Accessed 16 February 2024]. Available from https://www.sft.fr/sites/default/files/pdf/webinaire-resultats-enquete-interpretes-2023_SFT-AIIC.pdf

Yerevan Communiqué. 2015. [Accessed 11 August 2023]. Available from: https://www.ehea.info/media.ehea.info/file/2015_Yerevan/70/7/YerevanCommuniqueFinal_613707.pdf.

Yorke, M. 2006. Employability in Higer Education. What It Is, What It Is Not. *Learning and Employability* Series 1. [Online]. [Accessed 11 August 2023]. Available from: https://www.advance-he.ac.uk/knowledge-hub/employability-higher-education-what-it-what-it-not

Yorke, M. and Knight, P. 2006. *Embedding Employability into the Curriculum.* Higher Education Academy. [Online]. [Accessed 11 August 23]. Available from: https://www.advance-he.ac.uk/knowledge-hub/embedding-employability-curriculum

3
THE IMPORTANCE OF VISION IN INTERPRETER TRAINING

Jenny Wong

Introduction

This study involves an investigation of the relationship between various learner characteristics of interpreting trainees and their levels of learning success. It is hoped that higher levels of success can be shown at least in part to be the product of learners' capability to generate positive mental imagery of being competent interpreting learners (see literature review). It will then propose adjustments to the language learning experience involving the adoption of optimal motivating strategies within the educational context.

It has been argued that motivation is the main determinant of cognitive factors in determining foreign language learning success (Dörnyei 2014). Since the 1950s, research on language learning and motivation has been closely integrated (Gardner and Lambert 1959). At present the vast majority of motivation-oriented research relating to language learning is focused on European languages and studies focused on the Chinese language are still very limited, not to mention relating to English-Chinese interpreting learning. Our study will fill this gap by looking into the motivation aspect of language learning among Chinese students who enrol to interpreting training courses, by drawing on the latest research on vision.

The research objectives of this study are as follows:

- To investigate whether learner characteristics are related to their learning achievement in interpreting;
- To analyse how learners' vision of their desired interpreting competence affects their motivation.

- To study the importance of vision in the development of learners' future self-identities
- To suggest pedagogical approaches that incorporate elements of vision-related activities to motivate learning among Chinese interpreting students.

We seek to illuminate the relationship among learner characteristics related to sensory and mental imagery aspects and learning achievement. Our present focus is on the role images and senses play in shaping the motivation to learn through promoting a more vivid mental representation of one's self in future states. That is, the more positive one's self-image of himself/herself as an interpreter, the more they can achieve academic success in this discipline.

Literature Review

Vision, or mental imagery, is a unique capability that is involved in a variety of mental functions and it has been specifically associated with motivational enhancement in several fields in the social sciences, for example, in sports psychology and business management (Dörnyei 2019). Cattaneo and Silvanto (2015) define vision, or "mental imagery" (a term in cognitive science that refers to vision) as "a quasi-perceptual experience occurring in the absence of perceptual input", that is, it entails a mental representation in the brain but without actually seeing, or without any external sensory input. Dörnyei (2019) further defines the term vision in three distinct senses, drawing on contemporary English definitions: a) physical perception, which refers to one's eyesight; b) mental picture, which concerns various forms of internal images and visualizations such as memory images, daydreams, fantasies, creative imagination and spiritual revelations; c) future aspiration, which is frequently referred to ambitions of leaders. That said, vision can refer to seeing through one's physical eyes, or the mind's eye, without necessarily involving the visual sense.

Vision has also been widely applied in educational contexts, especially in second language acquisition over the past decade, through the L2 Motivational Self System developed by Dörnyei (2005, 2009). Previous studies by Dörnyei have demonstrated the various ways of using images and imagination to empower L2 learners in acquiring an L2. In short, visionary images can be used to boost motivation by visualising future scenarios that promote the motivation to reach an envisaged destination. In terms of language learning, the role of images and senses are integral components of learners' desired future self-images. In other words, those with a vivid and detailed ideal self-image of being a competent L2 learner are more likely to be motivated to take action in pursuing language studies than peers who do not have a desired future goal state for themselves. (Dornyei and Kubanyiova 2014).

In recent research by Dörnyei and his colleagues (You, Dörnyei, and Csizér 2016), based on a sample of 293 L2 English learners in China, they reported findings that offer a broad overview of the extent to which the capacity of vision contributes to the overall motivation of a whole language learning community. Through the use of three vision-related variables – visual style, auditory style, and vividness of imagery – their findings show that the majority of their participants reported that they had engaged in mental imagery in their L2 learning.

Methodology

We specifically focus on 10 interpreting students at the University of Birmingham (UoB) and collect self-reported evidence in the form of questionnaires as well as objective measures including their academic scores at interpreting exams over a one-year Master's programme. In particular, 18 graduates from the Master of Arts in Interpreting with Translation programme were contacted in 2021, and 10 replied by completing the questionnaires (refer to the Appendix for the questions). The questionnaires that we used are adapted from Dorynei's L2 Motivational Self System (L2MSS).

The L2MSS comprises three core elements proposed by Dörnyei in 2005 and 2009: the L2 ideal self, the L2 ought-to self, and the L2 learning experience. The L2 ideal self represents one's personal aspirations and desires for their language learning journey. In contrast, the L2 ought-to self reflects the expectations imposed by significant others or external influences. On a different note, the L2 learning experience encompasses one's immediate learning environment, including factors like the teacher, curriculum, and peers. In the following section, we will explore the empirical evidence for each of these three components.

The L2 Ideal Self

The L2 ideal self has garnered substantial attention in recent literature, yielding a diverse range of conclusions. Some researchers assert its strong predictive validity, describing it as a "straightforward" and "solid confirmation" of its significance (Dörnyei and Ushioda 2011: 87). They argue that it consistently aligns with desired outcomes. Conversely, there are reservations among other scholars (Kim & Kim, 2011). For instance, in one study of Korean secondary school students, the L2 ideal self failed to predict academic grades, suggesting a disconnect between motivation and achievement (Kim & Kim, 2011). In essence, the debate revolves around whether aspiring to an ideal self genuinely correlates with actual language proficiency. The complexity of this issue may be attributed to contextual variations and differing measurement approaches, warranting further analysis for a more comprehensive understanding.

The L2 Ought-to self

In contrast to the L2 ideal self, there is a greater consensus that the L2 ought-to self could benefit from refinement. It is acknowledged that while these external expectations play a role in shaping learners' motivation, they often lack the power to drive actual learning behaviours. Some researchers advocate for a distinction between one's own aspirations and those imposed by others within both the L2 ideal and L2 ought-to selves (Dörnyei 2014; Dörnyei and Kubanyiova 2014). For instance, the L2 ideal self can be divided into personal aspirations and significant others' expectations, while the L2 ought-to self can be bifurcated into obligations one personally wishes to fulfil and obligations imposed by external sources. This approach may offer a more nuanced understanding of motivation dynamics, and meta-analysis can serve as a benchmark for evaluating the effectiveness of such modifications.

The L2 Learning Experience

The L2 learning experience, also referred to as "attitudes toward language learning", focuses on present evaluations of the learning environment, setting it apart from the future-oriented self-guides of the ideal and L2 ought-to selves. Despite its potential significance, it has received relatively little attention, particularly in terms of theoretical development. Existing studies primarily employ observational designs, which can introduce biases and hinder the establishment of a clear causal relationship between course satisfaction and language learning outcomes (Al-Hoorie 2018). Experimental research in this area has challenged the assumed link between student satisfaction and success, calling into question the validity of course evaluations as reliable indicators of learning. Consequently, this study conducts a factor analysis to better understand the relationship between the L2 learning experience and language learning outcomes, shedding light on the complexities of this construct.

Adaptation of L2MSS

In our study, we adapted the Motivational Self System Questionnaire introduced by Dörnyei (2005, 2009) (See Appendix) to measure visionary components among Chinese interpreting students at the UoB at the beginning of the academic year, according to the following:

- The ideal self as an interpreter (representing a desired 'best-case' scenario, i.e. the best that one can conceivably be);
- The ought-to self as an interpreter (representing attributes that one believes one ought to possess to meet other people's expectations and to avoid possible negative outcomes);

- Three vision-related variables: visual style, auditory style, and vividness of imagery.

This questionnaire surveys students' self-image, with the 'image' aspect to be understood as mental imagery that the learner has of him/ herself as an interpreter projected in the future. Thanks to this questionnaire, we investigate how the students with mental imagery and vision of mastering interpreting in future states compare with those who do not. Their interpreting competence is then measured by collecting their actual grades at the end of the academic year.

The questionnaires were originally developed in English, which were then translated into Chinese. The Chinese version was then back-translated by a professional Chinese–English translator to amend the questionnaire to become more readable by Chinese students. Then two Chinese university students were invited to think aloud when completing the questionnaire and further minor amendments were made to the Chinese translation. The Chinese version of the questionnaire was then piloted among five Chinese interpreting learners who were in the same age range as the participants in the main study, to check if they had difficulties understanding the questions. Finally, we distributed the finalized version of the questionnaires to students doing their Master's in Interpreting with translation. The Statistical Package for the Social Sciences, also known as SPSS software version 29, was to be used for statistical analysis of questionnaire data.

Each questionnaire consisted of eight sections, each section comprising a set of statements on a Likert scale that serves to gauge their individual differences in mental imagery and learning attitude. Factor analysis was used to run the analysis. It should also be pointed out, however, that due to a small sample size, great caution had to be taken in interpreting quantitative data. Studies suggest a minimum sample of 10 (N=10) is sufficiently good for factor analysis, although there is not a consensus among statisticians as to how many samples are enough in a study. (MacCallum, Widaman, Zhang, and Hong 1999)

Findings

Factor Analysis

In this study, questionnaire items as well as their academic scores were subjected to a factor analysis. Factor analysis is used to find out the relationship, or correlation between variables. In this case, it measures the correlation between the individual differences of subjects and the extent to which they are related to their interpreting performance. It is a multivariate statistic where a number of variables are sorted and condensed into fewer factors. Simply put, variables that possess similar characteristics are clustered around a component that forms the factor. The contribution of each variable to the factor is revealed by its strength or loading. Loadings can be positive or negative, revealing the direction of the correlation of a particular variable with a factor. In other words, positive loadings imply a positive correlation with the factor, while negative loadings imply a negative correlation with a factor.

Some variables may be included in more than one factor, possibly due to the inter-correlation between variables. However, not every single variable may be included, or loaded, onto a particular factor. Their contribution to a particular factor may be too weak for meaningful interpretation. Studies suggest that strengths of variables, or loadings over 0.71 are considered excellent, 0.63 very good, and 0.55 good. In the present study, it was decided that factors with loadings 0.55 or higher are considered key variables, and the rest are presented to reveal the overall pattern or trend of the dataset.

Factor analysis is preferred to correlation, a more commonly used statistic, in this study because the latter gauges only the relationship between each independent variable and each dependent variable, without presenting the full picture to the researcher. In this light, factor analysis was used to take into account multiple effects between variables. In the present study, factors with loadings 0.5 or higher are considered key variables (see Table 3.1).

Four significant factors were extracted, accounting for 82.9% of the total variance:

- Factor 1 (34.5% of total variance) was termed "Attitude and mental vision". Key variables included here are attitude, visual style, auditory style, and ease of using imagery. It suggests that those students who have positive attitudes (i.e. high on the attitude score) were able to develop mental vision better.
- Factor 2 (20.9% of total variance) was termed "Ideal self versus intended effort". Key variables included here are ideal self and intended effort.

TABLE 3.1 Factors with Loadings 0.5 or Higher Considered as Key Variables

Variable	Factor 1	Factor 2	Factor 3	Factor 4	Communality
Ideal self	0.364	0.588	0.596	0.007	0.833
Ought to self	0.453	−0.509	0.283	−0.356	0.671
Vividness of Imagery	0.383	−0.395	0.558	−0.411	0.783
Attitude	0.938	0.000	0.000	0.348	1.000
Intended Effort	0.512	−0.836	−0.039	0.173	0.994
Visual Style	0.749	0.273	0.304	−0.167	0.755
Auditory Style	0.662	0.000	0.000	−0.750	1.000
Ease of using imagery	0.596	−0.533	0.560	0.049	0.954
Interpreting Score	0.354	0.246	0.528	−0.040	0.466
Variance	3.1037	1.879	1.4333	1.0407	7.4566
% Var	0.345	0.209	0.159	0.116	0.829

There is a negative correlation between ideal self (0.588) and intended effort (−0.836). It indicates that those who can imagine themselves as an ideal interpreter tend to spend less effort in interpreting.
- **Factor 3 (15.9% of total variance) was termed "Ease of vivid imagery and interpreting score"**. Key variables included here are ideal self, ease of use of imagery, vividness of imagery, and interpreting score. It suggests those who can develop vivid imagery of themselves as successful interpreters (i.e. high on the score of ideal self, ease of use of imagery, and vividness of imagery) do correlate with better interpreting scores (0.528).
- **Factor 4 (11.6%) was termed "auditory style"**. The predominant factor isolated here is the auditory style, which is not linked to other variables.

Discussion

Implications for Interpreting Training

Motivation Enhancement: The study underscores the importance of motivation in interpreter training. Educators and institutions should recognize the role of mental imagery and vision in motivating students. They can incorporate vision-enhancing strategies and activities to inspire learners and promote a more positive attitude towards their language studies. Teachers should particularly employ positive reinforcement strategies to encourage students further. Not only that, the programme leader should develop a collaborative peer-learning environment so that students can readily develop congenial relationships among themselves in order to motivate one another. While Chinese students gave the general impression that they tend to submit to the power and authority of teachers who are often viewed as the authoritative figure in the classroom, as Biggs (1999) and Littlewood (1999) argued, Asian students are also capable of benefiting from a cooperative learning environment despite such common misconception. A buddy system, for example, where trainees are paired up with a buddy for drills and practices, is a good way to cultivate a collaborative environment for students to motivate them further. Such pedagogy is informed by research as many scholars are aware of the importance of comparison and collaborative work in the teaching and training of translators (Kiraly 2000; Sainz 1992: 71). Not to be outdone, a mentoring scheme can be developed between graduates and incoming students so that the success stories of these mentors can help instil a positive image among students.

Individualized Learning: Understanding the factors that influence students' motivation and learning achievement, such as their ideal self-concepts and attitudes, allows for a more individualized approach to teaching. Douglas Robinson (1997) is amongst the first translation scholars who went to great lengths in stressing the importance of people-orientation in the practice of translation. Focusing on people, as he claimed, "will always be more productive and effective than a focus on abstract linguistics or cultural conventions (1995: 128)". As such, instructors can tailor their methods to address each student's unique motivational needs and goals. This can include, but not limited to, the use of peer models, as well as teacher models in motivating students in their interpreting performance. The research literature has shown that multiple modelling is more effective than modelling alone in improving self-efficacy (Bandura 1997: 99; Schunk 1998: 193). While mastery models are more competent at a particular task and thus are more influential, coping models who manage to overcome difficulties after times of struggles can be as motivating as (Schunk, 1985: 313–322), or even better (Schunk, 1987:54–61) than the former when observers found themselves more comparable with coping models than with mastery ones.

On the other hand, as self-evaluation constitutes an integral part of the learning of interpreting, self-models can be introduced to enhance a student's performance, especially when self-modelling is specially arranged where only the best performances of oneself are selected for evaluation (Bandura 1997: 87). This can be done by using video clips of one's performances featuring his/her best performances in the interpreting assignment or examination in order to reinforce the positive image one may have.

Effort Allocation: The finding that students who can imagine themselves as ideal interpreters tend to expend less effort suggests that students may benefit from guidance on how to balance their vision of success with the effort required to achieve it. Educators can help students set realistic goals and develop effective study habits. While interpreting exercises and drills are important in honing their skills, students should be encouraged to reflect on their self-image so that past failures in their interpreting performances and exercises will not discourage them from developing an ideal self.

Vivid Imagery of Being Successful Interpreter: The study highlights the positive correlation between the development of vivid imagery of themselves as successful interpreters and better interpreting scores. This suggests that training programmes can incorporate exercises to enhance students' mental imagery skills, such as mind mapping, positive thinking, creative thinking, potentially leading to improved interpreting performance. They can also incorporate experiential learning such as field exercises, company visits, or simulated environments for trainees in the programme so that they can visualize better how they can achieve success in real-life settings.

Auditory Style: The isolated factor related to auditory style provides an interesting avenue for further research. Understanding how auditory preferences relate to interpreting skills could inform teaching strategies and accommodations for students with different sensory strengths.

Cross-Cultural Implications: While the study focused on Chinese interpreting students in the UK, the findings may have broader applicability.

Interpreting educators worldwide can consider the role of mental imagery in motivating interpreting learners and adapting strategies accordingly. In Greater China, where interpreting drills are greatly emphasized as an integral part of the study programme, the inclusion of vision training will shift the emphasis from skill-based practice to a more balanced approach, making the interpreting learning experience less stressful and more enjoyable.

Conclusion

In conclusion, this study underscores the significance of mental imagery and vision in interpreter training and its implications for learner motivation and success. By recognizing and harnessing the power of mental imagery, educators can foster a more motivated and engaged cohort of interpreting students, ultimately contributing to their proficiency and success in the field. Further research in this area could expand our understanding of the relationship between vision, motivation, and interpreting learning outcomes.

Due to a relatively small sample size, it inevitably invites suspicion concerning the reliability of the study. Besides replicating on a larger sample data pool, it is suggested that the following recommendations be considered for future research.

Incorporating a focus group following the collection of questionnaires could further illuminate the degree of positive mental image exerted on individual interpreters. A limitation of this study is that students returned to Mainland China immediately after the academic year in 2021 due to the travel restrictions caused by COVID-19. As a result, many of them could not be contacted when their university email expired. A replication of this study can be done on future cohorts of MA students to include a more detailed discussion after data collection.

This research design is based on the adapted version of L2MSS which was given at the beginning of the academic year. As their confidence level would have changed over the course of the study, a replication of this current study along with questionnaire items that aim to gauge their motivation at the beginning and the end of the academic year is therefore suggested to monitor their feedback.

References

Al-Hoorie, A. (2018). The L2 motivational self system: A meta-analysis. *Studies in Second Language Learning and Teaching*, 8 (4). 2018. pp. 721–754.
Bandura, A. (1997). *Self-efficacy*. New York: W H Freeman and Company.
Biggs, J. (1999). What the student does: Teaching for enhanced learning. *Higher Education Research and Development*, 18(1), 57–75.
Cattaneo, Z., & Silvanto, J. (2015). Mental Imagery: Visual Cognition. *International Encyclopedia of the Social & Behavioral Sciences* (2nd ed.), pp. 220–227.

Dörnyei, Z. (2005). *Psychology of the language learner: Individual differences in second language acquisition.* Mahwah, NJ: Lawrence Erlbaum.

Dörnyei, Z. (2009). *Motivation, language identity and the L2 self.* Bristol: Multilingual Matters.

Dörnyei, Z. (2019). *Vision, mental imagery and the Christian life: Insights from science and scripture.* London: Routledge.

Dörnyei, Z., & Kubanyiova, M. (2014). *Motivating learners, motivating teachers: Building vision in the language classroom.* Cambridge: Cambridge University Press.

Dörnyei, Z., & Ushioda, U. (2011). *Teaching and researching motivation* (2nd ed.). Harlow: Pearson.

Gardner, R. C., & Lambert, W. E. (1959). Motivational variables in second language acquisition: An investigation using LISREL causal modelling. *Journal of Language and Social Psychology*, 2, 51–65.

Kim, Y.-K., & Kim, T.-Y. (2011). The effect of Korean secondary school students' perceptual learning styles and ideal L2 self on motivated L2 behavior and English proficiency. *Korean Journal of English Language and Linguistics*, 11(1), 21–42.

Kiraly, D. (2000). *A social constructivist approach to translator education-empowerment from theory to practice.* Manchester: St. Jerome Publishing.

Littlewood, W. (1999) Defining and developing autonomy in East Asian contexts. *Applied Linguistics.* 20/1:71–94.

MacCallum, R. C., Widaman, K. F., Zhang, S., & Hong S. (1999). Sample size in factor analysis. *Psychological Methods*, 4, 84–99

Robinson, D. (1997). *Becoming a translator.* London: Routledge.

Sainz, M. J. (1992). Developing translation skills. In Dollerup, Cay & Anne Loddegaard (Eds) *Teaching Translation and Interpreting 1: Training, Talent, and Experience.* Amsterdam: Benjamins, 71.

Schunk, D. H., & Hanson, A. R. (1985). Peer models: Influence on children's self-efficacy and achievement. *Journal of Educational Psychology*, 77, 313–322.

Schunk, D. H. (1987). Self efficacy and motivated learning. In Hastings & Schwieso (Eds.), *New Directions in Educational Psychology.* The Falmer Press, 54–61.

Schunk, D. H. (1998). Peer modelling. In Topping & Ehly (Eds.), *Peer Assisted Learning.* Lawrence Erlbaum Associates, Inc., Publishers, 93.

You, C., Dörnyei, Z., & Csizér, K. (2016). Motivation, vision, and gender: A survey of learners of English in China. *Language Learning*, 66(1), 94–123.

Appendix: A survey of learners of interpreting

Student ID: _____

Questionnaire Items Used to access your learning attitude in the Current Study.

Choose 1 for least Agree, 5 for strongly Agree

Ideal Self

- I can imagine myself interpreting in the future for foreign friends at meetings. 1 2 3 4 5

- I can imagine myself in the future interpreting successfully to the public in the future. 1 2 3 4 5
- I can imagine a situation where I am doing business with foreigners by interpreting. 1 2 3 4 5
- I can imagine myself in the future facilitating a discussion with foreign friends through interpreting. 1 2 3 4 5
- I can imagine that in the future in a conference, the speaker and I will be chatting casually. 1 2 3 4 5

Ought-to Self

- Studying interpreting is important to me in order to gain the approval of my teachers. 1 2 3 4 5
- Studying interpreting is important to me in order to gain the approval of my peers. 1 2 3 4 5
- Studying interpreting is important to me in order to gain the approval of the society. 1 2 3 4 5
- I study interpreting because close friends of mine think it is important. 1 2 3 4 5
- I consider learning interpreting important because the people I respect think that I should do it. 1 2 3 4 5
- My parents/family believe that I must study interpreting to be a successful person. 1 2 3 4 5

Vividness of Imagery

- If I wish, I can imagine how I could successfully interpret in the future so vividly that the images and/or sounds of the interpreting performance hold my attention as a good movie or story does. 1 2 3 4 5
- When imagining how I could interpret fluently in the future, I usually have a vivid mental picture of the scene. 1 2 3 4 5
- My dreams of myself interpreting successfully in the future are sometimes so vivid I feel as though I actually experience the situations. 1 2 3 4 5
- I can have several vivid mental pictures and/or sounds of situations when I'm imagining myself interpreting skilfully in the future. 1 2 3 4 5
- When I'm imagining myself interpreting skilfully in the future, I can usually have both specific mental pictures and vivid sounds of the situations. 1 2 3 4 5

Attitudes to Learning interpreting

- I really like the actual process of learning interpreting. 1 2 3 4 5
- I find learning interpreting really interesting. 1 2 3 4 5

- I really enjoy learning interpreting. 1 2 3 4 5
- I always look forward to interpreting classes. 1 2 3 4 5
- I think time passes faster while studying interpreting. 1 2 3 4 5

Intended Effort

- I am prepared to expend a lot of effort in learning interpreting. 1 2 3 4 5
- I would like to spend lots of time studying interpreting. 1 2 3 4 5
- I would like to concentrate on studying interpreting more than any other topic 1 2 3 4 5
- Even if I failed in my interpreting learning, I would still learn interpreting very hard. 1 2 3 4 5
- Interpreting would be still important to me in the future even if I failed in my interpreting course. 1 2 3 4 5

Visual Style

- I use colour coding (e.g. highlighter pen) to help me as I learn. 1 2 3 4 5
- Charts, diagrams, and maps help me understand what someone says. 1 2 3 4 5
- When I listen to a teacher, I imagine pictures, numbers, or words. 1 2 3 4 5
- I highlight the text in different colours when I study interpreting. 1 2 3 4 5
- I learn better by reading what the teacher writes on the screen. 1 2 3 4 5

Auditory Style

- When the teacher tells me the instructions, I understand better. 1 2 3 4 5
- I remember things I have heard in class better than things I have read. 1 2 3 4 5
- I learn better in class when the teacher gives a lecture. 1 2 3 4 5
- I like for someone to give me the instructions out loud. 1 2 3 4 5
- I remember things better if I discuss them with someone. 1 2 3 4 5

Ease of Using Imagery

- Sometimes images of myself interpreting successfully in the future come to me without the slightest effort. 1 2 3 4 5
- I find it easy to "play" imagined scenes and/or conversations in my mind. 1 2 3 4 5
- It is easy for me to imagine how I could successfully interpret in the future. 1 2 3 4 5
- I think I have a natural ability to visualize myself interpreting successfully in the future. 1 2 3 4 5
- I have always found it easy to visualize imagined situations. 1 2 3 4 5

4
TOWARDS EFFECTIVE INTERPRETER TRAINING

The Impact of Learning Environment Types and Students' Procedural Learning Abilities

Yinghua Wang

Introduction

The implicit learning environment, also known as the student-centred environment, has been widely advocated for interpreter training since the beginning of this century (Kim, 2013, p. 105). As opposed to the explicit (i.e. lecturer-centred) learning environment in which the lecturer plays an authoritative role in providing information, such as directly offering correct answers or solutions, the implicit learning environment encourages students to construct their knowledge by communicating what they know already to their colleagues (Serin, 2018, p. 165; Tao, 2012, p. 295). Lecturers only support this learning process by interacting with the students, such as by offering guidance for the students' reference (Kiraly, 2000, p. 47). Though scholars commonly endorse the implicit learning environment for interpreter training (e.g., Motta, 2016; Tikhonova et al., 2015), it has the drawback of being time-consuming (Chen, 2005; Fu et al., 2017; Wu, 2011), students' complaining about making slow progress (Fu et al., 2017), and of leading the students to seek rough solutions (Kain, 2003, pp. 104–106). These defects can arise from neglecting explicit instruction which can speed up students' learning (N.C. Ellis, 2005, p. 307) as knowledgeable lecturers can direct the class to focus on appropriate complex solutions (Serin, 2018, p. 165).

Literature focusing on balancing the implicit and explicit learning environments appears to be limited. Although a mixed learning environment exists, lecturers control it by having the final say on the answer to a question or a solution to a problem (González-Davies and Enríquez-Raído, 2016, p. 7). That is, the lecturers still dominate classes in the mixed learning environment, making it equivalent to the explicit learning environment, rather than a true balance of the implicit and the explicit. Nevertheless, some empirical interpreting studies (Tikhonova et al., 2015; Xu, 2010) offer a perspective on achieving balance for improving student interpreters' training. These studies indirectly suggest that student interpreters can better acquire interpreting skills according to the type of learning environment: explicit or implicit. Furthermore, the cognitive flexibility theory proposed by Spiro et al. (1987, 2013) supports the claim that different skills can benefit from either implicit or explicit learning environments (corresponding to ill-structured or well-structured domains, respectively) for better learning outcomes. Accordingly, my first hypothesis is that balancing the implicit and explicit learning environments can be achieved by adapting them to the different interpreting skills being taught.

In addition to the type of interpreting skill, an individual's procedural learning ability (PLA) also plays a role in determining the right balance in the learning environments. PLA underpins knowledge of how to perform a task (see reviews in Brill, 2012; Carpenter, 2008), and it measures individual differences in learning rather than psychometric intelligence (Kaufman et al., 2010). A number of studies (Brill, 2012; Carpenter, 2008; Granena and Yilmaz, 2019; Li, 2022; Tagarelli et al., 2016) find that the PLA can predict learning performance in the implicit learning environment. Although these studies mainly focus on lexical or grammatical learning, linguistic scholars outside these areas have similarly found that the PLA can affect an individual student's language-related learning (see reviews in Morgan-Short et al., 2022, p. 76). As interpreting is a linguistic activity, my second hypothesis is that the PLA can impact a student's learning of interpreting skills under different learning environments.

When testing the above two hypotheses, I focused on consecutive interpreting (CI) due to its wide applicability. Scholars have widely accepted CI as being versatile and popular in conference settings (e.g., Russell and Takeda, 2015, p. 103; Setton and Dawrant, 2016, p. 16), such as a government press conference, and non-conference settings (e.g., Setton and Dawrant, 2016, p. 16; Diriker, 2013, p. 364), such as a business negotiation. Furthermore, many interpreting instructors also view CI as the foundation of simultaneous interpreting training (Russell, 2002). The specific CI skills I examined include listening comprehension, expression, note-taking, note-reading, memory, shifted attention, and coping tactics.

To verify my hypotheses, my experiment investigated the impact of an implicit or explicit learning environment on student interpreters' learning of different CI skills. The results are further analyzed by considering individual student interpreters' PLA. This research contributes to proposing new training methods to match the learning environment type with the PLA, thereby helping student interpreters achieve optimum interpreting learning outcomes.

Method

Research Type and Approaches

The research conducted in this chapter adopts an ethnographic approach, a method widely utilized for studying groups through research participants (Hale and Napier, 2013, p. 84) and which works effectively for collecting data from various sources (Hammersley, 1990, pp. 2–3). Recruiting interpreting student participants from different educational institutions can mitigate the difficulty of obtaining a sufficient number of participants for statistical analysis. However, requesting these participants to commit to an additional CI class with controlled learning environments (in this case, half explicit and half implicit) alongside their intensive university courses was impractical. Therefore, investigating the participants' learning environments in their respective institutions worked out as the best alternative. This circumstance renders interviewing, a primarily qualitative approach in ethnography (Hale and Napier, 2013, p. 84), the most suitable method for my research. In addition to interviewing, my research incorporates quantitative CI and PLA scoring through statistical testing to ensure the research results can be generalized to a larger population beyond my participants.

Distinguishing Explicit and Implicit Learning Environments

Undetailed definitions of the explicit and implicit learning environments in current literature (e.g., Batterink and Neville, 2013; Berges-Puyó, 2018; Norris and Ortega, 2000) cannot serve as criteria for classifying participants' respective CI learning environments. These definitions merely describe the differences between explicit and implicit learning environments in terms of whether or not and how lecturers present the rules of a skill. Specifically, lecturers in the explicit learning environment point out rules (Batterink and Neville, 2013; DeKeyser, 1995; Norris and Ortega, 2000) or direct the students to deliberate on the underlying rules themselves (see also Berges-Puyó, 2018; R. Ellis, 2009; Housen and Pierrard, 2005) in an authoritative way. In contrast, lecturers in implicit learning environments neither provide rules nor guide the students to notice the rules (see also; Morgan-Short et al., 2012), rather they communicatively provide rules (Zhao and Ellis, 2020) to encourage students to find their rules.

Although the above definitions are vague, Zhao and Ellis (2020, pp. 2–4) concretize lecturers' specific practices in the explicit learning environment, including implicit and explicit corrective feedback (CF) with detailed strategies under each CF category: direct correction, explicit correction, elicitation, prescriptive clue, prescriptive explanation, recast, conformation check, clarification check, clarification request, and repetition. Additionally, merely informing students whether their answer is right or wrong without providing comments or corrections also falls under CF (Ai, 2017; Negro and Chanquoy, 2005). It is noteworthy that although CF can be implicit or explicit, CF intrinsically produces an explicit learning environment as it draws the student's attention to rules, such as guiding them to notice grammar (i.e., a language rule) or directly teaching students grammar (see also Adams et al., 2011; R. Ellis, 2006, 2008; Gashti, 2018; Shamiri and Farvardin, 2016; Zhao and Ellis, 2020). Therefore, I regarded CF as the guiding principle in determining an explicit learning environment.

I did not find a summary of detailed teaching approaches for implicit learning environments. Nevertheless, I considered exposure, memorization, feedback without embedded rules, and communicative feedback as typical practices, because they align with the overarching characteristic of implicit learning environments, which eschew explicit rules. The exposure approach involves immersing students in cases or examples, such as mock conferences and role plays, without providing rule-related feedback (see Reber, 1993; Sanz and Morgan-Short, 2005), or explanations that can lead students to discover the hidden rules themselves (see Batterink and Neville, 2013; Housen and Pierrard, 2005). The memorization strategy refers to asking students to memorize cases or examples with hidden targeted rules (R. Ellis, 2009; Norris & Ortega, 2000). For example, students memorize different translations of an expression. The lecturer does not offer rules directly or guide the students to focus on the embedded rule (e.g., they do not show the students that all the provided translations of an expression focus on functional rather than meaning equivalence). However, if a lecturer asks students to memorize rules directly, memorization belongs to a strategy under the explicit learning environment. In addition to exposure and memorization, feedback is an essential strategy in an implicit learning environment. Though I did not find studies summarizing specific strategies of feedback categorized under the implicit learning environment, the CF strategies summarized by Zhao and Ellis (2020) can be applied with modifications, according to which rules either should be excluded or provided communicatively.

Furthermore, vague rules given authoritatively fall under implicit rather than explicit. Vague rules refer to those that students cannot directly follow to resolve or answer a specific problem or question. Taking the note-taking skill as an example, merely instructing students to simplify their notes is vague while providing instructions to use acronyms and symbols along with presenting examples is not. Vague rules still require students to construct specific solutions or answers themselves (e.g., to find their own ways to improve their notes when told to simplify them). Since the implicit learning environment encourages students to construct their own knowledge (see Kiraly, 2000, p. 1), offering vague rules belongs under this category. Accordingly, offering vague rules, even if authoritatively, with exposure and memorization, feedback without embedded rules, and communicative feedback, constitute the criteria for judging an implicit learning environment.

Participants

A total of 39 student interpreters from nine different institutions from the UK and China participated in this research. They were all female and aged between 18 and 39 years (18–20: 2%; 21–29: 90%; 30–39: 8%), with Mandarin as their A language, including two with additional A languages (one Kazakh and one Uyghur), and English as their B language. All student participants received 10 weeks of CI training in their respective institutions during the experiment. Additionally, my research included seven CI lecturer participants from five institutions where the student participants received CI training.

Procedure

Each student participant completed two PLA tasks at their convenience via the Inquisit platform: the alternating serial reaction time (ASRT) task, and the weather prediction task (WPT). These tasks are commonly used in cognitive studies to measure PLA (e.g., Carpenter, 2008; Deroost and Soetens, 2006; Foerde et al., 2006; Howard and Howard, 1997; Poldrack and Packard, 2003). After completion, the student participants emailed back the automatically generated results of the two tasks.

CI tests and the post-CI-test interviews were conducted at the beginning and the end of the 10-week CI training via Zoom or VooV Meeting, depending on the student participants' accessibilities. The speech materials came from the English-to-Mandarin CI tests of the China Accreditation Test for Translators and Interpreters in November 2018 and June 2019, which were pre-video recorded by native English speakers. All the student participants received the time, the topic of the speech, and the Zoom or VooV Meeting link two days before every CI test. During a CI test, the student participants watched and listened to the pre-recorded speech via the screen-sharing function of the online communication platform. I manually paused the speech several times according to the original test design by the China Accreditation Test for Translators and Interpreters. After each pause, the student participants started interpreting, and they did not need to complete the interpreting within a specific time limit. Each student participant's interpreting performance was recorded with consent.

The post-CI-test interviews were carried out immediately after each CI test via Zoom or VooV Meeting when I played back each recording and pointed out CI errors on the spot. The student participant then explained the reasons for the errors. Interviews regarding the learning environment were conducted subsequently along with both the lecturer and the student to provide a comprehensive view of the in-class learning environment. During the interviews, both lecturer participants and student participants described the teaching practices involved in class. Additionally, student participants' CI practice time was asked and recorded to control for temporal influences on the research results during the statistical analysis.

Data Analysis

ASRT measured student participants' accuracy and reaction time across a series of trials. For my research, the overall reaction time score automatically calculated by Inquisit served as one indicator of the student participants' PLA, as recent research (Farkas et al., 2022) suggests its respectable reliability, compared to an overall accuracy score. WPT only measured student participants' accuracy in completing the task and served as another indicator of PLA. The calculation of the participants' overall PLA scores followed the practice by Brill (2012, pp. 27–28), which averaged the z-scores of ASRT and WPT.

The CI test speech materials were segmented into small chunks based on sense groups, defined as units of information interpreters can infer or understand the meaning of (Chernov, 2004, pp. 122–123), not necessarily complete sentences. Due to the absence of a specific procedure for dividing sense groups in interpreting that I could refer to, I performed this task based on my years of experience as an interpreter.

CI skill scoring was based on sense groups. When one or more CI errors within a sense group were attributed to an underperformed CI skill, the student participant received one-point deduction under that skill. When the errors were related to multiple CI skills within the same sense group, the student participant received separate deductions for each CI skill. This method ensured more accurate CI skill scoring compared to tallying errors directly. For instance, if one participant omitted an entire sentence due to a memory lapse, while another participant missed only one word for the same reason, counting errors alone would suggest both participants had equal mastery of the memory skill. However, segmenting the sentence into sense groups would reveal a more nuanced assessment.

The student participants completed two CI tests: one before and one after the ten-week CI training. Improvement in each CI skill was calculated by subtracting scores obtained in the post-training test from those in the pre-training test. Original scores for each CI skill were converted into percentages before calculating improvement to account for variations in the number of sense groups between tests.

CI errors were evaluated based on their completeness and accuracy, criteria widely accepted by interpreting scholars to assess interpreting quality (see reviews in Han, 2022, pp. 38–39; Pöchhacker, 2016, pp. 135–137; Xu, 2010, pp. 15–18). Completeness requires coverage of primary and secondary information from the source speech, such as main idea, modifiers, tense, and modals (Sun, 2010, pp. 53–59), while accuracy encompasses pronunciation, grammar, expression, and logic (Ouyang, 2018, pp. 204–205; Sun, 2010, p. 59). Interpreting styles, such as tone and wording, was excluded from the assessment criteria due to its questionable importance in interpreting (see Albl-Mikasa, 2012, p. 83).

The association between CI errors and underperformed CI skills was determined through student participants' self-explanations during post-CI-test interviews. In cases where participants were unable to explain their errors, I relied on a cognitive model of information processing developed in my PhD thesis (Wang, 2024, pp. 95–159) for analysis.

The student participant's learning environments for each CI skill were categorized as either explicit or implicit according to the criteria discussed in 'Distinguishing Explicit and Implicit Learning Environments'. A learning environment was classified as explicit when the teaching practices within a CI classroom satisfied some or all the explicit criteria listed in 'Distinguishing Explicit and Implicit Learning Environments'; for instance, if a lecturer offers students the 'correct' translation of a sentence instead of fostering translation discussion among them. Conversely, when teaching practices aligned with the implicit criteria specified in 'Distinguishing Explicit and Implicit Learning Environments', or when they constituted general practices unrelated to specific CI skills, the learning environment was considered implicit. For example, a lecturer instructs students to engage in gist interpreting without note-taking to bolster their memory skills, contrasting with an explicit approach that prompts students to primarily focus on the logical structure of a speech.

Results

This section presents the statistical results regarding the impact of learning environments and PLA levels on student interpreters. One student participant's note-taking score was excluded as they did not take notes during the pre-training CI test. Additionally, one participant's PLA score was omitted due to non-submission of the WPT result.

Due to an extremely small sample size for the note-reading skill in the implicit learning environment group (n = 2), these data were excluded from statistical analysis. Furthermore, the sample sizes for note-taking (n = 3) and coping tactics (n = 4) in the implicit learning environment group did not meet the minimum requirement of approximately eight for bootstrapping analysis (Chernick, 2008; Hall, 1997), which is the preferred statistical method for my data because it handles complex data with small sample sizes (Frost, 2018).

Consequently, I compared the improvement in these two skills between the purely explicit environment group and the mixed explicit environment group, rather than between the implicit and explicit environment groups.

Effects of Learning Environments on Improving Various Interpreting Skills

A one-way ANCOVA with bootstrapping (B = 2,000) was performed to compare the impact of implicit and explicit learning environments on student interpreters' improvement in each CI skill (i.e., listening comprehension, expression, note-taking, note-reading, memory, shifted attention, and coping tactics), controlling for PLA scores, pre-training CI test scores, and practice time. One-way ANCOVA works to assess significant differences between two independent groups, while also minimizing the impact of potential confounding factors (Laerd Statistics, 2017a).

Results indicated a statistically significant difference in memory performance between the two learning environments, $F(1, 33) = 6.59$, $p = .015$. Student interpreters trained in the implicit environment exhibited superior memory skill acquisition (estimate $M = 1.461$, 95% CI [−2.501, 6.182]) compared to those in the explicit environment (estimate $M = −5.001$, 95% CI [−8.772, −0.842]), with an estimate mean difference of 6.462, 95% CI [1.241, −11.476], $p = .019$. Additionally, the confidence interval from these results showed regression in memory skills among student interpreters following training in the explicit environment.

No statistically significant effect of learning environment type was found in student interpreters' learning of listening comprehension ($F(1, 33) = 2.601$, $p = .116$), expression ($F(1, 33) = 0.529$, $p = .472$), note-taking ($F(1, 29) = 0.263$, $p = .612$), shifted attention ($F(1, 33) = 0.012$, $p = .913$), and coping tactics ($F(1, 29) = 0.201$, $p = .657$). However, the estimated mean value of the expression skill was statistically significantly negative in the implicit learning environment (estimate $M = −2.633$, 95% BCa. CI [−5.178, −0.292]).

Effects of PLA on Improving Various Interpreting Skills Under Different Learning Environments

A Pearson Partial Correlation with bootstrapping (B = 2,000) was conducted to examine the relationship between PLA and student interpreters' improvement in each CI skill under different learning environments, while controlling for pre-training CI test scores and practice time. This statistical approach assesses the linear relationship between two sets of data, while minimizing the influence of potential confounding factors (Laerd Statistics, 2017b). Results indicated a positive partial correlation between the PLA and the improvement of listening comprehension skills, $r(9) = .762$, $p = .006$, 95% BCa. CI [.085, .933].

No statistically significant partial correlations were found between the students' PLA and the improvement in expression (r (5) = -.223, p = .630), note-reading (r (32) = -.244, p = .163), memory (r (12) = .253, p = .382), and shifted attention (r (7) = .492, p = .179) in the implicit learning environment. Similarly, no statistically significant correlations were found between PLA and improvement in listening comprehension (r (21) = .057, p = .797), expression (r (25) = .135, p = .501), memory (r (18) = -.394, p = .086), and shifted attention (r (23) = -.161, p = .442) in the explicit learning environment. Additionally, no statistically significant partial correlations were observed between the PLA and improvement in note-taking (pure explicit: r (3) = -.156, p = .802; mixed: r (24) = .041, p = .843) and coping tactics (pure explicit: r (22) = .035, p = .873; mixed: r (4) = .128, p = .809) under different learning environments.

Discussion

Scholars (e.g., Gillies, 2009; González-Davies and Enríquez-Raído, 2016; Kim, 2013; Moser-Mercer, 2008) have traditionally favoured the implicit learning environment for training student interpreters, yet my study shows that different interpreting skills can thrive in distinct learning environments. While memory skills benefit from the implicit learning environment, expression skills regress post-training if acquired in that environment. Conversely, memory skills regress after explicit training. Student interpreters with a higher PLA excel in acquiring listening comprehension skills in the implicit learning environment.

The preference for an implicit learning environment in memory skill acquisition is attributed to discrepancies in prior knowledge between students and lecturers. As observed in psychological literature, prior knowledge influences memory (Brod et al., 2013, p. 1), hindering memorization when incompatible with new information (Shing and Brod, 2016, p. 153; Umanath and Marsh 2014, p. 419). In the explicit learning environment, the lecturer authoritatively demonstrates how they link the new and prior knowledge to aid memorization. However, due to the nature of authoritative instruction, student interpreters tend to follow this information combination pattern for memorization. When the student interpreters lack shared prior knowledge with lecturers, authoritative instruction impedes memorization. For instance, if a lecturer instructs student interpreters to remember the logical word 'so' to memorize the sentence 'The UN launched the 2030 Agenda, so the organization continues striving for sustainable development', the student interpreters without prior knowledge of the 2030 Agenda's focus on sustainable development can struggle to effectively use 'so' as a link word for memorization.

The observed regression in expression skills among student interpreters in the implicit learning environment aligns with findings from Tikhonova et al. (2015). Their research revealed difficulties among student interpreters in utilizing sufficient vocabulary and transitioning between languages, indicative of inadequate expression skills after receiving CI training in an implicit learning environment. While current literature does not offer definitive explanations for this phenomenon, it is plausible that student interpreters struggle to find appropriate translations in the absence of authoritative guidance. In implicit learning environments, where lecturers do not provide standard answers, students can resort to selecting alternative but inappropriate translations. With repeated use, these incorrect translations become ingrained, leading to further challenges in accurate expression during other interpreting practices, particularly in the absence of corrective feedback.

The finding that student interpreters with a higher PLA benefit more from the implicit learning environment for improving listening comprehension skills is consistent with previous research by Brill (2012) and Carpenter (2008). These studies suggest that advanced language learners, such as interpreters, with a higher PLA may find implicit learning environments more conducive to enhancing non-native language skills, such as speech comprehension. The theoretical rationale behind this result lies in the reliance of advanced second language users on procedural memory, which the PLA tests assess (Brill, 2012, p. 36). Procedural memory serves as the foundation of implicit learning (Lum and Conti-Ramsden, 2013, p. 284), predominantly triggered by implicit learning environments (Khamesipour, 2015, pp. 1620–1621). Therefore, for interpreters with higher PLA, implicit learning environments offer optimal conditions for improving listening comprehension skills by leveraging their procedural memory abilities.

It's important to note that the statistical testing used in this study represents one approach among several possibilities. I have recently explored alternative methods, such as a combination of one-way ANCOVA and Quade test, as well as Kendall's tau-b partial test along with Pearson partial correlation. These alternative methods yielded varying results compared to those presented in this chapter: student interpreters only statistically significantly benefit from the implicit learning environment to improve memory skills. Such discrepancies are not uncommon, especially when dealing with sample sizes not above the range of dozens. However, despite the variations in results, the findings presented in this chapter remain robust. Rather than undermining the validity of the conclusions, the differing outcomes underscore the need for similar future research endeavours with larger sample sizes and more advanced statistical techniques to further validate the preliminary findings.

Conclusion

This research challenges the prevailing notion that the implicit learning environment is superior for training student interpreters. My findings suggest that the implicit learning environment leads to regression in the mastery of expression skills, but it highlights its continued importance in facilitating the acquisition of memory skills. Moreover, my research demonstrates that higher levels of PLA can significantly enhance improvement in listening skills within the implicit learning environment. These insights have significant implications for interpreting instructors, encouraging them to adopt a more nuanced approach to selecting learning environments based on individual interpreting skills and students' PLA levels. By tailoring the learning environment to specific CI skills and student characteristics, instructors can optimize the outcomes of interpreting education and better support student success.

References

Adams, R., Nuevo, A. M. and Egi, T. 2011. Explicit and Implicit Feedback, Modified Output, and SLA: Does Explicit and Implicit Feedback Promote Learning and Learner-Learner Interactions? *The Mordern Language Journal* 95, pp. 42–63.

Ai, H. 2017. Providing Graduated Corrective Feedback in an Intelligent Computer-Assisted Language Learning Environment. *ReCALL* 9(3), pp. 313–334.

Albl-Mikasa, M. 2012. The Importance of Being Not Too Earnest: A Process- and Experience-Based Model of Interpreter Competence. In: Ahrens, B. and Albl-Mikasa, M. ed. *Dolmetschqualität in Praxis, Lehre und Forschung: Festschrift für Sylvia Kalina*. Tübingen: Narr Verlag, pp. 59–92.

Batterink, L., and Neville, H. 2013. Implicit and Explicit Second Language Training Recruit Common Neural Mechanisms for Syntactic Processing. *Journal of Cognitive Neuroscience* 25(6), pp. 936–951.

Berges-Puyó, J. G. 2018 The Impact of Implicit/Explicit Instruction on the Learning Process of L2 Knowledge in Spanish. *Epos* 33, p. 185.

Brill, K. 2012. How Declarative and Procedural Memory Interact with Language Training Conditions. Master's thesis, University of Illinois.

Brod, G., Werkle-Bergner, M., and Shing, Y. L. 2013. The Influence of Prior Knowledge on Memory: A Developmental Cognitive Neuroscience Perspective. *Frontiers in Behavioral Neuroscience* 7, Article 139, pp. 1–13.

Carpenter, H. S. 2008. A Behavioral and Electrophysiological Investigation of Different Aptitudes for L2 Grammar in Learners Equated for Proficiency Level. Ph.D. thesis, Georgetown University.

Chen, G. 2005. Exploration on Student-Centered Interpretation Teaching Aided by Multimedia Methods. *Computer-assisted Foreign Language Education* 104, pp. 33–36.

Chernick, M. R. 2008. *Bootstrap Methods: A Guide for Practitioners and Researchers*, 2nd ed. Hoboken, NJ: Wiley.

Chernov, G. V. 2004. *Inference and Anticipation in Simultaneous Interpreting: A Probability-Prediction Model*. Amsterdam, PA: J. Benjamins Pub. Co.

DeKeyser, R. M. 1995. Learning Second Language Grammar Rules: An Experiment with a Miniature Linguistic System. *Studies in Second Language Acquisition* 17(3), pp. 379–410.

Deroost, N., and Soetens, E. 2006. Spatial Processing and Perceptual Sequence Learning in SRT Tasks. *Experimental Psychology* 53(1), pp. 16–30.

Diriker, E. 2013. Simultaneous and Consecutive Interpreting in Conference Situations (Conference Interpreting). In: Millán, C. and Bartrina, F. ed. *The Routledge Handbook of Translation Studies*. Milton Park Abingdon, New York: Routledge, pp. 363–376.

Ellis, N. C. 2005. At the Interface: Dynamic Interactions of Explicit and Implicit Language Knowledge. *Studies in Second Language Acquisition* 27(02), p. 177.

Ellis, R. 2006. Modelling Learning Difficulty and Second Language Proficiency: The Differential Contributions of Implicit and Explicit Knowledge. *Applied Linguistics* 27(3), pp. 431–463.

Ellis, R. 2008. A Typology of Written Corrective Feedback Types. *ELT Journal* 63(2), pp. 97–107.

Ellis, R. 2009. Implicit and Explicit Learning, Knowledge and Instruction. In: Ellis, R. ed. *Implicit and Explicit Knowledge in Second Language Learning, Testing and Teaching*. Bristol: Multilingual Matters, pp. 3–26.

Farkas, B. C., Krajcsi, A., Janacsek, K., and Nemeth, D. 2022. The Complexity of Measuring Reliability in Learning Tasks: An Illustration Using the Alternating Serial Reaction Time Task. *Behavior Research Methods* 55(1), pp. 1–17.

Foerde, K., Knowlton, B. J., and Poldrack, R. A. 2006. Modulation of Competing Memory Systems by Distraction. *PNAS* 103(31), pp. 11778–11783.

Frost, J. 2018. Introduction to Bootstrapping in Statistics with an Example. [Online]. [Accessed 25 April 2024]. Available from: https://statisticsbyjim.com/hypothesis-testing/bootstrapping/

Fu, S., Luo, Y., and Yang, J. 傅顺, 罗永驻, 杨劲松. 2017. Duo mo tai kou yi jiao xue: ji yu jian gou zhu yi de shi zheng yan jiu 多模态口译教学：基于建构主义的实证研究. *Journal of Higher Education* 17, pp. 101–103.

Gashti, Y. B. 2018. Explicit Feedback in Computer Assisted Reading Comprehension vs. Classroom Feedback. *European Journal of English Language Teaching* 4(1), pp. 35–60.

Gillies, A. 2009. Using Language Teaching Methods to Train Interpreters. In: Pellatt, V. and Minelli, E. ed. *Proceedings of the Bath Symposium*. Newcastle-upon-Tyne: Cambridge Scholars Publishing, pp. 118–130.

González-Davies, M., and Enríquez-Raído, V. 2016. Situated Learning in Translator and Interpreter Training: Bridging Research and Good Practice. *The Interpreter and Translator Trainer* 10(1), pp. 1–11.

Granena, G., and Yilmaz, Y. 2019. Corrective Feedback and the Role of Implicit Sequence-Learning Ability in L2 Online Performance. *Language Learning* 69, pp. 127–156.

Hale, S., and Napier, J. 2013. *Research Methods in Interpreting: A Practical Resource. Research Methods in Linguistics*. New York: Bloomsbury.

Hall, P. 1997. *The Bootstrap and Edgeworth Expansion*, 2nd ed. New York, Heidelberg: Springer.

Hammersley, M. 1990. *Reading Ethnographic Research: A Critical Guide*. London: Longman.

Han, C. 2022. Interpreting Testing and Assessment: A State-Of-The-Art Review. *Language Testing*, 39(1), pp. 30–55.

Housen, A., and Pierrard, M. 2005. *Investigating Instructed Second Language Acquisition.* In: *Investigations in Instructed Second Language Acquisition: Investigations in Instructed Second Language Acquisition.* Berlin, NY: Mouton de Gruyter, pp. 1–30.

Howard, J. H., and Howard, D. V. 1997. Age Differences in Implicit Learning of Higher Order Dependencies in Serial Patterns. *Psychology and Aging* 12(4), pp. 634–656.

Kain, D. J. 2003. Teacher-Centered versus Student-Centered: Balancing Constraint and Theory in the Composition Classroom. *Pedagogy* 3(1), pp. 104–108.

Kaufman, S. B., DeYoung, C. G., Gray, J. R., Jiménez, L., Brown, J., and Mackintosh, N. 2010. Implicit Learning as an Ability. *Cognition* 116(3), pp. 321–340.

Khamesipour, M. 2015. The Effects of Explicit and Implicit Instruction of Vocabulary through Reading on EFL Learners' Vocabulary Development. *Theory and Practice in Language Studies* 5(8), pp. 1620–1627.

Kim, M. 2013. Research on Translator and Interpreter Education. In: Millán, C. and Bartrina, F. ed. *The Routledge Handbook of Translation Studies.* Milton Park Abingdon, NY: Routledge, pp. 102–116.

Kiraly, D. C. 2000. *A Social Constructivist Approach to Translator Education: Empowerment from Theory to Practice.* Manchester, Northampton, MA: St. Jerome Publishing.

Laerd Statistics. 2017a. *One-way ANCOVA in SPSS Statistics.* [Online]. [Accessed 25 April 2024]. Available from: https://statistics.laerd.com/

Laerd Statistics. 2017b. *Pearson's Partial Correlation in SPSS Statistics.* [Online]. [Accessed 25 April 2024]. Available from: https://statistics.laerd.com/

Li, S. 2022. Explicit and Implicit Language Aptitudes. In: Li, S., Hiver, P., and Papi, M. ed. *The Routledge Handbook of Second Language Acquisition and Individual Differences.* London: Routledge, pp. 37–53.

Lum, J. A. G., and Conti-Ramsden, G. 2013. Long-Term Memory: A Review and Meta-Analysis of Studies of Declarative and Procedural Memory in Specific Language Impairment. *Topics in Language Disorders* 33(4), pp. 282–297.

Morgan-Short, K., Hamrick, P., and Ullman, M. T. 2022. Declarative and Procedural Memory as Predictors of Second Language Development. In: Li, S., Hiver, P., and Papi, M. ed. *The Routledge Handbook of Second Language Acquisition and Individual Differences.* London: Routledge, pp. 67–81.

Morgan-Short, K., Steinhauer, K., Sanz, C., and Ullman, M. T. 2012. Explicit and Implicit Second Language Training Differentially Affect the Achievement of Native-like Brain Activation Patterns. *Journal of Cognitive Neuroscience* 24(4), pp. 933–947.

Moser-Mercer, B. 2008. Skill Acquisition in Interpreting: A Human Performance Perspective. *The Interpreter and Translator Trainer* 2(1), pp. 1–28.

Motta, M. 2016. A Blended Learning Environment Based on the Principles of Deliberate Practice for the Acquisition of Interpreting Skills. *The Interpreter and Translator Trainer* 10(1), pp. 133–149.

Negro, I., and Chanquoy, L. 2005. Explicit and Implicit Training of Subject–Verb Agreement Processing in 3rd and 5th Grades. *L1-Educational Studies in Language and Literature* 5(2), pp. 193–214.

Norris, J. M., and Ortega, L. 2000. Effectiveness of L2 Instruction: A Research Synthesis and Quantitative Meta-Analysis. *Language Learning* 50(3), pp. 417–528.

Ouyang, Q. 2018. Assessing Meaning-Dimension Quality in Consecutive Interpreting Training. *Perspectives* 26(2), pp. 196–213.

Pöchhacker, F. 2016. *Introducing Interpreting Studies*. London, New York: Routledge.

Poldrack, R. A., and Packard, M. G. 2003. Competition Among Multiple Memory Systems: Converging Evidence from Animal and Human Brain Studies. *Neuropsychologia* 41(3), pp. 245–251.

Reber, A. S. 1993. *Implicit Learning and Tacit Knowledge: An Essay on the Cognitive Unconscious*. New York, Oxford: Oxford University Press, Clarendon Press.

Russell, D., and Takeda, K. 2015. Consecutive Interpreting. In: Mikkelson, H., and Jourdenais, R. ed. *The Routledge Handbook of Interpreting*. London: Routledge, pp. 96–111.

Russell, D. 2002. Reconstructing Our Views: Are We Integrating Consecutive Interpreting into Our Teaching and Practice? In: Swabey, L. A. ed. *New Designs in Interpreter Education: Proceedings of the 14th National Convention, 9–12 October 2002, Minneapolis/St. Paul, Minnesota*. [Online]. California: Conference of Interpreter Trainers, pp. 5–16. [Accessed 15 September 2023]. Available from: https://islandora.wrlc.org/islandora/object/cit%3A5

Sanz, C., and Morgan-Short, K. 2005. Explicitness in Pedagogical Interventions: Input, Practice, and Feedback. In: Sanz, C. ed. *Mind and Context in Adult Second Language Acquisition: Methods, Theory, and Practice*. Washington, DC: Georgetown University Press, pp. 234–264.

Serin, H. 2018. A Comparison of Teacher-Centered and Student-Centered Approaches in Educational Settings. *International Journal of Social Sciences & Educational Studies* 5(1), pp. 164–167.

Setton, R., and Dawrant, A. 2016. *Conference Interpreting – A Complete Course*. Amsterdam: John Benjamins Publishing Company.

Shamiri, H., and Farvardin, M. T. 2016. The Effect of Implicit versus Explicit Corrective Feedback on Intermediate EFL Learners' Speaking Self-efficacy Beliefs. *Theory and Practice in Language Studies* 6(5), pp. 1066–1075.

Shing, Y. L., and Brod, G. 2016. Effects of Prior Knowledge on Memory: Implications for Education. *Mind, Brain, and Education* 10(3), pp. 153–161.

Spiro, R. J., Coulson, R., Feltovich, P., and Anderson, D. 2013. Cognitive Flexibility Theory: Advanced Knowledge Acquisition in Ill-Structured Domains. In: Unrau, N. ed. *Theoretical Models and Processes of Reading*, 6th ed. Newark, Delaware: International Reading Association, pp. 544–557.

Spiro, R. J., Vispoel, W. P., Schmitz, J. G., Samarapungavan, A., and Boerger, A. E. 1987. *Knowledge Acquisition for Application: Cognitive Flexibility and Transfer in Complex Content Domains*. Champaign: University of Illinois Urbana-Champaign.

Sun, X. 2010. The Relation Between Linguistic Competence and Interpreting Competence During Information Processing in Consecutive Interpreting. Ph.D. thesis. Shanghai International Studies University.

Tagarelli, K. M., Ruiz, S., Vega, J. L. M., and Rebuschat, P. 2016. Variability in Second Language Learning. *Studies in Second Language Acquisition* 38(2), pp. 293–316.

Tao, Y. 2012. Towards a Constructive Model in Training Professional Translators: A Case Study of MTI Education Program in China. *Babel* 58(3), pp. 289–308.

Tikhonova, E. V., Gural, S. K., and Tereshkova, N. S. 2015. Consecutive Interpreting Training in Groups of Foreign Students by Means of LCT and ICT Technologies. *Procedia – Social and Behavioral Sciences* 215, pp. 243–249.

Umanath, S., and Marsh, E. J. 2014. Understanding How Prior Knowledge Influences Memory in Older Adults. *Perspectives on Psychological Science: A Journal of the Association for Psychological Science* 9(4), pp. 408–426.

Wang, Y. H. 2024. Tailoring Learning Conditions for Students with Different Procedural Learning Abilities to Improve Their Acquisition of 'Consecutive Interpreting Knowledge' with a Cognitive Model for Information Processing. Ph.D. thesis, Swansea University.

Wu, S. 2011. Application of Social Constructivist Model to the Interpretation Teaching. *Journal of Changchun Normal University (Humanities and Social Sciences)* 30(6), pp. 182–184.

Xu, H. 2010. An Empirical Study of the Skill-focused Approach to Undergraduate Interpretation Teaching for English Majors. Ph.D. thesis, Shanghai International Studies University.

Zhao, Y., and Ellis, R. 2020. The Relative Effects of Implicit and Explicit Corrective Feedback on the Acquisition of 3rd Person's By Chinese University Students: A Classroom-Based Study. *Language Teaching Research* 42(1), pp. 1–21.

PART II
Interpreting Training and the Profession

5
AN EXPERIMENTAL STUDY ON INTERPRETERS' EXPERIENCE OF RSI

Implications for Post-Pandemic Research and Practice

Clarissa Guarini

Introduction

The data reported in the present chapter was collected during an experimental study carried out using remote simultaneous interpreting (RSI). RSI will be addressed to highlight its benefits for research, implications for post-pandemic practice, as well as to stress the need to include it in interpreters' education.

As will be recalled in "Remote Simultaneous Interpreting (RSI): Development, Challenges, and Advantages", RSI was previously analysed by scholars to enlighten its challenges, its advantages, and how to further develop technologies and settings. The contribution of the present study in this regard is twofold: on one hand, the participants were asked to share their perspective on RSI. On the other hand, RSI was used as a research tool (the focus was anticipation in simultaneous interpreting), hence revealing how it can be useful not only in practice but in research as well. Individual sessions were scheduled with professional interpreters, during which they were tasked with the simultaneous interpretation of two 15-minutes speeches from German into English. After their performance, a structured discussion was carried out with the participants, using pre-determined questions. While most of the questions revolved around anticipation and strategies, one question was aimed at assessing their attitudes towards RSI: "do you particularly like or feel comfortable with RSI? Why/why not?". The question was purposely vague so that participants could reflect on their position towards RSI without being limited in their answer.

Before scheduling the sessions, a pilot study had been carried out with one student to test the methodology. Their feedback was valuable specifically to highlight the need to include RSI in training.

DOI: 10.4324/9781003440994-7

To avoid any confusion, it is worth noting that the term RSI will be mainly used to refer to an interpretation carried out from home as opposed to an interpreting hub with a hard console.

RSI: Development, Challenges, and Advantages

As defined by Braun (2015), the term *remote interpreting* refers to the use of communication technologies that have access to an interpreter located elsewhere. The interpreter could be in another room, building, or country, hence, the communication relies on information and communication technologies. This initial definition reveals an advantage of RSI: it allows one to have multilingual events with participants based anywhere. This in turn enables the organisation of more far-reaching events.

The systematic use of remote interpreting began in the 1970s in public service settings to ease access to public services, while reducing the cost of language support. The first audio-mediated interpreting service was established in the Australian immigration service in 1973 (Braun, 2019), and was later adopted in the 1980s and 1990s in the US and Europe, particularly in healthcare (Mikkelson, 2003 as cited in Braun, 2019). The first experiments with video-mediated interpreting in conference settings also date to the 1970s, when supra-national institutions were interested in ways to meet the language demands while mitigating the difficulties of having interpreters on-site (Braun, 2019).

For many years, this mode of interpreting was mainly used in healthcare and the judicial sector (Fantinuoli, 2018). However, the increased use of technology resulted in a greater use of remote interpreting, already pre-pandemic. Fantinuoli (2018) addressed technology in interpreting and stressed that we were on the edge of a 'technological turn'. The author mentioned how the rising demand for remote liaison and consecutive interpreters was already leading to the adoption of this mode of interpreting by many institutions and hypothesised (in fact, predicted) that this would soon apply to simultaneous interpreting. Moreover, the author identified three main drives that would explain the increased interest in (and use of) technology in interpretation. The first one is the anthropological drive, which refers to the reality that automation and human evolution run parallel to each other. This is followed by an economic drive based on the paradigms of productivity, optimisation, and cost reduction, which are the main reasons to incorporate or create new technologies. Finally, the psychological drive: we live in times when the adoption of technology in our private and professional lives is ever-increasing and this creates a psychological group pressure to use technology whenever there is the opportunity (Fantinuoli and Dastyar, 2022).

The adoption of technology saw an unprecedented rise during COVID-19. During the pandemic, several restrictions were introduced, prominent among them was social distancing with the consequent cancellation or shift to the online mode for all events, hence the need to rely on technology (Saina, 2021). In this scenario, RSI allowed multilingual events to be carried out remotely. Even post-pandemic, RSI allows us to be even more interconnected, as the use of a simultaneous interpreting delivery platform (SIDP) (ISO, 2022) can organise an event with participants from all over the world, who do not need to travel to the event location.

The increased use of RSI during COVID-19 revealed both its advantages and its challenges. First, in terms of input, to comply with technical standards the RSI equipment must ensure a high quality of sound and video and perfect synchronisation (Causo, 2011). During COVID-19, the difficulty of having high-quality video and audio was exacerbated by face masks (though this issue is clearly not attributed to the technology used). It would often happen that one speaker was in the same room with other colleagues, and had to respect the social distancing rules and wear a face mask. It is rather intuitive that face coverings make the sound less clear even in person, and working remotely only exacerbated this aspect. Although the requirement of wearing face masks and social distancing is no longer in place at the time of writing, it still shows how some aspects that make the input audio indistinct at an in-person event are amplified when working remotely. For this reason, it is necessary to pay appropriate attention to the quality of the audio and video input in order to ensure appropriate work conditions for interpreters.

As for the visual input, during an online meeting it is more difficult to rely on non-verbal cues, (Ziegler and Gigliobianco, 2018), hence (a high-quality) visual input is of primary importance (Seeber et al., 2019). This challenge however could be transformed into an advantage, as a zoomed-in view of the speaker allows interpreters to have a clear visual input, even clearer than it would be when working in-person in some cases. Ziegler and Gigliobianco (2018) have reported some possible solutions to use technology to compensate for the lack of a direct view of the speaker, for instance, using a camera remotely controlled by the interpreter to manage the visual input. This would eliminate the unpleasant feeling of not being in control and having to depend on camera operators, which was mentioned as a downside by interpreters in previous literature (Roziner and Schlesinger, 2010). A disadvantage sometimes reported by interpreters is the feeling of not really being 'there' and a feeling of alienation or isolation (Moser-Mercer, 2003). However, while still not being in the same room, using SIDPs interpreters could at least communicate with their 'boothmate' via chat.

As mentioned, the term 'remote interpreting' englobes all the situations where the interpreter, the speaker, and/or the audience are not in the same place. However, the place the interpreter is working from is a detail not to be overlooked. In fact, interpreters sometimes work from an interpreting hub (Saina, 2021) where they have a traditional interpreting booth and a hard console (Moser-Mercer, 2003). In other cases, and this was especially true during the pandemic, professionals work from home using SIDPs and rely on their own equipment. The above-mentioned difficulties related to the audio input are amplified when interpreters find themselves in non-professional working conditions, such as working from a place that is not soundproof, or relying on an unstable internet connection. Of course, a professional interpreter would ensure that their working environment, even if it is their home, is equipped to deliver a high-quality service. Nonetheless, during the pandemic, everyone was expected to shift to working from home quickly, even when the working conditions were not ideal. In fact, some of the interpreters who took part in the present study refused assignments because they did not have access to interpreting hubs and their home did not offer a professional working environment.

This emergency aspect revealed the need to include RSI in interpreters' education. Simultaneous interpreting is a cognitively taxing activity that runs on a very delicate balance of concurrent efforts (Gile, 2009). Interpreters constantly monitor their performance to ensure that their processing capacity is not overpowered by the task requirements. This shows how anything can threaten this delicate balance, especially having to cope with a new mode of delivery. In fact, what has become clear from the present study carried out during the pandemic, as well as from other research on this topic (Saina, 2021; Wang and Li, 2022), is that interpreters need to get accustomed to working remotely. This does not only entail knowing how to use Zoom or other platforms, but also being aware that the task might become more difficult when working remotely. Fatigue can arise sooner compared to in-person meetings as shown by Moser-Mercer (2003). The author carried out a study where interpreters were working remotely with hard consoles and traditional equipment. To this end, the present paper will provide a proposal to include RSI in interpreters' education, to give students the knowledge (and the awareness) necessary to accept remote assignments in the future. The inclusion of RSI in education will allow future interpreters to feel comfortable with this type of interpretation in their professional lives, as it is clear that RSI will continue to be used post-pandemic (Buján and Collard, 2022).

RSI for Research Purposes: How It was Used in the Present Study

There is no doubt that RSI can have some limitations, and that the fear of some interpreters to experience a worsening of their working conditions (e.g. lower remuneration) is legitimate (Fantinuoli, 2018). However, there is also no doubt that RSI is an extremely valuable tool under different aspects, and since it has achieved a central role during COVID-19, we should continue developing the technologies available and improving the working conditions for interpreters.

The main advantage offered by RSI for the present research was the possibility to have an experimental set-up and carry out an empirical investigation remotely with interpreters based elsewhere, which in general allows to increase the cohort of participants as they do not need to travel to the research location. RSI was the tool that made the present research possible.

The main goal of the investigation was to assess what strategies are used by simultaneous interpreters when working from German into English, particularly, when tackling syntactic features that are specific to the German language. The initial design (pre-pandemic) included individual in-person sessions with professional interpreters who had English as their A language and German as either A or B language. However, the methods and materials of the research were refined during the pandemic and the data collection took place in the final months of COVID-19. This is when RSI became an asset, as it allowed us to replicate real-life working conditions and to carry out the experiment online. RSI transcends geographical boundaries (Bryda and Costa, 2023), and this is an asset both in research and in practice. An added benefit of using RSI was that experiment set-ups can sometimes become too artificial, far from the real working conditions. Instead, organising an experiment online, especially at a time when interpreters could only work remotely, increased the ecological validity (Baekelandt and Defrancq, 2021) of the investigation, that is, its ability to reflect real-world conditions.

The use of RSI as a research tool was a new and original data collection method. For this reason, although the main focus of the investigation were strategies when interpreting simultaneously from German into English, attention was also paid to RSI both in itself and as a research tool.

Methodology

The data collection was carried out in two ways. RSI was used during individual sessions where participants were working from home and were asked to interpret two speeches from German to English simultaneously. After their performance, a structured survey with pre-determined questions was verbally conducted for them during which they were asked about their comfort level with RSI and to provide the reasons for their answer.

The platform chosen was Zoom. Although this platform was not originally designed for interpreting purposes (Chmiel and Spinolo, 2022), it was found to be widely used for interpreting during the pandemic (Frittella, 2021; Przepiórkowska, 2021; Buján and Collard, 2022). Moreover, on Zoom it is possible to hear the original speech in the background while listening to the interpretation, and this feature allowed (during the data analysis) an exact alignment of the source and target language speeches.

The source speeches were two political speeches that had been previously recorded by native speakers. One possible issue of this experiment design was the lack of visual input, which is not ideal when working remotely. However, since speech rate was one of the controlled variables to be analysed (alongside redundancy), it was necessary to manipulate the input tracks (using Audacity v. 2.4.2), and the manipulation of a video might have resulted in a less smooth source speech compared to a manipulated audio. All the participants were previously informed that the visual input would not be available. What helped in the set-up was a good audio quality that could compensate for the lack of video, as confirmed by the participants.

Finally, before carrying out the sessions with participants, a pilot study was organised with one student which mirrored the exact conditions of the sessions with professionals, in order to test the data collection and analysis methodology.

Participants

Nine professional interpreters were recruited from the websites of various professional associations, such as the International Association of Conference Interpreters The only requirement was for them to have English as A language and German as A or B language. It was necessary to include only professionals because the goal was to analyse their strategies, and the use of strategies develops over time because during the initial stages of learning more conscious control and selection are required (Moser-Mercer, 2010). The least experienced interpreter had five years of experience and the most experienced one was 43 years, with an average of 17,5 years (median = 10 years).

They took part in the experiment at the beginning of 2022; hence they had already worked pre-pandemic at in-person events but had shifted to working remotely after the outbreak of COVID-19.

Ethical approval was granted by the Faculty Research Ethics Committee at the University of Leeds (both for the pilot study and the sessions with professionals). All participants were provided with an information sheet and they signed a consent form. The documents clearly stated that they could withdraw from the study at any time without having to provide the reason why they chose to withdraw. They were aware of how the sessions were set up and that their performance would be audio-recorded.

Participants' Perspectives on RSI

Following their performance, participants were asked about their perspectives on RSI. Some of them had already clarified that they did not like working from home, either because they did not have a quiet space to work from, or because they found it stressful to cope with the technical side of the assignment, as opposed to working from interpreting hubs, where tech support would normally be available.

The perils of an unstable internet connection were also mentioned by one of the participants. They reported that, when working remotely, they request their clients to have a wired connection. Though it cannot always be possible, wired connections are traditionally more stable than wireless ones, and having the reassurance that their clients are using a wired connection allows the interpreter to focus on the assignment without worrying about possible internet-related glitches.

Another aspect mentioned by the participants, which has already been addressed in previous research, is remuneration. In fact, Fantinuoli (2019) underlined how one of the aspects that seem to preoccupy interpreters in relation to working remotely is a worsening of the interpreter's status, in this case, their salary. One of the participants in the current study openly stated "if the pay is not bad, I don't mind interpreting remotely". This aspect was raised because sometimes when working remotely the pay rates are lower compared to in-person assignments, though working remotely is as taxing as an in-person assignment. Moreover, though the increase in stress levels was not highly significant, professionals working remotely have been shown to feel on-site fatigue sooner compared to when working in person (Moser-Mercer, 2003).

All these issues, that is, having to attend to technical difficulties, issues with an internet connection, and the stress that derives from this are some of the factors that make some interpreters not entirely comfortable with remote interpreting. However, current literature on RSI as well as the feedback received in the present investigation can be used to improve RSI for future practice.

Implications for Post-Pandemic Practice

One aspect consistently mentioned by the participants in the study is the sound quality, and how it affects performance when working remotely. Sound has already been mentioned in the previous literature as one of the factors that can dramatically influence an RSI assignment (Fantinuoli, 2018). What was clear from the pandemic was that often clients are not aware of this. In fact, Buján and Collard (2022) carried out survey research on interpreters' perspectives of RSI during the pandemic, which revealed that active speakers do not always use an external microphone. This may result in a far worse audio quality.

Some of the participants in the current study were also aware of and worried about having to manage the technological aspects of working remotely when using SIDPs since they were working from home. This particular downside could be addressed by introducing training on RSI, especially on SIDPs, in interpreters' education as well as by providing remote IT support even when working from home and not just from interpreting hubs.

Clients need to be made aware of what the optimal conditions are when working remotely, and these can be summarised as follows based on the feedback received from participants in the present study:

- Adequate remuneration;
- High-quality input which involves audio and video. All the participants stressed the importance of having high-quality input when working remotely;
- Ideally, IT support not only in interpreting hubs, but also when interpreters work from home using SIDPs. Although clients normally organise meetings ahead of the event to test the set-up, it would be useful to have (remote) IT support available to interpreters throughout their assignment;
- A stable internet connection (both for interpreters and for clients, preferably a wired connection).

It is essential to shape RSI in order for it to be less challenging for interpreters, as it is a tool that has an unquestionable value and that will continue to be used post-pandemic, and we should strive to use it to its full potential.

RSI in Training Programs

Previous researchers (Braun, 2015; Fantinuoli and Prandi, 2018) advocated that training interpreters on remote interpreting is crucial. When educating future interpreters, technological competence needs to be developed so that students are prepared for their future careers (Wang and Li, 2022). Interpreters seem to share this desire to address RSI in training. In a survey carried out by Wang and Li (2022), 84.08% of interpreters agreed or strongly agreed that interpreting technology courses should be included in training. In order to avoid having to resort to external or private courses in interpreting technologies, the respondents suggested that such courses should be included in the curricula of higher education institutions.

Before detailing why RSI needs to be included in training programs, a clarification is due. In most cases, student interpreters already interpret remotely during their classes, as they are often asked to interpret a speech in the form of a video, where the speaker is not physically present. However, when referring to RSI in training in this case, what is meant is interpreting remotely from home using online interpreting platforms, hence simulating real-life RSI assignments, as it has been suggested that education and training should mirror professional practice (Fantinuoli and Prandi, 2018).

Familiarising with RSI

Interpreters feel more confident when they have had previous experiences with RSI during training. Before carrying out the core experiment for the present research, a pilot study was organised with an interpreting student. The objective of the pilot study was to test the methodology, specifically the session set-up and data collection, therefore, having a student as a participant would not have had a negative influence on the outcome. The pilot study was carried out in 2021 and the student had already shifted to remote teaching due to COVID-19 restrictions. When asked whether they felt comfortable with remote interpreting, they confirmed that they did not find RSI challenging at all as they were used to it and felt confident using it.

Aside from feedback from this student, the reasons behind their perspective on RSI can be found in the previous research on interpreters' training. In terms of training, Moser-Mercer (2010) clarified how brain plasticity plays an essential role in learning processes. When students learn something new, their brains create new pathways to acquire and keep that information, and novice interpreters rely largely on consciously controlled processing. This entails that exposure to remote interpreting during their learning phase enables a considerable degree of adaptation to that particular scenario thanks to the plasticity of their brain. Willss (1978) also underlined how only what can be systematised is truly learnt, hence novice interpreters cannot be expected to learn how to cope with RSI on their own during their first remote assignment. In relation to RSI specifically, Moser-Mercer (2005) argued that experienced interpreters may find it more difficult to adapt to remote interpreting because they rely on automated processes whereas novice interpreters, especially when they are subject to this new method during their training, have a greater potential for adaptation. Finally, Saina (2021) discussed how the participants in his investigation expressed the need to have classes on RSI to become familiar with systems and set-ups.

Therefore, both previous research and the experience of the COVID-19 pandemic, highlighted the need to include RSI in training programs to allow future interpreters to be exposed to this different type of interpreting during their education.

Stress Management and Feedback

Another reason that makes RSI training necessary is stress management. Simultaneous interpreting is widely known to be a cognitively taxing activity (Setton, 1999; Seeber and Kerzel, 2011), and previous research reported a perception of higher on-site fatigue and stress compared to working in-person (Moser-Mercer, 2005; Roziner and Schlesinger, 2010). This stress might be amplified for novice interpreters, as they are facing these difficulties for the first time. The inclusion of RSI in training programs can provide students with the opportunity to interface with this new type of interpreting and tackle RSI-related stress in a protected environment.

In fact, it should not be underestimated that Universities, or training programs in general, are 'test benches'. While making mistakes or not being able to manage stress during a professional performance bear serious consequences, when these issues arise in training they become optimal learning opportunities. In this regard, it would be useful for students to interpret remotely from home, because interpreters do not always have access to an interpreting hub. During training, having their tutor as an 'audience' allows the student to receive valuable feedback on their performance, including how appropriate is the sound quality at their place of work, their home equipment, their internet connection, etc. This may all seem self-explanatory and even basilar to a professional interpreter, but it might not be for students.

Empowerment

One can conclude from the pandemic that it is necessary to spend more care and effort to design optimal working conditions for interpreters working remotely so that the remote element does not become a further source of stress for them. However, when defining the details of an RSI assignment, interpreters need to be aware of what the optimal conditions are. Including RSI in training programs is not only a chance for the trainer to provide feedback to students and to teach them how to interface with working remotely, but also for students to understand what *their* optimal working conditions should be. For instance, some interpreters do not rely greatly on visual input because they close their eyes when interpreting, as was the case for some of the participants in the present study, hence not having a visual input would not be an issue for them. Knowing what working remotely entails, and more specifically being aware of what details are important to make the assignment less daunting for them, helps students feel empowered and more aware when starting their careers.

Moreover, knowing that interpreters often lament over a higher level of perceived stress and fatigue when working remotely (Moser-Mercer, 2003) would allow students (i.e. future interpreters) to request shorter turns, as it has been proven (Moser-Mercer, 2003) that there is a worsening of the quality of interpreting after 15 to 18 minutes of working remotely. Instead, when working in person, errors tend to increase past the 30-minute mark on average (Moser-Mercer et al., 1998).

Training Ideas

The inclusion of RSI in training programs should entail theoretical and practical approaches. In this regard, a training module on RSI can be moulded starting from the pattern identified by Anderson (1995, cited in Moser-Mercer, 2008) and elaborated by Moser-Mercer (2008). This pattern includes three main stages:

1 Cognitive stage: a learner acquires the basic information about the task.
2 The associative stage: during which a learner engages in trial-and-error learning.
3 Autonomous stage: a learner engages in further practice to fine-tune strategies, automate responses etc.

The cognitive stage would be the theoretical part of the training, during which students are provided with theoretical information on RSI. It is essential to have a first approach and (theoretical) knowledge of this kind of interpreting before tackling it in practice. As part of the theoretical overview on RSI, it would be useful to help students familiarise themselves with the different ways of working remotely mentioning that it could be carried out from an interpreting hub using a hard console or SIDPs. The latter would need to be explained further to help students understand what SIDPs are, which ones are available, and how they are operated. During the theoretical explanation of RSI, it would be useful to address previous research on the topic so that students have an overview of how RSI has been analysed thus far so they understand that it is a viable tool to use.

The associative stage, also defined by the author as 'trial-and-error learning', is the practical phase when students can use SIDPs from their homes. In this phase, after being shown how the different platforms work, tutors can organise some classes from home so that the students are able to use the SDIPs on their own. This would also allow them to become more aware of whether the environment they have at home would be appropriate to accept remote interpreting assignments. During this phase, it would be beneficial to provide students with input speeches both with and without visual input, in order for them to be prepared to work with both.

While the theoretical aspects of RSI can be addressed in one class, the trial-and-error learning could be divided into two classes, so that students have time to become familiarised with RSI without feeling overwhelmed.

The associative stage in training has to lead to the autonomous stage. After some practice with RSI, students can approach RSI with more awareness, hence being able to fine-tune their approach and find ways that make them more comfortable with this type of interpreting.

The training on RSI can be divided into three classes (at least) for the tutor to be able to address the basic aspects of RSI and for the students to have a basic knowledge of it. As with any other interpreting practice, the work done in class with the tutor should be followed by further autonomous practice.

Engaging students in actual RSI from home differs from working in a class, as in a class they would be able to either interpret their tutor who is in their presence or interpret a video using a professional booth and hard console. Instead, working from home they would have to rely on their own equipment. Moreover, while at the basis of RSI there is still a form of interpreting, both the working conditions and the input speech are inevitably different when working remotely. The audio and video signal quality can vary in input and output; therefore, they have to be addressed during training. Finally, the training specific to RSI should be inserted in training programs after students become comfortable with simultaneous interpreting, otherwise it might become overwhelming to learn simultaneous interpreting and, at the same time, how to master the technological and remote aspects of RSI.

This training idea is proposed specifically as part of a training course on simultaneous interpreting, but the same structure could be applied to training on consecutive or dialogue interpreting.

Conclusion

Based on what has been discussed so far (both in the present investigation and previous research on the topic), RSI can be a great asset and seems to be here to stay. However, it can only truly be an asset if we use its full potential, while being aware of its challenges.

The pandemic caused an unprecedented increase in the use of RSI, and since the shift to use RSI exclusively was so abrupt, it also highlighted its downsides. Based on the experience of using RSI during COVID-19, it is necessary not only to adjust the remote work environment for future professionals, but also to include RSI in training programs. Although the technique at the basis of RSI is still simultaneous interpreting, which is already taught to students, all the features that are added when working remotely (i.e. different types of input, internet connection, having to operate a SIDP, etc.) need to be addressed during training so that future interpreters are aware and can feel empowered. Fantinuoli was already addressing this technological turn before the pandemic, in 2018, and in this post-pandemic world, it is even more urgent to learn from our past experiences and draw on them to design adequate working conditions for professionals as well as training programs for students, so that everyone can continue with this profession in a fast-changing landscape. Finally, RSI seems to be a valuable asset not only in practice, but also in research, as it allows to organise (simultaneous) interpreting sessions remotely which increases the number of participants and maintains a high ecological validity.

References

Anderson, J.R. 1995. *Cognitive Psychology and Its Implications*, New York: W.H. Feeman, 4th edition.

Baekelandt, A., Defrancq, B. 2021. Elicitation of particular grammatical structures in speeches for interpreting research: Enhancing ecological validity of experimental research in interpreting. *Perspectives*, 29(4), 643–660. [Online] [Accessed 10/11/2023] Available from: https://doi.org/10.1080/0907676X.2020.1849322

Braun, S. 2015. Remote interpreting. In: Holly Mikkelson, Renée Jourdenais (eds.) *Routledge Handbook of Interpreting*. New York: Routledge, pp.352–367.

Braun, S. 2019. Technology and interpreting. In M. O'Hagan (ed.), *The Routledge Handbook of Translation and Technology*. New York: Routledge, pp. 271–288.

Bryda, G., Costa, A.P. 2023. Qualitative research in digital era: Innovations, methodologies and collaborations. *Social Sciences* 2023, 12(10), 570. [Online] [Accessed on 20/11/2023] Available from: https://doi.org/10.3390/socsci12100570

Buján, M., Collard, C. 2022. Remote simultaneous interpreting and COVID-19: Conference interpreters' perspective. *Translation and Interpreting in the Age of COVID-19*, 9, Springer Nature Singapore, pp. 133–150, 2022, Corpora and Intercultural Studies. [Online] [Accessed 10/01/2024] Available from: https://dx.doi.org/10.1007/978-981-19-6680-4_7

Causo, J.E. 2011. Conference interpreting with information and communication technologies. Experiences from the European Commission DG Interpretation. In: S. Braun, J. L. Taylor (eds.), *Videoconference and Remote Interpreting in Criminal Proceedings*. Guilford: University of Surrey, pp. 199–203.

Chmiel, A., Spinolo, N. 2022. Testing the impact of remote interpreting settings on interpreter experience and performance. Methodological challenges inside the virtual booth. *Translation, Cognition & Behavior*, 5(2), 250–274 (2022). [Online] [Accessed 08/01/2024] Available from: https://doi.org/10.1075/tcb.00068.chm

Fantinuoli, C. 2018. Interpreting and technology: The upcoming technological turn. In: C. Fantinuoli (ed.), *Interpreting and Technology*. Berlin: Language Science Press, pp. 1–12.

Fantinuoli, C. 2019. The technological turn in interpreting: The challenges that lie ahead. In: W. Baur, F. Mayer (eds.), *Proceedings of the Conference Übersetzen und Dolmetschen 4.0.—Neue Wege imdigitalen Zeitalter*. Bonn: BDÜ-Fachverlag, pp. 334–354.

Fantinuoli, C., Dastyar, V. 2022. Interpreting and the emerging augmented paradigm. *Interpreting and Society: An Interdisciplinary Journal*, 2(2), 185–194.

Fantinuoli, C., Prandi, B. 2018. Teaching information and communication technologies: A proposal for the interpreting classroom. *Journal of Translation and Technical Communication Research*, 11(2), (2018), 162–182.

Frittella, F.M. 2021. Computer-assisted conference interpreter training: Limitations and future directions. *Journal of Translation Studies*, 02, 103–142.

Gile, D. 2009. *Basic Concepts and Models for Interpreter and Translator Training*. Amsterdam & Philadelphia: John Benjamins.

ISO 24019. 2022. Simultaneous Interpreting Delivery Platforms. Requirements and Recommendations.

Mikkelson, H. 2003. Telephone Interpreting: Boon or bane? In L. Pérez González (ed.) *Speaking in tongues: language across contexts and users*. València: Universitat de València, 251–69.

Moser-Mercer, B. 2003. Remote interpreting: Assessment of human factors and performance parameters. *Joint Project International*. [Online] [Accessed on 12/09/2022] Available from: https://www.academia.edu/117177384/Remote_interpreting_Assessment_of_human_factors_and_performance_parameters

Moser-Mercer, B. 2005. Remote interpreting: issues of multi-sensory integration in a multilingual task. *Meta*, 50(2), 727–738.

Moser-Mercer, B. 2008. Skill acquisition in interpreting: A human performance perspective. *The Interpreter and Translator Trainer*, 2(1), 1–28.

Moser-Mercer, B. 2010. The search for neuro-physiological correlates of expertise in interpreting. In: E. Angelone, G. Shreve (eds.), Translation *and* Cognition. Amsterdam & Philadelphia: John Benjamins, pp. 263–287.

Moser-Mercer, B., Künzli, A., Korac M. 1998. Prolonged turns in interpreting: Effects on quality, physiological and psychological stress (Pilot study). *Interpreting*, 3(1), 47–64. [Online] [Accessed 04/01/2024] Available from: https://doi.org/10.1075/intp.3.1.03mos

Przepiórkowska, D. 2021. Adapt or Perish: How forced transition to remote simultaneous interpreting during the COVID-19 pandemic affected interpreters' professional practices. *Między Oryginałem a Przekładem*, 4(54), 137–159. [Online] [Accessed 20/10/ 2022]. Available from: https://journals.akademicka.pl/moap/article/view/3980

Roziner, I., Shlesinger, M. 2010. Much ado about something remote: Stress and performance in remote interpreting. *Interpreting*, 12(2), 214–247.

Saina, F. 2021. Remote interpreting: Platform testing in a university setting. *Proceedings of the Translation and Interpreting Technology Online Conference*, pp. 57–67, Held Online. INCOMA Ltd. [Online] [Accessed 12/11/2022]. Available from: https://acl-bg.org/proceedings/2021/TRITON%202021/pdf/2021.triton-1.7.pdf

Seeber, K.G., Keller, L., Amos, R., Hengl, S. 2019. Expectations vs. experience. *Attitudes towards video remote conference interpreting*. Interpreting, 21(2), 270–304. [Online] [Accessed 03/01/2024]. Available from: https://doi.org/10.1075/intp.00030.see

Seeber, K.G., Kerzel, D. 2011. Cognitive load in simultaneous interpreting: Model meets data. *International Journal of Bilingualism*, 16(2), 228 –242. [Online] [Accessed 16/08/2023] Available from: https://doi.org/10.1177/1367006911402982

Setton, R. 1999. *Simultaneous Interpretation. A Cognitive-Pragmatic Analysis*. Amsterdam & Philadelphia: John Benjamins.

Wang, H., Li, Z. 2022. Constructing a competence framework for interpreting technologies, and related educational insights: An empirical study. *The Interpreter and Translator Trainer*, 16(3), 367–390.

Wilss, W. 1978. Syntactic anticipation in German-English simultaneous interpretation. In D. Gerver, H.W. Sinaiko (eds.), *Language Interpretation and Communication*. New York: Plenum Press, pp. 335–343.

Ziegler, K., Gigliobianco, S. 2018. Present? Remote? Remotely present! New technological approaches to remote simultaneous conference interpreting. In: C. Fantinuoli (ed.), *Interpreting and Technology*. Berlin: Language Science Press, pp. 119–139.

6

INTERPRETING FOR MINORS IN LEGAL ENCOUNTERS IN IRELAND DURING THE COVID-19 PANDEMIC

A Case Study of Patterns of Practice and Implications

Eddie López-Pelén

Introduction

Article 3(1) of the *United Nations Convention on the Rights of the Child*,[1] states that 'In *all actions concerning children*, whether undertaken by [...] courts of law, administrative authorities or legislative bodies, the *best interests of the child* shall be a primary consideration' (my italics). In line with this, *General comment No. 24 (2019) on children's rights in the child justice system*[2] by the UN Committee on the Rights of the Child, for which the *United Nations Convention on the Rights of the Child* constitutes the basis, encourages that 'Consideration should also be given to the possible use of new technologies such as video "court appearances"' (Paragraph 112) so that the minor is not unnecessarily exposed to the daunting environment of the court or forced to be in the same room as their victimiser. In accordance with this, the Children Act, 2002,[3] the Irish piece of legislation specific to children, states that 'where a judge of the District Court is satisfied on the evidence of a registered medical practitioner that the attendance before a court of any child, in respect of whom an offence [...] is alleged to have been committed, would involve serious danger to the safety, health or wellbeing of the child, the judge may take the evidence [...] through a *live television link*' (Part 12, Section 255.b. My italics). Similarly, the Criminal Evidence Act, 1992,[4] determines that in cases involving a sexual offence, violence or a threat of violence to a person, a minor can provide evidence through a television link, a video recording or an intermediary. In fact, for the examination of the evidence to be less intimidating to the minor, if a television link is being used, the Criminal Evidence Act, 1992, (Part III, Section 13.3) adds that 'neither the judge, nor the barrister or solicitor concerned in the examination of the witness, shall wear a wig or gown'.

DOI: 10.4324/9781003440994-8

The aforementioned pieces of legislation acknowledge a universally recognised fact: that minors are vulnerable for the mere fact that they are minors (Balogh and Salaets, 2015). Consequently, measures such as being able to provide evidence through a television link are taken to protect minors and lessen the emotional impact that going through legal procedures can have on them. However, in some instances, minors do not speak the language of the legal proceeding. For this, *General comment No. 24 (2019)* states that 'A child who cannot understand or speak the language used in the child justice system has the right to the free assistance of an interpreter at all stages of the process' (Paragraph 64). In the European context, the right to the free assistance of an interpreter is made explicit in Directive 2010/64/EU[5] *on the right to interpretation and translation in criminal proceedings* where it is stated that the use of 'communication technology such as videoconferencing, telephone or the Internet' (Article 2.6) is a valid medium for the provision of the interpreter.

However, the COVID-19 pandemic 'forced the use of remote interpreting as the default' (Hale et al., 2022, p. 222) and brought along 'the closure or limited access to public buildings, such as courts and tribunals' (Rossner et al., 2021, p. 94) and most legal encounters with both adults and minors including police investigations, international protection application interviews and appeals had to be held remotely to prevent parties from contracting COVID-19. Interpreter-mediated legal encounters with minors held remotely during the COVID-19 pandemic is the context in which this study is framed.

The next section provides an overview of the advantages and disadvantages of remote interpreting and discusses relevant research that has been carried out on it.

Remote Interpreting

Remote interpreting refers to 'the use of communication technology for gaining access to an interpreter who is in another room, building, city or country and who is linked to the primary participants by telephone or videoconference' (Braun, 2015a, p. 346). The term remote interpreting is sometimes used to refer to an interpreting task where the interpreter is not present in the same room with the primary participants but linked to them via videoconference, whereas videoconference interpreting is used to refer to an interpreting task for a videoconference where the interpreter is co-located with one of the participants or in a separate site (Braun, 2015b, p. 437). However, in this chapter, the term remote interpreting will be used to refer to both videoconference and telephone interpreting for simplification purposes.[6]

Remote interpreting has been argued to offer advantages such as 'convenience for users of the service, access to interpreters in minor languages or specialised areas who are not available for face-to-face interpreting, removal of distance even across countries, and presumably increased cost effectiveness for both service users and interpreters' (Ko, 2006, p. 325). However, several disadvantages have been identified with the use of remote interpreting. For example, telephone interpreting can result in 'potential technical issues, lack of visual cues, possible physical discomfort, inconsistent or non-existent protocols, [...], [and] can be very challenging for interpreters and those who use their services' (Xu et al., 2020, p. 18). On the other hand, in addition to technical issues and poor-quality equipment, videoconference interpreting can 'entail a reduction in the quality of the intersubjective relations between the participants and a greater fragmentation of the discourse' (Braun, 2016, p. 177). Moreover, it has been asserted videoconference interpreting can 'result in making translation more difficult and less accurate' and in making it 'hard to make eye contact and communicate through body language' (Haas, 2006, p. 63). In fact, it has been argued that testimony provided via videoconference may be less credible than testimony provided in person and that proceedings held via videoconference may 'result in an ineffectual court system, in which individuals gain speedier entrance, but fewer receive the opportunity to be heard in a meaningful manner' (Harvard Law Review, 2009, p. 1193).

In several countries, in public service settings, telephone interpreting has been gradually replaced with video links (Braun et al., 2023, p. 91). Research on legal remote interpreting has discouraged the use of telephone interpreting and recommends its use as a last resort and for emergencies (Wang, 2018; Hale et al., 2022). For example, in the context of international protection hearings, Ellis recommends that 'there should be a direct telephone link [...] [only] when the video portion of the proceedings is going wrong' (2004, Conclusions and Recommendations, Point 11). In addition, it has been found that international protection hearings held via videoconference have an impact not only on the mutual trust and understanding among parties, amplifying cultural differences in non-verbal communication, but also increases the inclination to deceive while reducing the ability to detect falsehoods (Federman, 2006).

As pointed out by Braun et al. (2018), government entities 'have turned to videoconferencing to minimise delays in legal proceedings, reduce costs and improve access to justice' (p. 144). Similarly, Shaffer and Evans argue that 'the staffing and budget constraints experienced by many law enforcement agencies—as well as the ease and efficacy of telephone translation' are reasons for the increase in the use of telephone interpreting (2018, p. 159). Research has also found that legal professionals such as police officers are more confident in conducting a thorough interview when the interpreter is in the same room as opposed to when the interpreter is over the phone (Wakefield et al., 2015, p. 67) and that adequate telephone interpreting 'is related to use of the appropriate equipment and relevant practice or training' (Ko, 2006, p. 336).

On the other hand, experimental research on videoconference interpreting compared to face-to-face interpreting in police interviews has found an increase in issues with message content rendition, non-verbal elements, faster decline in performance over time, turn-taking and omissions, among others, when videoconference interpreting is used (Braun, 2013).

Regarding interpreting quality, a major study conducted by Hale et al. (2022) in which face-to-face interpreting was compared with both videoconference and telephone interpreting found that videoconference interpreting can be almost as effective as face-to-face interpreting, provided the interpreters are equally skilled and experienced. Hale et al. (2022) found the negative impact of telephone interpreting on interpreter performance, emphasising the importance of using telephone interpreting as a last resort.

The next section delves into the methodological considerations of this study.

Methodological Approach

This study aims to identify patterns of practice in interpreter-mediated legal encounters with minors held remotely. The data used in this study was collected as part of a larger-scale doctoral project (López-Pelén, 2024) which included feedback from twelve interpreters and twelve professionals who have worked in legal encounters with minors. The feedback included here deals exclusively with the feedback provided by participants with experience in working in interpreter-mediated legal encounters with minors held over the phone or on videoconference.

Although I recognise that the sample used in this case study cannot count as qualitative research as it is too small,[7] I will still use a qualitative approach to illustrate my work as it fits the purpose of my study. The qualitative approach this study adopts is phenomenology, whereby the main goal is to 'get to the truth of matters, to describe phenomena, in the broadest sense as whatever appears in the manner in which it appears, that is as it manifests itself *to consciousness, to the experiencer*' (Moran, 2000, p. 4. My italics). Edmund Husserl asserts that phenomenological analysis aims at the '*pure essence of experiences*' through discarding 'all empirical facticity and individuation' (1970, p. 170. Italics in original).

Conversely, for Martin Heidegger, one of Husserl's former students, it is not a realistic endeavour to expect that the researcher put aside empirical facticity and individuation. Instead, he acknowledges that it is inevitable that researchers bring their own personal experiences and understanding to the study of phenomena (Mapp, 2008, p. 308). For Heidegger, there is always 'an *assumption*' regarding the nature of phenomena under study (1962, p. 192. My italics). Heidegger states that an 'interpretation is never a *presuppositionless* apprehending of something presented to us' (1962, pp. 191–192).

My italics). As opposed to Husserlian phenomenology, Heidegger states that the 'methodological meaning of phenomenological description is *interpretation*' and that his approach to phenomenology is '*hermeneutics* [...] which designates the work of interpretation' (Heidegger, 1996, p. 33. Italics in original).

This study utilises a Heideggerian approach to understand remote legal encounters involving minors and interpreters. This choice is based on the premise that uncovering the practice patterns and their implications requires a methodology rooted in interpretivism. As Paley stresses, the uniqueness and distinctiveness of phenomenology is that 'it aims at *meaning attribution*, not [just] common themes or causal hypotheses' (2017, p. 17).

Method

To obtain feedback on how participants experience phenomena, either in Husserlian or Heideggerian phenomenological research, interviews are 'by far the most dominant method for data collection' (Bevan, 2014, p. 137). For this, semi-structured interviews were implemented as they 'allow for variation in the order in which questions are asked as well as to introduce new questions' (Saldanha and O'Brien, 2014, p. 172).[8]

Conceptual Framework

As examined in the section "Methodological Approach", phenomenology aims at meaning attribution. For this, to determine the implications of the patterns of practice in interpreter-mediated legal encounters with minors held remotely in Ireland, this study also draws on Sofía García-Beyaert's concept of *communicative autonomy*. This concept was first introduced by Bancroft et al. (2015) and refers to the service providers' (legal professionals') and service users' (minors') 'capacity to be in control of, and responsible for, [their] own communication' (Bancroft et al., 2015, p. viii). Under the concept of communicative autonomy, the interpreter allows interviewers and interviewees to communicate as if they share a 'common language' (Bancroft, 2017, p. 201) and be in control of the 'flow of communication' (Bancroft, 2017, 211). Consequently, the implications of the patterns of practice in interpreter-mediated legal encounters with minors held remotely in Ireland are identified based on the extent to which these patterns allow minors and legal professionals to be communicatively autonomous.

Participants

The participants that were interviewed for this study are two interpreters, three solicitors and one social worker who worked with minors in

TABLE 6.1 Interpreters' Experience with Minors

#	Participant	Interpreter experience	Experience with minors (times)	Average age of minor(s)	Mode	Condition of minor
1	Interpreter 1	8 years	2	15 y/o	1 in person/ 1 over the phone	No data
2	Interpreter 2	3 years	1 girl (investigation of rape)	No data	Over the phone	Child victim

TABLE 6.2 Lawyers' Experience in Interpreter-Mediated Encounters with Minors

#	Participant	Experience in legal encounters with minors (times)	Average age of minor(s)	Training on how to work with an interpreter	Mode
1	Solicitor 1	No data	15–17	No data	In person and online
2	Solicitor 2	15–20	14–17	No data	All over phone because of COVID-19
3	Solicitor 3	6	15	No	All over phone because of COVID-19

legal encounters held remotely during the COVID-19 pandemic in Ireland. Table 6.1 shows the profile of the interpreters.

Interpreter 1 interpreted in one legal encounter with an unaccompanied minor held over the phone in a case involving family reunification whereas Interpreter 2 interpreted for a very young child in a case with the police involving an investigation of rape.

On the other hand, this study includes the feedback provided by three solicitors who gave legal advice to unaccompanied minors seeking international protection in Ireland prior to their first instance application interview. Table 6.2 shows the profile of the solicitors whose feedback is included in this study.

In addition, this study includes the feedback of one social worker from Tusla's Separated Children Seeking International Protection (SCSIP)[9] unit who works with unaccompanied minors in Ireland and accompanies them throughout the international protection application process. The SCSIP social worker who participated in this study has accompanied over 100 separated minors (ranging between 16 and 17 years of age) to international protection proceedings in person and remotely.

Findings

This section presents the findings of the study based on four themes identified during the data analysis: training, briefings, rapport building and non-verbal communication.

Training

When a minor needs to provide evidence through an interpreter in legal proceedings, the added layer of relying on a third party to communicate (the interpreter) can leave them in a more vulnerable position. Taking this into consideration, *General comment No. 24* (2019) on children's rights in the child justice system by the UN Committee on the Rights of the Child states that in all legal proceedings where minors may experience communication barriers, 'interpreters should be trained to work with children' (Paragraph 64). However, previous research has shown that legal interpreters are often not trained in how to work with minors (Balogh and Salaets, 2015).

The feedback provided by the participants of this study shows that the use of untrained interpreters is a pattern in legal settings in Ireland. In fact, none of the interpreters whose feedback is included here had accredited interpreter training nor training in how to work with minors. For example, when asked what would help them be better prepared to interpret for minors, Interpreter 1 asserted:

> I think to have a training (sic) really… and to know the protocols of the [police].

However, the interpreter training highlighted by the professionals in this study is not so much in interpreting skills, but about their linguistic proficiency in English. For example, Solicitor 1 stated:

> the [interpreting] standards [in Ireland] are really variable. […] I have had issues with the interpreters where I don't think they're interpreting appropriately.

Similarly, Solicitor 2 regretted the following:

> interpreters don't have an official training and there's nobody that monitors them […]. […] I think the training part is really necessary and some kind of regulation as well.

The pattern of lack of training of interpreters stems from the fact that in Ireland the spoken language interpreting profession lacks proper regulation and interpreters are currently not required to undergo accredited training. Historically, translation agencies serving government entities have recruited interpreters without needing to demonstrate language proficiency or possess interpreting qualifications. However, in late 2022, a new mandate was introduced, requiring interpreters to prove their English proficiency, a requirement previously unspecified in the request for tenders. Still, accredited interpreter training is not yet required.

In addition to the usual serious consequences of inadequate interpreting, that is, rejection of international protection applications, contamination of evidence, among others, the minors' lack of trust in the interpreter being able to transmit their ideas into the language of the encounter can make them feel 'unsafe and disempowered' (Bancroft, 2017, pp. 199–200). In fact, since the interpreter 'controls the message' (Bancroft, 2017, p. 211. Italics in original) with poor interpreting, the minor's communicative autonomy is greatly affected. In addition to that, sound and video quality can vary in remote interpreting settings (Braun et al., 2018), resulting in even lower interpreting quality. As Powell et al. (2017) note, 'having one's language interpreted is often unfamiliar and stressful for children who have not previously used an interpreter' (p. 95). Therefore, if the use of an on-site interpreter can result in increased 'cognitive load on children' and the heightening of 'fatigue and the risk of communication errors' (Powell et al., 2017, p. 95), the use of remote interpreting technologies combined with the deployment of untrained interpreters can result in increased cognitive load and higher levels of stress on minors. This makes the case for the establishment of regulations and standards for interpreters working in legal settings, especially for interpreters working with minors.

However, lack of interpreter training or in how to work with minors is not the only issue in interpreter-mediated legal encounters with minors. As the social worker who participated in this study notes, interpreter training in the use of communication technologies has also been an issue. They stated that it 'can be difficult if the interpreters maybe struggle to understand how to get onto Microsoft Teams or whatever platform they're using. And maybe that's caused stress, delays…'.

Briefings

Prior studies have shown that briefings with interpreters in legal settings are an exception and that interpreters are often 'the least prepared participant in the case' (Laster and Taylor, 1994, p. 17). As part of the CO-Minor-IN/QUEST (Part I) project, among the 230 interpreters who responded, only 41 interpreters, which accounts for 18% of the total, reported that they consistently received briefings (Amato and Mack, 2015, p. 252). This finding is significant because it aligns with the belief held by many legal professionals that interpreters should maintain complete impartiality and neutrality and should not possess any prior knowledge about the cases they are called upon to interpret (Amato and Mack, 2015, p. 251). When asked if they are ever briefed before an interpreting job with a minor, Interpreter 2, who took part in an investigation of the rape of a very young child responded:

> Never with this... never given to us.

Interestingly, Interpreter 2 added the following:

> I don't mind [to be briefed], to be honest with you. Because you don't build expectations [...]. So, for me, it doesn't really make a difference if they tell me or not.

Interpreters may not want to learn about the case details before the interpreting job to protect themselves from the emotional stress of hearing about the traumatic experiences that minors have endured. As Bancroft asserts, 'interpreting traumatic content can be *more* stressful and traumatic for interpreters than for many service providers' (2017, p. 213. Italics in original), particularly when interpreting for minors. However, being aware of the specifics of the minors' background can help interpreters mentally prepare for the encounter since the element of surprise and resulting stress is mitigated (Bancroft et al., 2016, p. 86). In fact, briefings can assist interpreters in effectively managing stress since they could agree to 'set up a pre-arranged signal' (Bancroft et al., 2016, pp. 88, 100) or 'a potential "interpreter distress signal"', with the legal professional, so that the legal professional can call for a break without the interpreter disrupting the session' (Bancroft, 2017, p. 216), be it an audible or a visual signal, depending on the communication technology in use. This would enable legal professionals to have control over the flow of communication, ultimately fostering communicative autonomy.

On the other hand, when asked if they provide background information to interpreters before a legal consultation with a minor, Solicitor 1 reported:

> there's no personal information provided to the interpreter or any of the interpreters we work with. [..]. They can't pass information about the clients and yeah.

On the same lines, Solicitor 2's answer was:

> No, and what normally happens is we just phone the interpreter first before we would add them and the rest of the party to call. I might let the

> interpreter know that [...] I'm having a consultation with an applicant for international protection. I might get in their name and that's probably it.

As can be seen, the legal professionals' rationale for not providing interpreters with background information about the case appears to be confidentiality concerns. However, it needs to be borne in mind that interpreters will learn about the specifics of the case during the encounter anyway. Hence, the interpreter's confidentiality has to do more with their ethics and professionalism and less with being briefed.

Fortunately, Interpreter 2 who interpreted for a minor in a family reunification case stated:

> the officer prepared me... he... I had brief (sic) of the situation and he said to me it's important that [...] he will feel (sic) comfortable with you and me because he then will call back other times [...].

In both face-to-face and remote interpreting, the absence of interpreter briefings has a significant impact on the ability of minors and legal professionals to share a 'common language' and communicate effectively (Bancroft, 2017, p. 201). Without briefings, interpreters lack vital information about the minor's context and background (Kelly, 2008, p. 270), leading to increased risks of mistranslations and inaccuracies as interpreters are prevented from anticipating culturally sensitive expressions and preparing terminology specific to the case. In addition, the lack of briefings in legal encounters held remotely prevents legal professionals from foreseeing and discussing with interpreters the alternatives on what to do if issues with the communication technology medium in use arise.

Rapport Building

From April 2018 to June 2018, the United States ran the "zero tolerance" policy, whereby minors were separated from their parents at the US-Mexico border to deter illegal immigration. After hundreds of minors were separated from their parents, many unaccompanied minors had to appear before immigration authorities. Separated minors as young as three and eight years of age have appeared before an immigration judge with the help of an interpreter to make their case, sometimes over the telephone. Concerns have been voiced over the minors' ability to trust the interpreter on the other end of the phone (Stillman, 2018). In cases like this, rapport-building with the interviewer *and the interpreter* is essential. For this, it is advised that the interpreter 'be introduced to the child and that the interpreter's role should be explained' to them as this 'would enable the interpreter to build rapport with the child and possibly notice problems with communication' (Balogh and Salaets, 2015, p. 65). In fact, 'being clear about the interpreter's role can eliminate a child's lack of trust in the interpreter, or at least decrease any distrust' (Balogh and Salaets, 2015). In line with this, when asked if they ever introduce the interpreter to the minor, Solicitor 2 answered:

> I would usually start a consultation with (sic) saying to my client, "I have a – and whatever the language is – interpreter on the phone.

Solicitor 2's approach can have a positive effect on the communicative autonomy of the minor and the legal professional since developing trust in the interpreter would allow the minor to disclose the information requested by the legal professional and, at the same time, the latter can have control over 'the flow of communication' (Bancroft, 2017, p. 211). As a result, the minor would be able to 'receive more support' because when the minors disclose the information that is requested by the legal professional 'it is easier and more natural for [them] to provide the support [minors] need' (La Rooy et al., 2015, p. 118).

On the other hand, although they reported to not give any background information on the case to interpreters, Solicitor 3 acknowledged the following:

> they'd [interpreters] just be told the name of the person and where they're from, and then they would be asked to have a brief conversation with the person to make sure that they can both understand each other.

As can be seen, Solicitor 3's approach (as it is also Solicitor 2's approach) consists of introducing the interpreter and allowing the interpreter and the minor to interact before the legal encounter begins so it can be made sure that they understand each other. Although this practice might make sense at first, the legal professional is not necessarily aware of the content of the interaction between the interpreter and minors, thus it is being taken for granted that the interpreter is 'able to say things which do not originate from the person who is leading the exchange' and that they are capable of striking a delicate balance, determining the appropriate level of coordination and initiative needed to uphold their role as interpreters (Böser and Wilson, 2015, p. 238). In fact, this practice has been advised against as with 'some clients it may be difficult to avoid the conversation becoming more personal' (Phelan, 2020, p. 106). As a result, if the legal professional wants to make sure that the interpreter and the minor understand each other, an adequate alternative could be that the legal professional uses the initial phase of the encounter as a building rapport phase by asking questions to the minor through the interpreter as the interpreter makes sure the minor and they understand each other, and asking the minor directly if they understand the interpreter.

Non-Verbal Communication

As examined in the section "Remote Interpreting" above, a recurrent issue about remote interpreting in research outputs, particularly so with telephone interpreting but also videoconference interpreting (Braun et al., 2018), is the lack of non-verbal communication and visual cues such as body language. According to Ahrens, body language makes 'a significant contribution towards the constitution of the meaning of the spoken word' (2015, pp. 36–37). However, in legal encounters held via remote interpreting, especially via telephone, neither the legal professionals nor the interpreters are able to monitor the minors' body language. For instance, when asked if they felt the environment was appropriate for a child in an investigation of rape with the police held over the telephone, Interpreter 2 said:

> To be honest with you, it is difficult for me to talk because I wasn't there personally and I find it difficult to read the setting when I'm not there. I am not able to see their eyes and I cannot really read their body language.

In addition, when asked if in consultations over the phone they had been able to identify that a minor was having an emotional reaction, Solicitor 3 reported:

> So, there's been a few times where the minor will start crying, then you can't continue [...] where the interpreter has flagged to me that the minor is distressed.

As can be noticed, the interpreter can be a valuable ally in alerting the interviewer about anything wrong with the minor during the encounter. In Solicitor 3's account, although the consultation was over the phone, the interpreter was able to spot, perhaps through the minor's tone of voice, that they were getting distressed. However, noticing signs of distress or anxiety in encounters held over the phone can be extremely difficult. This is worsened by the fact that in the Irish legal context, briefings, where the legal professional can agree with the interpreter on what to do if the interpreter notices that something is happening to the minors, are the exception rather than the norm.

In like manner, when Solicitor 3 was asked if they find consultations with minors via telephone challenging, they answered:

> I do, yeah, and it's just very hard because, you know, when people start getting stressed [in person] you can see it before anything else. You can't see it through their body language, so I sort of depends on the person who's there with the minor to tell me [...].

Solicitor 3's answer on the unlikelihood of spotting visual cues in encounters over the telephone stresses the fact that interpreter-mediated legal encounters with minors over phone is used only and exclusively as a last resort and for emergencies where videoconferencing and face-to-face interaction are not an option (Wang, 2018; Hale et al., 2022).

Although the social worker who participated in this study acknowledges that 'it's always better to have [the interpreter] in the room, [...] [because] the interpreter can pick up on the nuances and you can make eye contact with the interpreter [...] [and] it's more personable', they also state that 'telephone interpreting [has] actually become more the norm now. Before in our offices, we would always have in-person interpreters. Now our go-to is maybe to have the interpreter over the phone'.

However, the social worker also pointed out the advantages of the interpreter not being in the same room as the minor. They stated the following:

Maybe for the young people in some ways, maybe it might actually be easier for them if the interpreter is not in the room for them and maybe having another person in the room can be stressful just for them, so it can work two different ways. [...] I think it makes it easier for a young person who really needs to have counselling but has no English, that the interpreter is on the phone. That makes them removed. That's a positive thing. (Social worker)

Conclusions

This study aimed to shed light on patterns of practice in interpreter-mediated legal encounters with minors held remotely in Ireland during the COVID-19 pandemic. The patterns of practice identified in the feedback provided by 2 interpreters, 3 solicitors and 1 social worker are the lack of interpreter training, lack of briefings with interpreters, inadequate rapport-building strategies and the lack of non-verbal communication elements in remote settings. These have a detrimental effect on the communication autonomy of legal professionals and minors. Based on participant feedback in this study, recommendations for legal encounters with minors held remotely are the use of qualified interpreters, the provision of clear guidelines and background information about the case to interpreters through briefings and using telephone interpreting only and exclusively as a last resort.

Notes

1 Available at https://www.ohchr.org/en/instruments-mechanisms/instruments/convention-rights-child
2 Available at https://tinyurl.com/y7n5ncyu
3 Available at https://revisedacts.lawreform.ie/eli/2001/act/24/revised/en/html
4 Available at https://www.irishstatutebook.ie/eli/1992/act/12/enacted/en/print.html

5 Available at https://eur-lex.europa.eu/LexUriServ/LexUriServ.do?uri=OJ:L:2010:2 80:0001:0007:en:PDF
6 Video interpreting is the term commonly used to refer to sign language interpreting via video.
7 While this sample appears small, it is noteworthy that interpreting for minors is uncommon in Ireland due to the low number of unaccompanied minors seeking international protection compared to other European countries. Moreover, non-native English-speaking minors have often attained a proficient level of English by the time they provide evidence in court or police investigations. As the head of a translation company that provides interpreters for Irish government institutions stated, 'Less than 3% of interpreters we work with have had any experience in interpreting for minors in legal settings'. As a result, it was not possible to recruit more interpreters and professionals who have worked in legal encounters with minors held remotely for the present study.
8 See Appendix for the structure of the interview.
9 Tusla – Child and Family Agency is the Irish government entity established to support children's welfare and protection in Ireland.

References

Ahrens, B. 2015. Body Language. In: Pöchhacker, F. *The Routledge Encyclopedia of Interpreting Studies*. London and New York: Routledge, pp. 36–38.
Amato, A. and Mack, G. 2015. Briefing, Debriefing and Support. In Balogh, K. and Salaets, H. *Children and Justice: Overcoming Language Barriers*. Cambridge, Antwerp and Portland: Intersentia, pp. 247–280.
Balogh, K. and Salaets, H. eds. 2015. *Children and Justice: Overcoming Language Barriers*. Cambridge, Antwerp and Portland: Intersentia.
Bancroft, M. A. 2017. The Voice of Compassion: Exploring Trauma-Informed Interpreting. In: Valero-Garcés, C. and Tipton, R. *Ideology, Ethics and Policy Development in Public Service Interpreting and Translation*. Bristol and Blue Ridge Summit: Multilingual Matters, pp. 195–219.
Bancroft, M. A, Allen, K., Green, C. E. and Feuerle, L. M. 2016. *Breaking Silence: Interpreting for Victim Services*. Washington, DC: Ayuda.
Bancroft, M.A., Beyaert García, S., Allen, K., Carriero-Contreras, G. and Socarrás-Estrada, D. 2015. *The Community Interpreter®: An International Textbook*. Columbia, MD: Culture and Language Press.
Bevan, M. T. 2014. A Method of Phenomenological Interviewing. *Qualitative Health Research* 24(1), pp. 136–144.
Böser, U. and Wilson, C. 2015. Issues of Role in Interpreting for Minors. In Balogh, K. and Salaets, H. *Children and Justice: Overcoming Language Barriers*. Cambridge, Antwerp and Portland: Intersentia, pp.228–246.
Braun, S. 2013. Keep Your Distance? Remote Interpreting in Legal Proceedings: A Critical Assessment of a Growing Practice. *Interpreting* 15(2), pp. 200–228.
Braun, S. 2015a. Remote Interpreting. In: Pöchhacker, F. *Routledge Encyclopedia of Interpreting Studies*. London and New York: Routledge, pp. 346–348.
Braun, S. 2015b. Videoconference Interpreting. In: Pöchhacker, F. *Routledge Encyclopedia of Interpreting Studies*. London and New York: Routledge, pp. 437–429.
Braun, S. 2016. The European AVIDICUS Projects: Collaborating to Assess the Viability of Video-Mediated Interpreting in Legal Proceedings. *European Journal of Applied Linguistics* 4(1), pp. 173–180.

Braun, S., Davitti, E. and Dicerto, S. 2018. Video-Mediated Interpreting in Legal Settings: Assessing the implementation'. In: Napier, J., Skinner, R. and Braun, S. *Here or There: Research on Interpreting via Video Link*. Washington, DC: Gallaudet, pp. 144–179.

Braun, S., Sharou, K. A. and Temizöz, Ö. 2023. Technology Use in Language-Discordant Interpersonal Healthcare Communication. In: Laura Gavioli and Cecilia Wadensjö *The Routledge Handbook of Public Service Interpreting*. London and New York: Routledge, pp. 89–105.

Ellis, S. R. 2004. Videoconferencing in Refugee Hearings. [Accessed 13 September 2023]. Available from https://irb.gc.ca/en/transparency/reviews-audit-evaluations/Pages/Video.aspx

Federman, M. 2006. On the Media Effects of Immigration and Refugee Board Hearings via Videoconference. *Journal of Refugee Studies* 19(4), pp. 433–452.

Haas, A. 2006. *Videoconferencing in immigration proceedings*. University of New Hampshire Scholars' Repository. https://scholars.unh.edu/unh_lr/vol5/iss1/5

Hale, S., Goodman-Delahunty, J., Martschuk, N. and Lim, J. 2022. Does Interpreter Location Make a Difference? A Study of Remote vs Face-to-Face Interpreting in Simulated Police Interviews. *Interpreting* 24(2), pp. 221–253.

Harvard Law School. 2009. Access to Courts and Videoconferencing in Immigration Court Proceedings. *Harvard Law Review* 122(1151), pp. 1181–1193.

Heidegger, M. 1962. *Being and Time* [Translation by John Macquarrie and Edward Robinson]. Oxford and Cambridge: Blackwell.

Heidegger, M. 1996. *Being and Time* [Translation by Joan Stambaugh]. Albany, NY: SUNY Press.

Husserl, E. 1970. *Logical Investigations* [Translation by J. N. Findlay]. London and New York: Routledge.

Kelly, N. 2008. *Telephone Interpreting: A Comprehensive Guide to the Profession*. Bloomington: Trafford Publishing.

Ko, L. 2006. The Need for Long-Term Empirical Studies in Remote Interpreting Research: A Case Study of Telephone Interpreting. *Linguistica Antverpiensia* 5, pp. 325–338.

La Rooy, David J., Ahern, E. C. and Andrews, S. J. 2015. Developmentally Appropriate Interviewing of Highly Vulnerable Children: A Developmental Psychology Perspective. In Balogh, K. and Salaets, H. Children *and* Justice: *Overcoming Language Barriers*. Antwerp and Portland: Intersentia, pp. 113–131.

Laster, K. and Taylor, V. 1994. *Interpreters and the Legal System*. Sidney: The Federation Press.

López-Pelén, E. 2024. *Interpreting for Minors in Legal Settings*. Dublin City University [Unpublished PhD thesis].

Mapp, T. 2008. Understanding Phenomenology: The Lived Experience. *British Journal of Midwifery* 16(5), pp. 308–311.

Moran, D. 2000. *Introduction to Phenomenology*. London and New York: Routledge.

Paley, J. 2017. *Phenomenology as Qualitative Research: A Critical Analysis of Meaning Attribution*. London and New York: Routledge.

Phelan, M. 2020. Codes of ethics. *Ethics in Public Service Interpreting*. London and New York: Routledge, pp. 85–146.

Powell, M. B., Manger, B., Dion, J. and Sharman, S. J. 2017. Professionals' Perspectives about the Challenges of Using Interpreters in Child Abuse Interviews. *Psychiatry, Psychology and Law* 24(1), pp. 90–101.

Rossner, M., Tait, D. and McCurdy, M. 2021. Justice Reimagined: Challenges and Opportunities with Implementing Virtual Courts. *Current Issues in Criminal Justice* 33(1), pp. 94–110.

Saldanha, G. and O'Brien, S. 2014. *Research Methodologies in Translation Studies*. London and New York: Routledge.

Shaffer, S. A. and Evans, J. R. 2018. Interpreters in Law Enforcement Contexts: Practices and Experiences According to Investigators. *Applied Cognitive Psychology* 32(2), pp. 150–162.

Stillman, S. 2018, June 21. Trump's executive order creates a new border crisis. *The New Yorker*. https://www.newyorker.com/news/news-desk/the-new-border-crisis-following-trumps-executive-order

Wakefield, S. J., Kebbell, M. R., Moston, S. and Westera, N. 2015. Perceptions and Profiles of Interviews with Interpreters: A Police Survey Australian & New Zealand. *Journal of Criminology* 48(1), pp. 53–72.

Wang, J. 2018. Telephone Interpreting Should Be Used Only as a Last Resort: Interpreters' Perceptions of the Suitability, Remuneration and Quality of Telephone Interpreting. *Perspectives* 26(1), pp. 100–116.

Xu, H., Hale, S. and Stern, L. 2020. Telephone Interpreting in Lawyer–Client Interviews: An Observational Study. *Translation & Interpreting* 12(1), pp. 18–36.

Appendix

Structure of the Interview

1. For how long have you been an interpreter?
2. Have you ever received any interpreting or translation training?
3. Have you ever received any training on how to interpret for children?
4. Have you ever interpreted for children?
5. Where did these interviews happen?
6. Can you tell me an approximate number of the times you have interpreted for children? Ever interpreted for unaccompanied children seeking asylum?
7. What is the average age of children you have interpreted for?
8. Who is normally present during these interviews? Where do you normally stand/sit in interviews with children? What is the room like? Do you find the room and environment suitable for an interview with a child?
9. Do interviewers normally introduce you to the child (function, name)? Do interviewers usually use the child's name when they address them? What about you?
10. Have you ever been given background information about the case prior to the interview?
11. In your opinion, should interviews with children be different from interviews with adults? What differences should there be?
12. Could you tell me about your approach when interpreting for children.

- Do you have special considerations in interviews with children? What about the interviewers?
- Have you noticed any differences in the way interviewers talk to children compared to adults? Is it like that in all settings? Which settings?
- Do you make any adaptations to your work when interpreting for children? (Tone, language, body language, gestures, etc).
- Is your approach when interpreting for children different to your approach with adults? If so, in what way?
- To what extent do you replicate the way interviewers talk to children?
- Do you ever try to build rapport with the minor or put them at ease? What about the interviewer? Why so?
- What have you noticed about the way interviewers speak to children?
- Who do children tend to look at the most when they speak (you, the interviewer, the parents, solicitor)?
- Who do you look at when you interpret for the child (to them, to your notes)?
- Are you happy with the way interviews with children are conducted?
- Looking back, would you change anything about your approach with children?

13 How do you decide what is ethical or not when interpreting for children? Do you abide by a code of ethics? Are you given any guidelines when interpreting for children?
14 Have you ever interpreted in a situation where a child showed emotional reactions?

- signs of trauma? If so, what did you do? If not, what would you do in such a situation?
- unresponsiveness? If so, what did you do? If not, what would you do in such a situation?
- emotional responses? If so, what did you do? If not, what would you do in such a situation?

15 Are there any challenges you face when interpreting for children? What challenges?
16 What would help you feel better equipped to interpret for children?

7
IMPLEMENTING HIGHER EDUCATION TRAINING FOR INTERCULTURAL MEDIATORS IN SCHOOLS

Letizia Leonardi

Introduction

The introduction of distance education during the pandemic-induced lockdowns posed many challenges to foreign pupils with limited language proficiency. By curtailing human exchanges, remote teaching modalities caused social exclusion and considerably increased communication difficulties. Furthermore, online education made students' academic progress largely dependent on parental engagement (Garbe et al., 2020, p. 45). In the case of migrant students, however, families' support was often unavailable due to parents being uncollaborative with educators (Proietti, 2020) or having an inadequate language level to assist children's learning activities. The COVID-19 emergency highlighted the importance of intercultural mediators as vital resources in areas with high migrant presence to ensure that education is not hindered by linguistic and cultural diversity. Nevertheless, the role of the intercultural mediator is not officially recognised in the UK (Casadei and Franceschetti, 2009, p. 67). Indeed, while in other countries the intercultural mediator is a third figure mediating between public service operators and migrants (Catarci, 2016, p. 130), in Britain, intercultural mediation is regarded as an extension of civil mediation (Olympic Training and Consulting Ltd, 2016, p. 9). This means that intercultural mediation activities are carried out by 'advisers' operating within the system itself and often working on a voluntary basis (Casadei and Franceschetti, 2009, pp. 67–72). As a result of a lack of professionalisation, these figures do not possess proper mediation skills and are called by different names depending on the type of support they provide (Casadei and Franceschetti, 2009, p. 76). Consequently, training opportunities for intercultural mediators are unavailable in the country, especially at higher education levels. Previous

DOI: 10.4324/9781003440994-9

studies highlighted the important functions performed by intercultural mediators in educational contexts and how their intervention can facilitate migrant pupils' language acquisition process and inclusion in the classroom (Chiofalo et al., 2019; Sani, 2015). However, the British education system does not include the presence of mediators in schools, whose functions are generally carried out by teachers themselves (Casadei and Franceschetti, 2009, p. 79). In a multiethnic society like the British one, the support of mediators in a school setting is advisable for better migrant social inclusion. For this to be possible, however, adequate training opportunities should become available.

Against this background, this chapter proposes a pedagogical model for the introduction of university courses in intercultural mediation in Britain. Special emphasis shall be given to educational settings. This is because, as discussed later, the functions performed by mediators in schools are multifaceted. Therefore, tailored training has to be provided. It also purports to show that the implementation of these courses may have positive repercussions for both language service users (migrants) and language service providers (recruiters and mediators).

This study was conducted through a systematic review of existing intercultural mediation practices across different countries. The sources reviewed include research outputs and documentation regulating the provision of intercultural mediation services throughout Europe. These analyse the duties of intercultural mediators in relation to the different social spheres where these intervene and discuss the available training opportunities.

The review enabled identification of a number of university training programmes that could be used as the starting point to implement future courses in intercultural mediation in Britain. However, some structural amendments should be made to ensure that training is tailored to the specific competencies required in migrant services. Based on these observations, it was possible to design a model for the introduction of intercultural mediation as a university subject across the UK. Results also evidenced that, in order to provide effective mediation services in educational settings, trainees need to develop a wide range of abilities beyond pure linguistic skills. Training, therefore, needs to be interdisciplinary and take into account the whole gamut of sociocultural and psychological implications that working with migrant pupils entails. The chapter concludes with the observation that, apart from fostering migrant social inclusion, the implementation of university modules in intercultural mediation may promote the definition of a clear code of conduct for intercultural mediators, thus encouraging professional recognition.

Literature Review

The cultural turn of the 1990s directed increasing scholarly attention to the intercultural dimension of translation and interpreting (Liddicoat, 2016,

p. 354). This is because, as a culturally shaped activity, any type of linguistic transference inevitably involves a certain degree of cross-cultural negotiation. In previous studies, the topic of intercultural mediation was tackled from both an academic perspective and a practical one.

From the academic standpoint, research has been mainly focused on the degree of overlap existing between intercultural mediation and other akin professions it is often assimilated to, such as community interpreting (Baraldi, 2014; Pokorn and Južnič, 2020; Wang, 2017). Starting from the assumption that interpreting always involves a certain degree of mediation between cultures, some scholars claim that the two profiles entirely coincide (Wang, 2017). Against this argument, this chapter asserts that the type, modality, and context in which mediation occurs might not be exactly the same for interpreters and intercultural mediators. Hence, a distinction between the two professions is necessary. This consideration is supported by a simple observation. Had the two roles been equivalent or completely interchangeable, there would have been no reason for the rise of intercultural mediation as a new and highly requested profession across Europe. Whilst the profession has started emerging only in recent years, the practice of intercultural mediation, intended as dispute resolution, conflict management, and translation, has existed for decades (Erdilmen, 2021, p. 6). The need for intercultural mediation originated in response to the increasing flows of migrants and refugees who spoke languages not traditionally taught by established translation and interpreting European institutions (Pokorn and Južnič, 2020, pp. 100–101). In lack of qualified interpreters, organisations working with migrants turned to anyone who could speak and understand the languages of newly arrived immigrants. To bridge the linguistic gap, ad hoc interpreters began to be trained and professionalised under the term 'intercultural mediators'. Although a similar identifiable figure already existed in the market, the community interpreter, the two roles started to be differentiated on the grounds of the duties performed, with the role of the community interpreter being reduced to communicative and linguistic functions (Pokorn and Južnič, 2020, p. 101). On the contrary, the duties performed by an intercultural mediator are not limited to interpreting but encompass cultural brokerage, negotiation, conflict prevention and resolution, trust and relationship building between parties, and advocacy, when necessary (Erdilmen, 2021 p. 6). This implies that the required skills and competencies of an intercultural mediator transcend mere linguistic transference and include empathy, the ability to recognise body language, a basic understanding of legal procedures, and a certain knowledge of disciplines like psychology, sociology, and political science, among others (Theodosiou and Aspioti, 2015, p. 17). A clear differentiation between the two roles can also be traced by looking at industry requirements (Wang, 2017, p. 94), and ethical positioning (Pokorn and Južnič, 2020). In general, institutions' codes of conduct support the principles of neutrality and impartiality, also named 'equal distance', for interpreters and emphasise advocacy and conflict resolution for intercultural mediators (Pokorn and Južnič, 2020). A distinction between the roles is also necessary in terms of service suitability. English-speaking countries and Northern European countries favour interpreting in public services (Baraldi, 2014, p. 18). Conversely, the institutions of some countries, like healthcare in Italy, tend to prefer mediators as they are better qualified to manage conflicts and intercultural relations with migrants (Baraldi, 2014, p. 18).

As a practice, intercultural mediation has been foregrounded in research publications issued at the European level, where it is discussed in connection with the broader burning issue of migrant integration. As a premise, it is necessary to specify that different types of intercultural mediation exist (*in business*, *in tourism*, and *for immigrants*) (Olympic Training and Consulting Ltd., 2016, p. 6) and that this chapter exclusively focuses on the latter. Intercultural mediators for immigrants can intervene in different fields including healthcare, education, police and legislative services, housing, state service, and labour (Olympic Training and Consulting Ltd., 2015, pp. 18–22). As for the specific case of education, which is the social area taken into consideration in this chapter, previous research highlighted that the school system of several countries theoretically includes the presence of linguistic-cultural mediators in educational settings. For instance, France operates on a role distinction between interpreters, whose primary task is that of promoting migrants' cultural alterity, and mediators, or *adultes-relais*, who intervene, instead, in case of marginalisation and communication problems between teachers and students (Casadei and Franceschetti, 2009, p. 27). Similarly, a wide range of services, including guidance, assistance, translation, and interpreting, are offered to migrant students in Germany (Casadei and Franceschetti, 2009, p. 47). In Italy, apart from working in schools, mediators serve as additional teaching support in Provincial Centres for Adult Education (CPIA), and autonomous institutions providing training and Italian language courses for foreign adults in local areas (Loprieno et al., 2019, p. 9).

In practice, intercultural mediation in education is nonetheless insufficiently provided (Chiofalo et al., 2019). The introduction of remote teaching modalities during the COVID-19 emergency highlighted this deficiency in the school systems of many countries, but a shortage of mediators in education and other public services was already registered in pre-pandemic times. Evidence shows, in fact, that in lack of appropriate support, the role of intercultural mediators is frequently taken up by unqualified figures: teachers, as it happens in Italy (Chiofalo et al., 2019), and parents or voluntary students themselves, as is the case in Spain (Casadei and Franceschetti, 2009, p. 94). Despite being cost-effective, this practice can have some negative consequences. First, parents and pedagogical educators may not possess the necessary linguistic and cultural skills to effectively support migrant pupils' inclusion and language-learning process. For example, in a study conducted by Chiofalo et al. (2019), teachers reported using certain forms of non-verbal communication, such as gestures, to overcome language barriers. However, this does not allow students to develop linguistic abilities autonomously and establish interactions. Second, in lack of appropriate mediation practices, the foreign pupil's culture risks getting completely absorbed into the host country (Chiofalo et al., 2019). For example, in Greece, where the presence of migrant students in schools has never been properly tackled, the promotion of the Greek identity ended up eclipsing any form of multiculturalism (Casadei and Franceschetti, 2009, pp. 60–62). This runs counter to the scope of intercultural education, whose aim should be that of valorising cultural diversity. As discussed by Casadei and Franceschetti (2009, p. 79), in the UK, major emphasis is placed on equality of access to learning opportunities rather than on the need for mediation. The British school system does not officially include the professional figure of the intercultural mediator, with the role being generally fulfilled by teachers themselves. Unlike the case of Spain, Greece, and Italy, the UK tends to favour the recruitment of teachers with a migratory background as a measure to ease foreign students' inclusion in the education system (Casadei and Franceschetti, 2009, p. 79). As a result of increasing immigration flows, a rise in the number of teachers of Indian, Pakistani, and Caribbean origin has occurred (Casadei and Franceschetti, 2009, p. 79). They perform both teaching and mediation tasks, thus replacing figures like the Multicultural Adviser and the Home Maison Teacher, who used to facilitate school-migrant communication in the past (Casadei and Franceschetti, 2009, pp. 79–80). As will be discussed below, this peer-to-peer approach, where intercultural mediation is carried out by migrants themselves, can have multiple benefits. Nevertheless, this chapter claims that it may not adequately supply the type of assistance required by migrant pupils, especially newly arrived ones. Therefore, a separation between the two roles (teachers and intercultural mediators) is desirable. The main argument against an exclusive reliance on migrant teachers is that they may not be able to effectively cater to foreign students' needs while simultaneously teaching the rest of the class detrimental consequences for both inclusion and learning outcomes.

Studies specifically focusing on mediators working in school settings evidenced the significant role played by these professional figures in migrant students' integration. The functions of intercultural mediators in schools can be analysed from the perspective of both migrants and teachers. The former group can be divided into two further categories: families and children. As observed by Sani (2015, p. 2584), on what concerns families, mediators perform a threefold function: mediation (they facilitate communication between educators and parents, and solve conflicts arising from cultural differences), assistance (they provide information about the host country's education system), and translation of written documentation and notices from the school. Towards children, the mediator works as a guide, providing orientation and psychological support during the inclusion process (2015, p. 2584). When it comes to teachers, the abovementioned study by Chiofalo et al. (2019) demonstrated that the intervention of cultural mediators is deemed necessary by pedagogical educators. In fact, although their role does not coincide with that of a teacher, mediators complement tutoring activities and support foreign pupils' language acquisition process (Sani, 2015, p. 2584). Learning the host country's language is indeed an essential prerequisite to complete migrant integration as this allows them to become active members of the society (Leonardi, 2022, p. 81). The mediator also cooperates in the planning and organisation of intercultural projects. These serve to illustrate the foreign pupil's source culture to the native classmates and, at the same time, help the migrant appreciate the culture of the host country (Sani, 2015, p. 2584).

Based on the above considerations, this chapter stresses the importance of including professionally recognised intercultural mediators as a systemic part of the school system (Leonardi, 2022, p 81). Similarly, to special educational needs teachers, these figures could complement pedagogical activities by working closely with foreign students and guiding them throughout the different stages of the integration process. However, for this to be possible, adequate training opportunities should be provided. From previous studies, it has emerged not only that educational opportunities for mediators are currently unavailable in the UK but also that clear guidelines for the implementation of these courses in the country have not been issued yet. In this light, this chapter argues that training in intercultural mediation may be introduced at higher education levels in the UK through the adaptation and improvement of existing training practices in Europe.

Methodology

As seen from the above observations, this chapter has two main objectives: (a) providing a pedagogical model for the implementation of courses in intercultural mediation at higher education levels in the UK, and (b) showing how both migrant communities and the language industry may benefit from the introduction of university training for intercultural mediators.

The methodological approach adopted to conduct this study consists of a review of existing intercultural mediation and training practices across different European countries. The countries taken into consideration include Italy, France, Spain, and Germany as these are some of the main areas where both training opportunities and intercultural mediation services are provided. To this aim, different sources were scrutinised. These can be divided into two broad categories: the first group encompasses publications issued at the European level where the profession of intercultural mediation is discussed.

These offer an overview of the different fields where mediators operate as well as discuss available training opportunities. These include Casadei and Franceschetti's 'Il mediatore culturale in sei Paesi europei' (2009) (focusing on Italy, France, Germany, Greece, the UK, and Spain), Erdilmen's 'Frameworks and good practices of intercultural mediation for migrant integration in Europe' (2021) (offering a comparative analysis of intercultural mediation models in Bulgaria, Germany, Italy, and Spain), the research outputs of the TIME Project (Train Intercultural Mediators for a Multicultural Europe) (2015), and the research reports on intercultural mediation published in the European Commission Website. As for training opportunities, the web pages of different higher education institutions providing courses in intercultural mediation in Europe were also checked to see and compare how programmes and contents were organised. In view of the scope of this chapter, the second group comprises publications specifically focusing on problems linked to migration in education. The main one is 'Integrating migration into education interventions', published by the International Organization for Migration (2021).

This review activity revealed that different courses in intercultural mediation are currently available throughout Europe. Considering the purpose of this chapter, attention was predominantly devoted to training programmes offered at higher education levels. It was observed that, although specialists argue that specific training should ideally result in a bachelor's or master's degree (Olympic Training and Consulting Ltd, 2015, p. 5), courses in intercultural mediation at the university level are not uniformly available throughout Europe. The countries currently offering degree programmes in intercultural mediation include Austria, Finland (at the undergraduate level), Italy, France (at both undergraduate and postgraduate levels), Spain, Belgium, Germany, Lithuania, Poland, Portugal, and Switzerland (at the postgraduate level) (Olympic Training and Consulting Ltd, 2016, pp. 18–20). By checking the different programmes through university web pages, it was possible to identify some good practices that could be used as a model to structure training courses in the UK. Some examples include the 'Master in Intercultural Mediation and Social Intervention' offered by Politécnico de Leira in Portugal and the 'Máster en Migraciones, Mediación, y Grupos Vulnerables' offered by Universidad de Almería in Spain, both providing modules focussing on mediation, negotiation, and migrant integration. Similarly, a series of weaknesses were noticed. First, many courses tendentially consider intercultural mediation as an extension of translation and commuting interpreting rather than a discipline on its own. This is the case, for instance, of the 'Máster Oficial en Traducción y Mediación Intercultural' offered by the University of Salamanca and the undergraduate 'Degree Programme in Public Service Interpreting' offered by the Diaconia University of Applied Sciences in Finland. Consequently, many courses neglect migration issues and the type of competencies needed to work in migratory contexts. Analogously, undergraduate programmes in intercultural mediation in Italy have a strong linguistic and literary focus. The outcomes of this piece of research thus confirmed the results of the study conducted by Amato and Garwood (2011), claiming that bachelor's degrees in intercultural mediation in Italy are often an adaptation of pre-existing courses in foreign languages and literature. Second, many programmes offer either homogeneous training or exclusive focus on a single area of intervention—such is the case, for example, of the 'Postgraduate diploma in interpreting-mediation in social and medical settings' offered by the University Paris Diderot (Mayr et al., 2015, p. 42). In other words, courses do not necessarily offer a specialisation in different areas and generally overlook the diversified and context-specific duties performed by mediators in different service sectors. Results thus suggested that European degree programmes in intercultural mediation can provide valuable indications for the development of university training in the UK. Nevertheless, some changes are imperative if training is to take into account the diversified migratory settings in which mediators operate.

Discussion

Based on the above considerations, it was then possible to design a more comprehensive pedagogical model for the introduction of higher education courses in intercultural mediation. These may be implemented at the postgraduate level and could have a bipartite structure consisting of both mandatory modules and optional ones. Compulsory modules should focus on specific subjects pertinent to the profession. Along the lines of the above-discussed training practices, core modules should impart theoretical knowledge relating to migrants' history and legislation as well as help develop mediation skills and tension resolution techniques. Following the observation that mediators' functions slightly vary depending on the specific social sphere in which they operate, courses should allow specialisation in one or more fields of intervention (healthcare, education, asylum centres, etc.) to raise role awareness in different sectors. Since, as discussed, most European university programmes do not provide specialised modules, in this case, most training suggestions were retrieved from the guide entitled "Intercultural Mediator Profile and Related Learning Outcomes" (2015) available on the TIME project website. As explained above, the mediators' role in educational settings is hybrid and multifaceted as these figures stand between a language expert, a tutor, and a supportive figure in foreign pupils' integration process. Further difficulties may be posed by the fact that communication is not simply mediated between two parties but entails the participation of multiple groups (foreign children, native classmates, migrant families, and teachers). Based on these considerations, this chapter claims that specialisation courses for mediators in education should be interdisciplinary and combine elements of the following disciplines: didactics and pedagogy, with a special focus on second-language learning and children-centred methodological approaches, essential to effectively support foreign pupils' language acquisition process; psychology, focusing on the psychological and sociocultural characteristics of vulnerable groups (especially refugees), special issues applying to mediation with children, body language (to recognise signs of stress or discomfort in children's behaviour), and techniques to be collaborative with teachers and other pedagogical educators; knowledge of education systems (similarities and differences between the host country's education system and that of the pupil's country of origin in relation to aspects such as types of school, levels of education, attitudes to schooling and teachers' role, etc.); knowledge of exclusion and discrimination mechanisms, necessary in the presence of hostile or bullying behaviours due to racism and stereotyping (Olympic Training and Consulting Ltd, 2015). Furthermore, the theoretical component may be complemented by practical training (e.g., an internship) of variable length. This would give students a realistic view of the mediator's role in educational settings as well as the opportunity to apply theoretical knowledge to real-life work scenarios.

In practical terms, the implementation of new degree programmes specifically focusing on intercultural mediation may be, nonetheless, obstructed by several issues. First, the creation of new courses has significant financial implications. Indeed, the viability of such a project would largely depend on institutions' funding accessibility and may not be concretised in the lack of proper budgetary support. Second, the point of a new course endeavour is that this meets a highly demonstrated demand from both employers and prospective students. Employment possibilities generally respond to specific social urges. In a multiethnic society like Britain, for example, effective intercultural mediation practices in school environments would help ensure equal access to education. The removal of linguistic barriers in teaching contexts became a pressing need, especially after the Ukrainian emergency, during which 9,900 foreign pupils were offered admission to schools (GOV.UK, 2022). However, whilst proper training for mediators may have advantages from the social perspective, students' interest in educational opportunities of this kind is yet to be assessed. An indication in this sense may be provided by attendance levels and enrolment numbers in language and Translating and Interpreting (T&I) programmes across British universities. For decades, the UK has attracted hundreds of students hailing from EU countries. However, the post-Brexit drop in applications from European students reported in the academic year 2021–2022 (O' Carrol and Adams, 2023), probably caused by the concomitant temporary suspension of in-person teaching during the COVID-19 emergency, has negatively impacted this trend. Against this backdrop, the implementation of degree programmes in intercultural mediation may encounter the resistance of institutions and funding bodies that may be reluctant to approve courses with scarce prospective attendance.

To streamline the process from both the financial and logistical perspective, intercultural mediation may be, therefore, incorporated as a separate module in existing T&I programmes. By drawing upon students' linguistic and communicative skills, it would be possible to train future professionals for intercultural mediation in a wide range of social spheres, thus offering trainees broader job possibilities. Additionally, the practice may facilitate the discrimination between interpreting and intercultural mediation, which, as discussed above, are often erroneously considered interchangeable professions. From an academic perspective, it may also foster a multidisciplinary approach and cross-faculty collaborations. Students wishing to pursue a career as mediators in school settings, for instance, may benefit from teachings in didactics or child psychology.

Another problem relates to language selection since the minoritarian languages and dialects spoken by migrants are generally excluded from university curricula. This concern had already been raised by Amato and Garwood (2011) in their article on intercultural mediation in Italian universities, but the consideration can be extended to language courses in the UK as well. If the introduction of a wider language selection would theoretically lead to increased course efficiency, on the practical level, factors like students' demand and unavailability of academic staff properly qualified to teach these subjects may work as a deterrent for the concrete realisation of such a project. An alternative solution could be one that entails migrants' active participation in the provision of intercultural mediation duties. Recruiting mediators from within migrant communities is an approach already used in different EU countries including Italy, France, and Spain, (Casadei and Franceschetti, 2009, p. 101). This practice, whose controversial political implications go beyond the scope of the present chapter, is grounded on the assumption that migrants' own experiences can be utilised as a sound resource to provide tailored assistance to immigrant communities in public services (Mayr et al., 2015, p. 79). Prompting migrants' active engagement in the process can indeed have some advantages from both the sociocultural and professional perspectives. By giving them access to an intellectual occupation, this measure would encourage migrants' inclusion and participation in the host country's society (Casadei and Franceschetti, 2009, p. 34). In addition to that, hailing from a similar background, the migrant mediator can better empathise with fellow immigrants when problems of linguistic-cultural diversity arise. For instance, by facilitating physicians' understanding of immigrant women's cultural beliefs, female mediators with a migratory background can be an asset in healthcare settings. Their assistance can favour patient-doctor relationship building and prove to be crucial in situations where a lack of understanding of gender issues may potentially result in delayed or inadequate medical treatments. Roma Health Mediators exemplifies this. The programme employs female mediators with migratory origins to facilitate communication in those contexts where, for example, women are prevented from discussing health-related topics with men (Open Society Foundations, 2011, p. 26). With regard to the educational sphere, an efficient application of the peer-to-peer approach is Campus Rütli, a school-based project aimed to encourage schooling and integration of socially disadvantaged children and adolescents in the Berlin area. The approach adopted by the school is that of hiring intercultural mediators from the same background as migrant students to mediate between parties. The intervention of migrant mediators had a positive impact, easing dialogue and mutual understanding between teachers and students (Erdilmen, 2021, p. 16). The peer-to-peer methodology involves two different categories of participants: socially integrated migrants, who have been living long in the host country, and newly arrived migrants with lower levels of integration (European Website on Integration, no date). Migrants from the first category are those who can be recruited to act as mediators between underprivileged migrant communities and public services. A suggestion could be promoting university courses in intercultural mediation amongst migrant communities. Such a measure could not only potentially increase the number of prospective students in new degree programmes in intercultural mediation but also be advantageous from the perspective of social inclusion. In this way, migrants could be offered university education and later employed as intercultural mediators. Moreover, in a multiethnic society like the British one, this may be beneficial to the different social groups involved: newly arrived communities may receive assistance tailored to their needs; well-integrated migrants could help bridge the gap between the host country and migrant communities, thus becoming a valuable asset to society. If the teaching of minoritarian languages at the university level cannot be logistically and financially sustainable, the peer-to-peer approach may thus offer an alternative solution to ensure migrant communities are still provided with intercultural mediation support from qualified professionals.

As a final word, apart from fostering migrant inclusion, the implementation of training opportunities may be advantageous from the perspective of the language industry in general. With regard to service providers, the introduction of degree courses in intercultural mediation might increase the number of available workers in the language sector. Moreover, a standardised job description may prevent the generation from distorted expectations (Pokorn and Južnič, 2020, p. 100) about the responsibilities and ethical positioning of mediators, whose role, as explained above, is often confused with that of a community interpreter or other akin professions. It has been discussed above that in the UK intercultural mediation duties are provided by civil mediators. From their standpoint, the introduction of proper training courses in intercultural mediation may lead to a clearly defined set of competencies and professional standards, thus setting the basis for the recognition of the intercultural mediator as a professional. Indeed, the fact that mediation activities are often carried out on a voluntary or ad hoc basis seems to contribute to the long-standing devaluation of the profession and to minimise its essential social function. In this sense, defining a clear code of conduct might also help mediators better identify themselves in their social role, thus producing higher satisfaction levels and performance standards.

Concluding Remarks

As a prerequisite to employability, education is paramount to migrant socioeconomic inclusion. However, access to equal learning opportunities can be guaranteed only when linguistic and cultural barriers are appropriately removed. Accordingly, the presence of intercultural mediators should become a systemic part of the education system of countries with high migrant presence. For this to be possible, the role of the intercultural mediator should be professionally recognised and proper training should be made available. Results evidenced that university training for intercultural mediation in the UK could be modelled on the degree programmes offered by other European institutions. However, this paper suggests that these should first be subject to some improvements, advocating the need for role specialisation in different fields of intervention and a greater focus on the specific skills needed when working in migratory contexts. Starting from these premises, it was possible to design a pedagogical model for the introduction of courses in intercultural mediation in Britain, with a strong emphasis on school settings. Considering the different functions performed by mediators in educational contexts, training should be interdisciplinary and aim to develop a wide range of competencies beyond linguistic ones, including mediation skills, migrant legislation in the host country, basic pedagogical principles, and the ability to psychologically support foreign pupils in difficult situations. Furthermore, given the practical focus of this profession, courses should be complemented by an internship of variable length in schools. Nevertheless, the implementation of courses in intercultural mediation may encounter financial and logistical constraints. To overcome this limitation, this chapter suggests that intercultural mediation could be introduced in existing T&I courses as elective modules. Another limitation may be the unavailability of qualified staff for teaching these modules, especially in the case of minoritarian languages which are generally left out of university curricula. As an alternative, this chapter proposes a peer-to-peer approach where migrants of the second generation could be trained and hired to provide intercultural mediation assistance to those newly arrived. This measure could have multiple advantages: on the one hand, it would provide migrants with university education and employment possibilities; on the other hand, it would highlight the important social contribution they can bring to the host country's society. The chapter concludes with the observation that the introduction of training at the university level in the UK would be beneficial to both the language industry and migrant communities. In the former case, the provision of specialised training might help the definition of a code of conduct for intercultural mediators, thus encouraging their professional recognition. In the latter case, given the high number of migrants in the country, the support of intercultural mediators in schools may be an effective measure to foster migrant education and inclusion in society at large.

The main limitation of this piece of research consists in the fact that, as discussed, it was predominantly based on the review of current practices across Europe. In other words, the pedagogical model proposed in this chapter is not based on empirically collected data but rather stems from theoretical assumptions. In this light, future studies may be conducted, for example, by collecting verbal data (through questionnaires or interviews) from intercultural mediators operating in schools across different countries. Their replies may be used to identify the daily challenges they encounter and how these could be addressed by training. For example, it may be interesting to explore how mediators practically face issues such as relationship-building with children, interfacing with parents, and activity coordination with pedagogical educators. In this way, the factual experiences of professional mediators working in educational settings could be leveraged to improve the potential weaknesses of the pedagogical model offered in this chapter and improve its efficiency.

References

Amato, A. and Garwood, C. 2011. Cultural mediators in Italy: A new breed of linguists. *Intralinea Online Translation Journal*, 13, [no pagination].

Baraldi, C. 2014. An interactional perspective of interpreting as mediation. *Languages, Cultures, Mediation*, 1(1–2), pp. 17–36.

Casadei, S. and Franceschetti, M. 2009. *Il Mediatore culturale in sei Paesi europei (Italia, Francia, Germania, Grecia, Regno Unito e Spagna). Ambiti di intervento, percorsi di accesso e competenze*. [Online]. Strumenti ISFOL. [Accessed 27 August 2023]. Available from: https://inapp.infoteca.it/ricerca/dettaglio/il-mediatore-culturale-in-sei-paesi-europei-risorsa-elettronica-italia-francia-g/16125.

Catarci, M. 2016. Intercultural mediation as a strategy to facilitate relations between the school and immigrant families. *Revista Electrónica Interuniversitaria de Formación del Profesorado*, 19(1), pp. 127–140.

Chiofalo, T. A., Fernández-Martínez, M. d. M., Luque-de-la-Rosa, A. and Carrión-Martínez, J. J. 2019. The role of L2 and cultural mediation in the inclusion of immigrant students in Italian schools. *Education Sciences*, 9(4) [no pagination].

Erdilmen, M. 2021. *Frameworks and good practices of intercultural mediation for migrant integration in Europe*. [Online]. International Organization for Migration

(IOM). [Accessed 27 August 2023]. Available from: https://eea.iom.int/resources/frameworks-and-good-practices-intercultural-mediation.

European Website on Integration [no date]. Mimi – *With Migrants for Migrants*. [Online]. [Accessed 27 August 2023]. Available from: https://ec.europa.eu/migrant-integration/integration-practice/mimi-migrants-migrants_en.

Garbe, A., Ogurlu, U., Logan, N. and Cook, P. 2020. COVID-19 and remote learning: Experiences of parents with children during the pandemic. *American Journal of Qualitative Research*, 4(3), pp. 45–65.

GOV.UK. 2022. *Thousands of Ukrainian Refugees Offered School Places around the Country*. [Press release]. [Accessed 27 August 2024]. Available from: https://www.gov.uk/government/news/thousands-of-ukrainian-refugees-offered-school-places-around-the-country.

International Organizer for Migration. 2021. *Integrating Migration into Education Interventions. A Toolkit for Interventional Cooperation and Developmental Actors*. [Online]. ION UN MIGRATION, publications platform. [Accessed 8 February 2024]. Available from: https://publications.iom.int/books/integrating-migration-education-interventions-toolkit-international-cooperation-and

Leonardi, L. 2022. Overcoming Linguistic Inequities: Strengths and Limitations of Translation during the Pandemic. *International Journal of Translation and Interpreting Studies*, 2(2), pp. 74–84.

Liddicoat, A. J. 2016. Intercultural mediation, intercultural communication and translation. *Perspectives*, 24(3), pp. 354–364.

Loprieno, D., Elia, A. and Di Maio, C. 2019. *Language Education for Asylum Seekers and refugees in Italy: Provision and Governance*. [Online]. Zenodo. [Accessed 27 August 2023]. Available from: https://zenodo.org/record/5082298.

Mayr, S., Wittgen G. A., Theodosiou, M., Coune, I., Verrept, H., Cruz, C., Diniz, M., A.I. Panagiotopoulou, A. I., Papagiannopoulou, M. T., Bianconi, L., Raguso, C., Kaczmarczyk D. 2015. *Description of 10 Good Practices in Intercultural Mediation for Immigrants (IMfI) throughout Europe and Suggestions for Transfer*. [Online]. European Website on Integration. [Accessed 27 August 2023]. Available from: https://ec.europa.eu/migrant-integration/library-document/description-10-good-practices-intercultural-mediation-immigrants-imfi-throughout_en.

O'Carrol, L. and Adams, R. 2023. *Number of EU Students Enrolling in UK Universities Halves post-Brexit*. [Online]. The Guardian. [Accessed 27 August 2023]. Available from: https://www.theguardian.com/education/2023/jan/27/number-eu-students-enrolling-uk-universities-down-half-since-brexit.

Olympic Training and Consulting Ltd. 2015. *Intercultural Mediator Profile and Related Learning Outcomes*. [Online] TIME. Train Intercultural Mediators for Europe. [Accessed 27 August 2023] Available from: https://mediation-time.eu/index.php?option=com_content&view=article&id=3&Itemid=122&lang=en.

Olympic Training and Consulting Ltd. 2016. *Self-Study Course for Trainers of Intercultural Mediators. Module 7, Resources on Intercultural Mediation*. [Online]. TIME. Train Intercultural Mediators for Europe. [Accessed 27 August 2023]. Available from: https://mediation-time.eu/index.php?option=com_content&view=article&id=3&Itemid=122&lang=en.

Open Society Foundations (OSF). 2011. *Roma Health Mediators: Success and Challenges*. [Online]. [Accessed 19 February 2024]. Available from: https://www.opensocietyfoundations.org/publications/roma-health-mediators-successes-and-challenges.

Pokorn, N. K. and Južnič T. M. 2020. Community interpreters versus intercultural mediators. Is it really about ethics? *Translation and Interpreting Studies*, 15(1), pp. 80–107.

Proietti, S. 2020. *Didattica a distanza e alunni stranieri: le problematiche*. [Online]. [Accessed 26 August 2023]. Available from: https://www.piuculture.it/2020/04/alunni-stranieri-dad/.

Sani, S. 2015. The Role of Intercultural Mediation in the Integration of Foreign Students. *Procedia – Social and Behavioural Sciences*, 191, pp. 2582–2584.

Theodosiou, A. and Aspioti, M. (eds.) 2015. *Research Report on Intercultural Mediation for immigrants in Europe*. [Online]. European Website on Integration. [Accessed 27 August 2023]. Available from: https://ec.europa.eu/migrant-integration/library-document/research-report-intercultural-mediation-immigrants-europe_en.

TIME Project (Train Intercultural Mediators for a Multicultural Europe). 2015. *Intellectual outputs*. [Online]. [Accessed 28 September 2023]. Available from: https://www.mediation-time.eu/index.php?option=com_content&view=article&id=3&Itemid=122&lang=it.

Wang, C. 2017. Interpreters = Cultural mediators? *TranslatoLogica*, 1, pp. 93–115.

PART III

Live Subtitling Training, the Classroom and the Profession

8
REDEFINING RESPEAKERS' TRAINING

A Practical Approach to Diamesic Translation Tactics and Respeaking Skills

Martina A. Bruno

Introduction

Bridging the gap between Simultaneous Interpreting (SI) and subtitling, Live Subtitling (LS) makes live events accessible to diverse audiences, including d/Deaf and hard-of-hearing people, via the reformulation, the transcription or the translation of a live speech into real-time intralingual or interlingual subtitles (Eugeni, 2007). In order to perform their task, live subtitlers, or respeakers, utilise Automatic Speech Recognition (ASR) software, which they train to recognise their voices (Marsh, 2006). A crucial part of the respeaking task, and thus of respeakers' training, is familiarisation with the ASR software, which is an essential co-worker of respeakers (Remael and Van der Veer, 2006).

The training of respeakers, including their familiarity with ASR software, is pivotal given the range of abilities and skills they must possess, as highlighted in research on LS performance. Such abilities include enunciation, psycho-cognitive, metalinguistic, and diamesic skills, and both textual (Eugeni, 2008a, pp. 91–94; Romero-Fresco, 2011, p. 52; Eugeni and Gambier, 2023, pp. 72–73) and translation skills (Gambier, 2007) during an LS performance. However, research has left a gap in the didactic of respeaking concerning the strategies students need in order to cope with this complex process's various cognitive challenges.

With the final aim of establishing a novel training approach, this paper will first draw on the similarities that respeaking has in common with SI and Subtitles for the d/Deaf and the Hard-of-Hearing (SDH). Later, the LS effort model will be defined to guide us through the set of abilities and respeaking strategies that need to be used to cope with the challenges posed by the

Source Text (ST) and that students need to be made aware of and trained in before they enter the professional practice.

Similarities between Respeaking, SI and SDH

Respeaking is at the crossroads of SI and SDH. It has in common with SI what Seeber (2011, p. 185) defines as the intralingual or interlingual transfer of meaning in real-time. On the other hand, respeaking and SDH have features such as adding punctuation and character identification in common. This hybrid nature of respeaking is reflected both in practice and in theory. In practice, this discipline is part of course modules within interpreting and subtitling training programs (Arumí-Ribas and Romero-Fresco, 2008, p. 123; Eugeni, 2008b, pp. 357–382; Eugeni et al., 2021, pp. 217–218). In theory, the current academic programs show that several skills respeakers need in their profession intersect with those of SI and SDH (Arumí-Ribas and Romero-Fresco, 2008, pp. 114–116; Eugeni, 2008b, pp. 357–382; Romero-Fresco, 2011, pp. 51–54; Pagano, 2020, pp. 33–35).

Similar to interpreters, respeakers produce LS with little margin for their output's correction or improvement and exert constant control over their voice while listening (Romero-Fresco, 2011, p. 46). An extensive *ex-ante* glossary and relevant terminology preparation characterise both professions. In SI, this kind of preparation accelerates information retrieval without further burdening the interpreters' Working Memory (WM) during their performance (Gile, 2021, p. 153). Finally, both professionals operate in similar working conditions: in a booth, with a microphone and headset, and often with a colleague (Arumí-Ribas and Romero-Fresco, 2008, p. 110; Eugeni, 2008b, pp. 357–382; Pagano, 2020, p. 32; Eugeni et al., 2021, pp. 218–219).

On the other hand, respeaking and SDH aim to create comprehensible intralingual or interlingual subtitles deemed usable by their audience, namely d/Deaf and hard-of-hearing viewers. Both professionals apply reduction, reformulation or expansion tactics on the ST to achieve this. Moreover, they add punctuation and deal with difficulties such as overlapping dialogue, multiple turn-takings and *realia* (Romero-Fresco, 2011, p. 48). Finally, like subtitlers, respeakers must be aware of their audience's needs and expectations, providing extralinguistic information when needed (Eugeni, 2008a, p. 15).

In an attempt to outline the effort model of respeaking, Eugeni finds that the efforts involved in the respeaking process are very similar to those encountered in SI, both from a sociolinguistic and a psycho-cognitive perspective (Eugeni, 2008a, p. 65). The respeaking task requires a listening and decoding effort that takes place during the ST reception and comprehension; a memory effort that is responsible for stocking phonetic, grammatical, semantic, pragmatic and conceptual units for the necessary time to produce the Target Text (TT);

a production effort concerned with the TT's stylistic and grammatical quality; and a delivery effort which they share with the ASR software for the generation of potential mistakes in the TT. The effort model seems to confirm respeaking's similarity to SI, with the former mainly differing from the latter in linguistic directionality, as far as Intralingual Live Subtitles (ILS) are concerned. However, research conducted by Romero-Fresco (2011, pp. 46–47) shows how this aspect is compensated by the additional effort procured by the respeaker's interaction with the ASR software, which requires an extra monitoring effort to counter the latter's potential lexical and semantic misrecognitions that could hinder the audience's comprehension.

Respeakers Skills

The efforts involved in the LS process call for a set of competencies, enunciation and psycho-cognitive skills and text and translation-related strategies, on the part of respeakers. Hence, prospective professionals need to be first trained to develop enunciation skills, pronouncing each word as clearly as possible and trying to avoid misrecognitions from the software (Eugeni, 2008a, p. 26). On the psycho-cognitive front, respeakers must deal with the simultaneity of ST reception and TT process and product (Eugeni, 2008a, p. 25). Additionally, prospective respeakers should also be trained in text and translation-related strategies. Text-related strategies refer to 'genre,' which reunites a series of conventionalised or institutionalised textual products with characteristics specific to contexts, practices and cultures (Bhatia, 2002, p. 6). The multimodality of Audio-Visual Translation (AVT), with the co-presence of the acoustic and visual–verbal and non-verbal components, conveys a broader sense of the notion of 'genre' applied to respeaking where factors such as the translation production time, the type of audience for which the translation is intended and the time taken to access the translation need to be considered (Eugeni and Gambier, 2023, pp. 72–73). When it comes to translation-related strategies, quality becomes paramount. The TT must answer to several criteria such as grammatical and linguistic acceptability, legibility, semantic comprehensibility, synchronicity and pertinence in relation to the ST, and assimilation strategies related to cultural aspects and values to be conveyed in the TT (Eugeni, 2008a, pp. 87–88). A further criterion for determining AVT quality is considering the end users as vectors of all the stylistic and linguistic decisions (Nord, 2000, p. 195). A translation must answer the latter's needs and expectations if it has a specific end user as an addressee. For a d/Deaf and hard-of-hearing audience, this entails being aware of their deafness degree, age, education and whether they use Sign Language (SL) or oralism. However, it is impossible to produce a text that can satisfy the needs of all receivers, and only a text conceived for a specific purpose can be considered satisfactory (Nord, 2000).

From this notion of quality in AVT, several authors – Gottlieb (1992), Lambert and Delabastita (1996), Chesterman (1997) and Gambier (2007), among others – have tried to outline a framework for the translation strategies to be used. Drawing on the notion of LS as a form of Diamesic Translation (DT) because of the shift from the spoken to the written form, Eugeni and Gambier (2023, pp. 83–91) design a taxonomy tailored to the four sets of strategies that respeakers employ during their task, namely *litteratim*, for dealing with phonetic elements, *verbatim*, for lexical items, *sensatim*, for semantic components and *signatim*, for non-verbal features.

Data Collection

As stated in the Introduction, this paper aims to establish a novel training approach for the didactic of respeaking. In order to do so, it will be necessary to identify the strategies and best practices that professionals employ during their tasks to include them in a respeaking training program. For this purpose, we will outline the criteria for choosing the ILSed conference used for this research, the interview to the LS providers and the research tools and method for transcribing the conference and the subtitles.

The Conference

We chose an ILSed accessibility conference named *Les Assises Régionales de l'Accessibilité* ('The Regional Accessibility Conference') for this purpose. The conference was accessed online from its YouTube channel[1] and was 3h 38' 22" long. The portion chosen for the present analysis corresponds to the last 50,' characterised by spontaneous and prepared speeches. This conference was deemed appropriate for our scope because of 1) the discourse authenticity, 2) the speakers' fast speech rate of 179 words per minute (Romero-Fresco, 2009, pp. 127–128), 3) the combination of impromptu and scripted speeches, and finally 4) the conference's topic, whose focus on accessibility is central to the ILS field. The accessibility service to the event was provided by *Le Messageur*, a French cooperative whose activity revolves around LS and inclusive communication. For the aims of the present paper, Bruno (2023, pp. 389–390) interviewed *Le Messageur* on their work modality and best practices during LS tasks, and their answers helped define the respeaking strategies that will be discussed later in the chapter.

Transcription and Alignment Method

The transcription of the oral speech of the conference is *verbatim*, hence word-for-word (including repetitions, interruptions and overlapping dialogues, among others), and literal (Szarkowska et al., 2011, p. 363), hence words are transcribed as they are pronounced, in order to highlight any pronunciation errors made by the speakers. The conference's ILS were transcribed as they appeared on the screen of the dedicated YouTube channel. The method adopted for chunking the transcripts relied on what Eugeni (2008a, p. 108) defines as idea units, namely, each proposition expressing a finite idea. Afterwards, we executed the segmentation and alignment of the spoken and the respoken parts of the conference via ELAN (2023), a programme developed specifically for transcription and extraction of oral data and, as such, has several advantages. Amongst these, ELAN allows for the annotation of the interactions among the speakers, such as overlapping dialogue or multiple turn-takings (Niemants, 2020, pp. A65-A66). In ELAN, each speaker had an allocated slot, called *tier*. Each *tier* contained a number of annotations filled with either the spoken or the respoken transcripts for a total of 747 idea units that were later analysed using Eugeni and Gambier's (2023, pp. 83–91) new taxonomy for DT analysis.

Teaching Respeaking Skills

Building on the taxonomy by Eugeni and Gambier (2023) through the DT analysis and the interview with *Le Messageur* to be found in Bruno (2023, pp. 389–390), we will give a brief overview of the main tactics used by the respeakers to deal with the conference's spoken text. The analysis will show the importance of a respeaking training tailored towards a *sensatim* approach. Consequently, by employing the lessons learnt from such analysis, we propose a novel didactic of respeaking skills to allow students to develop a comprehensive skillset. In particular, we will start with the techniques respeakers and interpreters have in common, namely *understanding strategies*, to overcome the translating task's potential challenges (Kohn and Kalina, 1996, pp. 120–132). Consequently, we will look at the *production strategies* derived from Eugeni (2008a, p. 69) and further implemented thanks to the DT analysis and the interview with *Le Messageur*. Finally, from the *neutralisation and evasion strategies* (Kohn and Kalina, 1996, p. 127), designed to tackle ST difficulties, we will look at the *exit strategies* (LTA, 2018) for dealing with the challenges arising during ILS.

Diamesic Translation Analysis

We studied the data using Eugeni and Gambier's (2023, pp. 83–91) new taxonomy for DT analysis. The following review of the main tactics found in the analysis is intended to illustrate the main ILS characteristics that emerged. The taxonomy comprises four strategies, *litteratim*, *verbatim*, *sensatim* and *signatim*, each containing ten tactics. Specifically, the *litteratim* strategy concerns phonetical, phonological and orthographical tactics, rendering the ST phonemes into graphemes in the TT. During the analysis, we found that the main *litteratim* tactic used was omitting phonetic sounds such as hesitations, as in the case of *euh* ('uh') or *hmm*.

The *verbatim* strategy contains tactics dealing with the ST's lexical and morphological aspects aimed at delivering word-for-word subtitles. Besides adding punctuation, the analysis showed that respeakers were mainly concerned with omitting lexical repetitions, filler words, false starts and autocorrections, as in the case of *qui sont... qui ont* ('who are... who have').

The *sensatim* strategy comprises tactics that focus on the ST's syntactic, semantic and pragmatic aspects and are concerned with delivering each idea unit's meaning. The analysis showed that the main tactic used is the omission of semantic information, as in the example:

ST: *on va euh commencer cette **dernière** table ronde* ('we are uh going to begin this last round table')

TT: *On va commencer cette table ronde.* ('We are going to begin this round table.')

Another widespread ILS *sensatim* tactic is the reformulation of idea units via condensation or expansion. Interpreting Studies (IS) show that reformulation is essential for the instantaneous rendition of a speech we are simultaneously listening to (Seeber, 2011, p. 189). This is because in SI two different languages are involved in the translation process, thus leading to a cognitive overload for the interpreters. Consequently, the latter will either anticipate or postpone information in the TT to free up their information processing capacity and WM. In the same way, in respeaking the ST – too fast or complex from a syntactic perspective – and the need to keep up with the speaker's speech rate, together with the additional ASR software monitoring effort, does not allow for a *verbatim* rendition. Hence, a reformulation becomes a suitable coping mechanism in such instances. In the following example, the respeaker chose to reformulate the repetition *même s'il leur manque* ('even if they miss') with a shorter *ou* ('or'):

ST: *même s'il leur manque un bras **même s'il leur manque** une jambe* ('even if they miss an arm even if they miss a leg')

TT: *même s'il leur manque un bras **ou** une jambe.* ('even if they miss an arm or a leg.')

This strategy also includes a tactic that accounts for cohesion or coherence changes from the ST to the TT. A case for coherence changes is connected to LS mistakes generated either by a dictation error from the respeaker or by a misrecognition from the software. Errors are almost inevitable because of the human-machine interaction and the nature of the ST, whose content can be unpredictable and delivered at varying speeds. A respeaking course should teach students to recognise and evaluate errors to develop mistake-coping mechanisms during their ILS production. Three mistakes emerged from the ILS DT analysis: minor, standard and serious (Romero-Fresco and Pérez, 2015, p. 33). A minor mistake, such as a grammatical one, can cause a cohesion and coherence issue. Such is the case in the following example, where there is a lack of grammatical agreement between the verb and the gender of the subject:

ST: *manager technique **retraité** de l'industrie* ('technical manager [m.] retired from the industry')

TT: *manager technique **retraitée** de l'industrie,* ('technical manager [f.] retired from the industry,')

Here, 'retired' becomes feminine in the TT even though the subject is male. However, this does not hinder the subtitles' readability and comprehensibility. On the other hand, a standard mistake can hinder the TT reception. Usually, the audience can notice a standard mistake and tries to fill in the gaps by inferring from the context:

ST: comme le disait **Marc** tout tout à l'heure et en introduction ('as Marc said just just before and in the introduction')

TT: Comme **marque** le disais tout à l'heure, en introduction, ('As [sic] the brand said just before, in the introduction')

In the previous example, the mistake is quite evident. The audience could compensate for the lack of correct semantic information thanks to the knowledge they acquired by attending the conference and their knowledge of the attending speakers. However, without a reception study, it is impossible to determine whether the participants at the event inferred the information from previous knowledge or whether the semantic content was inaccessible. Finally, a serious mistake alters the proposition's meaning without the public being able to notice it who will, therefore, receive incorrect information. In the following case, it is hardly possible to determine that the word *interpoler* ('include') is an error – it does not pose any semantic or grammatical problems – and to recover the meaning of the word *interpeller* ('address'):

ST: elle a besoin de nous demain pour nous **interpeller** sur un sujet qu'elle souhaite évoquer ('she needs us tomorrow to address us on a topic she wants to talk about')

TT: Si elle a besoin de nous demain pour nous **interpoler** sur un sujet qu'elle souhaite évoquer, ('If she needs us tomorrow [sic] to include us on a topic she wants to talk about,')

The *signatim* strategy aims to deliver the ST's paraverbal, non-verbal and semiotic elements. The present analysis found that character identification, employing an underscore, is the main tactic used, as shown in the following exchange between two speakers at the conference:

ST: *bah oui j'suis de nature positive* ('well yes I'm of a positive disposition')
TT: _ *Oui, je suis de nature positive!* ('_ Yes, I am of a positive disposition!')
ST: *ouais c'est bien ça fait du bien ça fait du bien* ('yeah that's good that is a good thing that is a good thing')
TT: _ *Ça fait du bien.* ('_ That is a good thing.')

The DT analysis found a prevalence of *verbatim* tactics, with the word-for-word repetition or with the punctual manipulation of isolated lexical elements, and of *sensatim* tactics, through semantic changes in the ST. These trends are revealing of the respeakers' approach during their task and the *exit strategies* they employ to deal with the difficulties they encounter (LTA, 2018). The interview with *Le Messageur* sheds light on their respeakers' approach towards a more *verbatim* versus *sensatim* approach. The main goal is to remain faithful to the speaker's intention without omitting semantic information. If the speech rate is moderate, there are no particular difficulties, the subject of the conference is well-mastered, and the sound conditions are optimal, they are encouraged to produce word-for-word subtitles. However, respeakers paraphrase dense or fast speech, removing superfluous elements when needed. Finally, some repetitions are retained when they are used as a rhetorical device. With these elements in mind, let us look at the respeaking skills students should be trained in during a live-subtitling course.

Understanding Strategies

Starting from Kohn and Kalina's (1996, p. 124) notion that SI is a *strategic discourse processing* with many aspects in common with the comprehension and production of a foreign language text, the two German researchers developed a model that builds on the *strategic model of discourse comprehension* of van Dijk and Kintsch (1983, p. 96) according to which text comprehension depends on the implementation of six different strategies.

In *propositional strategies*, the phonetic and morpho-syntactic input is translated in the listener's mind into the ST structure's lexical and grammatical comprehension. Next, in the *local coherence strategies,* the single propositions establish logical connections in the listener's mind that favour the text's lexical and grammatical comprehension. The *macrostrategies* used by the speaker construct the ST's macro-structure that allows the listener to understand its evolution in time and space. Furthermore, they speak of *schematic strategies* referring to the textual genre the ST belongs to, whose previous knowledge allows the listener to anticipate or infer textual elements. In addition, *production strategies* are the general strategies implemented by the speaker to convey the message, and that can be selected based on the communicational framework within which the text is produced. Last, *other strategies for comprehension and production* comprise a whole series of stylistic, rhetorical, non-verbal and conversational strategies that are part of the shared language knowledge and help the audience understand the essence of a text.

Based on these strategies, Kohn and Kalina (1996) define a model to overcome the translating task's potential challenges. This model relies on a broad shared knowledge base, encompassing linguistic expression, world and subject knowledge, discourse context, mental modelling and procedural knowledge (Kohn and Kalina, 1996, p. 121). This shared knowledge allows for a bottom-up or a top-down inferencing approach where the former stands for inferring from data, and the latter corresponds to an *ex-ante* interpretation based on expectations and prior knowledge. In respeaking, a bottom-up versus top-down approach takes on a particular meaning when dealing with ASR software (Arumí-Ribas and Romero-Fresco, 2008, p. 117). While humans adopt a top-down inferencing process to recognise speech, using concepts and their knowledge of the world to identify words, machines use a bottom-up approach, analysing sound structures from phonemes, the most basic unit, to recognise speech (Keyes, 2007). Based on shared knowledge of the world and the language used in a specific communicational framework, let us now look at the *production strategies* that respeakers need to produce meaningful subtitles.

Processing and Production Strategies

Understanding strategies must be accompanied by a set of *processing strategies* adapted by Eugeni (2008a, p. 69) from Kalina (1992, pp. 254–255). Respeakers must enact *elaborative inferencing* strategies through the anticipation of lexical, grammatical and conceptual elements, thus deriving a better stylistic rendition. Moreover, *memorising* strategies lead to better stylistic results by postponing the memorised lexical, grammatical and conceptual elements. Such efforts will require *monitoring strategies*. Respeakers must monitor their output for the entire task to counter or correct lexical, grammatical and conceptual mistakes via delay reduction, syntactic reformulation, chunking and editing. Respeakers will be called upon to adopt *adaptation strategies* to adapt the ST content to the TT. In light of the linguistic, conceptual, and cultural differences that arise during this task, respeakers can count on tactics such as disambiguation, explanation, reformulation, generalisation, substitution and paraphrasing. Respeakers must also adopt *neutralisation and evasion strategies*, such as omission and generalisation, to preserve the text's coherence and cohesion (Kohn and Kalina, 1996, p. 127).

However, for these *processing strategies* to be activated during the respeaking task, live subtitlers must first be familiar with a series of *production strategies*, identified and implemented, thanks to the DT analysis results and the interview with *Le Messageur*. To be defined, such approaches are enunciation, psycho-cognitive, diamesic, genre and accessibility skills (Eugeni, 2008a, pp. 165–167).

Enunciation skills are paramount for a quality TT delivery. Respeaking students must become familiar with the ASR software. To do so, refer to exercises for dictating with clear and flat pronunciation, avoiding non-verbal sounds, and setting clear boundaries between words (Eugeni, 2008a, p. 26; Russello, 2010; Eugeni and Bernabé Caro, 2019, p. 97). Moreover, students must create domain-specific vocabularies and macros by identifying technical and uncommon terms present in the ST (Arumí-Ribas and Romero-Fresco, 2008, p. 117). Making a list of all those words that could not be included in their voice profile and training the ASR software will be helpful to minimise misrecognitions and mistakes. The interview with *Le Messageur* found in Bruno (2023, pp. 389–390) confirms the importance of this kind of preparation in the professional market. Their respeakers conduct internet research, analyse customer documents, create shared-use glossaries, optimise ASR software dictionaries, and establish voice shortcuts for customer-specific jargon. Training varies, with known topics mainly requiring updating the vocabulary in the ASR software and specialised events demanding more time to familiarise with the new topic and domain-specific terms. The DT analysis showed that many domain-specific terms to the conference could not be present in the ASR software language model, thus requiring previous preparation and training. Such terms are proper names (*Stéphane Bourdon*, *Yvette Molina*), associations (*UNIACCES*, *SENSOCOM*), places (*Langoëlan, Morbihan*) and domain-related terms (*audioprothésistes* 'audiologists,' *presbytie* 'farsightedness').

Psycho-cognitive or *multitasking skills* are essential to a respeaking training program. Respeakers must master the ability to speak and listen at the same time, reformulate, edit and correct their respoken output while simultaneously listening, remember complete sentences while lagging and deal with extralinguistic elements such as slides and videos (Eugeni and Bernabé-Caro, 2019, p. 96). Delay is a paramount *production strategy*. Respeakers cannot dictate at a faster pace to reduce delay, as subtitles are displayed on screen according to the speed of dictation (Russello, 2010). Additionally, dictating at a quicker pace would make sentences appear on screen at a faster rate, thus compromising the TT's accessibility and the audience's readability capacity. So, respeakers must resort to omissions, reformulations and an even dictation pace (Russello, 2010).

Diamesic skills comprise synthetic and metalinguistic skills. Where the former is concerned, in cases of high ST speech rate or difficulty, respeakers will have to make a qualitative and quantitative synthesis of the ST in the TT to avoid skipping some important elements of the original, thus respecting the event's multimodality (Eugeni, 2008a, p. 27). To make the TT accessible and comprehensible, respeakers need to develop some metalinguistic skills for formatting, dictating punctuation and implementing non-verbal elements for each working context by applying different techniques such as changing colours or font size for plays-on-words, music and extradiegetic sounds, or by inserting labels or character identification tags (Eugeni, 2008a, p. 95; LTA, 2018). The DT analysis showed extensive use of punctuation, which follows French syntactic rules, for 820 occurrences (Bruno, 2023). During their ISL production, the DT analysis showed, and the interview confirmed, that the respeakers consistently chose to break the line only when there was a change in the speaker and to render character identification in the subtitles using an underscore. When segmenting speech, respeakers need to consider the subtitles' display mode, synchronicity with the ST and permanence on screen. In *Les Assises*, the subtitles are no longer than three lines and the on-screen display mode is scrolling.

Genre skills require students' training in genre analysis. Each genre will require diverse preparation and strategies to tackle difficult moments. A respeaking training program must focus on identifying the programme genre, training on speakers' speech rate, the image succession speed and the video components' role in the overall semantic and semiotic system (Eugeni, 2008a, p. 167). With this information, the student can decide which approaches to adopt. By analysing several texts of the same genre in detail, it will also be possible to determine a register, terminology and structures that are repeated and can even be anticipated. Given these elements, it is paramount that a respeaking training program prepares students in various speeches and genres.

Accessibility skills are critical in a respeaking training program, as every speech needs to be adapted to the target audience's needs and expectations. The conference analysed in this paper revolved around accessibility, and the *criteria* adopted during ILS production were tailored with a straightforward recipient design in mind. Accessibility also comprises the notion of inclusion, and the following is an example that *Le Messageur*'s respeakers attempt to employ inclusive language when gender representation is concerned:

ST: un bon retour pour **celles et ceux** qui sont dans la salle // et une bonne déconnexion pour **celles** qui sont euh derrière derrière leur petit écran ('a good return trip for the female and male attendants in the room // and a good disconnection for the female attendants who are uh behind behind their screen')

TT: un bon retour pour **ceux** qui sont dans la salle // et une bonne déconnexion pour **ceux et celles** qui sont derrière leurs écrans. ('a good return trip for the male attendants in the room // and a good disconnection for the female and male attendants who are behind their screen.')

In the first ST proposition, the speaker uses the male and female form (*celles et ceux qui sont dans la salle* 'female and male attendants in the room') to address the audience. The corresponding segment in the TT flattens the rendition by employing the male variant *ceux* only to retrieve both forms (*ceux et celles*) in the following proposition. Bearing in mind the efforts involved in the LS process, the rendering of both the male and the female variations may not always be possible due to lack of time or the need to keep up with the speaker as well as the overall deontological requirement to stay faithful to the speaker's intended message. Hence, respeakers can hardly produce inclusive subtitles when the ST is not gender inclusive. However, teaching LS skills to prospective professional respeakers could incorporate aspects such as gender representation and inclusivity, opting for methods that reflect gender-neutral forms of language (Ludbrook, 2022, pp. 20–23).

Exit Strategies

Once *production strategies* are mastered, it will be necessary to focus on *neutralisation and evasion strategies* to tackle ST difficulties (Kohn and Kalina, 1996, pp. 127). Several situations may cause trouble to respeakers during a LS task, such as fast, incomprehensible, low-volume, impromptu, plays-on-words speeches (LTA, 2018).

When trying to subtitle a fast speaker, live subtitlers encounter three problems: they cannot produce an accurate rendition at the same speed; they find it hard to memorise or to understand what is being said; and, even if they were able to keep up with the speaker's pace, the audience would have a hard time reading the subtitles, especially if they are visible as two-line subtitles. One of the *exit strategies* that can be applied is the *gordian knot strategy* (LTA, 2018), which means subtitling every other sentence while trying to keep coherence and providing understandable subtitles:

ST: SURDICOM **avec les services UNIACCES SENSOCOM MBA Mutuelle Askoria les PEP Bret'ill Armor et et l'APAMO et son président Jean Migot euh ont été aussi des** partenaires qui nous ont soutenu tout au long de la démarche ('SURDICOM with the services UNIACCES SENSOCOM MBA Mutuelle Askoria the PEP Bret'ill Armor and and APAMO and its president Jean Migot uh were also partners who supported us throughout the process')

TT: Surdicom, MBA Mutuelle, Askoria, Sensocom, nos partenaires qui nous ont soutenu tout en haut de la démarche. ('Surdicom, MBA Mutuelle, Askoria, Sensocom, our partners who supported us at the very top of the process.')

In the above example, the respeaker kept the overall coherence and cohesion of the text even though some crucial idea units went missing in the process, such as organisations' names (*UNIACCES, PEP Bret'ill Armor, l'APAMO*) and proper names (*Jean Migot*). Another strategy for a fast speaker is the *garwood strategy*, namely 'when in doubt, leave it out,' resuming back from the first intelligible sentence. The following example represents an overlapping exchange between two speakers. In this case, the respeaker decided to apply the *garwood strategy* by omitting the propositions in bold and preserving only clear sentences that make sense in the TT:

ST: oui c'est pour ça qu'on parlait de formation tout à l'heure // **c'était ça hein?** // **ça veut dire** // oui absolument // **absolument** // **oui oui oui oui** // voilà // un bénévole se forme // tout à fait ('yes that's why we were talking about training earlier // that was it eh? // it means // yes absolutely // absolutely // yes yes yes yes // that's it // a volunteer gets trained // definitely')

TT: _ C'est pour ça que l'on parlait de formation tout à l'heure. // _ Tout à fait. ('_ That's why we were talking about training earlier // _ Definitely.')

If respeakers do not understand one or more sentences, they can opt for the *generalisation strategy*. They do so by providing the correct information via a reformulation or by saying something general or logical when the context and the topic are known. In this example, the second proposition is repeated *verbatim* in the TT. Instead, the first one is incomprehensible and characterised by stuttering, repetitions and false starts that lead the respeaker to reformulate it, keeping only the necessary elements.

ST: euh et au final **pour donner un exemple 6 6 allant à rendre accessible je vais pas dire bêtises euh… 6 euh… y avait euh…** // les 6 salles étaient remplies complètement ('uh and in the end to give an example 6 6 going to make accessible I am not talking nonsense uh… 6 uh… there were uh… // all 6 theatres were completely full')

TT: Au final, // les 6 salles étaient remplies complètement. ('In the end, // all 6 theatres were completely full.')

For incomprehensible speech, the *garwood strategy* is still applicable. In this proposition, eliminated by the respeaker in the TT, even the orthographic transcription is uncertain. Hence, it was put in between brackets, per the transcription standards outlined in Groupe ICOR (2007).

ST: (*qui est au su apparu*) ([*sic*] 'who is at the known appeared')
TT:

When live subtitlers try to caption a low-volume speech, their voice might cover that of the speaker. Hence, the problem is not at the understanding level. Additionally, allocating more effort to grasping what the speaker is saying reduces the live subtitler's dictation abilities. They can resort to the *gordian knot strategy*, hearing and repeating a sentence as fast as possible, compressing it, skipping the second sentence and resuming on the third to maintain cohesion and coherence with the first sentence. In the following example, the respeaker implemented this strategy by repeating and compressing the first statement and cutting out the proposition reported in bold. The overall result is coherent, and it conveys the essential semantic elements useful for communication:

ST: le respect des uns et des autres quel que soit euh son projet de vie ou quelles que soient les situations de handicap **qu'on peut vivre au jour le jour** ('respect for each other whatever uh one's life plan or whatever disability conditions one may experience on a day-to-day basis')

TT: Le respect des un et des autres, quel que soit son projet de vie ou la situation de handicap? ('Respect for each other, whatever one's life plan or disability condition' ?).

The features of orality characterise impromptu speeches. When deciding between a *verbatim* or a *sensatim* approach in LS, one must consider that impromptu speeches are an obstacle to the subtitling process due to the presence of mispronunciations, for speakers who have a disability, or even calques, and for foreign speakers (LTA, 2018). One option is to correct the speaker's bad grammar, mispronunciations, wrong words, mumblings, hesitations, self-reformulations, and extra sounds. In an impromptu speech, the subtitles need to be consistent with what the speaker says. For this reason, it is recommended that the ST manipulation is only done at the grammatical level; otherwise, those who read the subtitles will not access the same content as those who listen to the speaker. In this example, the ST presents the typical features of orality in the form of the subject's anaphoric retrieval (*elle* 'it'), a hesitation (*euh* 'uh') and a grammatical mistake (*au* 'at the'). For respeakers to perform their duty, namely ensuring the accessibility within a communication event, they produce the necessary corrections to foster readability:

ST: la communication **elle** se fait tout simplement **euh au** [sic] bouche-à-oreille ('communication it is done simply uh at the [sic] word of mouth')

TT: La communication se fait **du** bouche-à-oreille tout simplement. ('Communication is simply done by word of mouth.')

Live subtitlers typically interrupt respeaking for plays-on-words which they type in uppercase letters, exclamation points, or ellipses. These are all devices to draw the audience's attention. In this instance, the respeaker omitted a play-on-words, *allez les merlus* ('Go, Hakes!'), referring to FC Lorient, a soccer team from the French Morbihan department. Several reasons could explain this choice: relevance in the TT, unfamiliarity, or avoidance of ASR recognition issues. This case exemplifies the challenges in handling wordplay within the transcribed conference segment.

ST: dans le Morbihan **allez les merlus** eh et référent handicap ('in Morbihan go hakes eh and disability referent')
TT: dans le Morbihan et référent handicap ('in Morbihan and disability referent')

Finally, *exit strategies* come into play when there is a comprehension problem on the part of respeakers, which is also why *understanding strategies* are paramount. When respeakers understand the ST, they apply a *sensatim* tactic that fosters readability. When they do not understand, they use a tactic that allows them to produce a coherent text which misses some critical idea units. In addition to *exit strategies*, each professional entity has its standards for dealing with problematic speech. *Le Messageur* pointed out some of their coping mechanisms to also integrate into a respeaking course. They usually insert an explanation inside square brackets such as: 1) Off-mic speech; 2) Poor sound reception; 3) Incomprehensible speech; 4) Overlapping dialogue; 5) Background noise; 6) * which stands for a word or a proper noun whose spelling is uncertain; and 7) ** which stands for a missing proposition. Of course, such devices are bound to create inequalities between the hearing audience and the d/Deaf audience and need to be used carefully, preferring generalisations or downright omissions as in the *gordian knot strategy* (LTA, 2018).

Conclusions

This contribution aimed to show how studies on the didactic of respeaking have stressed the need for live subtitlers to develop textual and linguistic strategies to cope with the diamesic nature of LS. Focusing on the intralingual aspect of this discipline and drawing from previous literature, we have come to define the need to work on *understanding strategies* by Kohn and Kalina (1996) to develop those skills that respeakers have in common with SI to foster their *production strategies* acquisition. We defined such strategies thanks to previous contributions – Kalina (1992) and Eugeni (2008a) – and implemented them thanks to the DT analysis, using Eugeni and Gambier's (2023) suggested DT strategies and tactics, and to the interview with *Le Messageur* found in Bruno (2023) for the best practices that professional respeakers deploy in the professional market. Finally, focusing on the *exit strategies* (LTA, 2018), we have come to see which strategies respeaking students need to be trained on to cope with difficult moments in the ST, and that allows us to deliver a quality TT in a communication-based approach where all parties participating in an event have access to the information.

All factors considered, this study confirmed that respeakers work close to their saturation threshold because of the pool of cognitive skills, text and translation-related strategies they must allocate during their task. However, likewise with SI, if students practice a lot, they can expect to expend less processing capacity, thus taking less time for each effort and eventually becoming less vulnerable to processing capacity deficits and their consequences, such as attention fluctuations and errors (Gile, 2021, p. 143).

The proposed parameters for the didactic of respeaking skills need further research on the respeaking tools to use during a course, the stages and the exercises it should comprise. Such training programs should inform students of the respeaking modalities best suited to a specific audience and their accessibility needs (Eugeni, 2008a, pp. 109–110). Moreover, training should be tailored to learning objectives (Eugeni, 2008a, p. 158; Russello, 2010; LTA, 2018; Eugeni et al., 2021, pp. 219–221). In class, prospective respeakers should be given a general hint of the topic to autonomously conduct the research and create glossaries with the relevant terminology. They should train the ASR software with domain-specific terms to avoid overloading their WM during their task by increasing the retrieving availability of such items. Given the similar efforts allocated to both SI and respeaking, Eugeni (2008a, p. 158) suggests teaching LS students *verbatim* skills during the 1st year course – with shadowing being a good exercise for the ST word-for-word repetition – and *sensatim* skills during the 2nd year.

Finally, respeaking training should always be tailored to the current and changing professional market's best practices, as highlighted by the interview with *Le Messageur*, with different tools used during the task as technology improves, such as software for displaying subtitles and for working *in tandem* and adapting to in-person or on-remote modalities according to the clients' needs, as during the COVID-19 pandemic.

Note

1 Assises Régionales de l'Accessibilité. [Online]. [Accessed 24 August 2023]. Available from: https://www.youtube.com/watch?v=yIZhZr-nZoE.

References

Arumí-Ribas, M. and Romero-Fresco, P. 2008. A practical proposal for the training of respeakers1. *Journal of Specialised Translation*. [Online]. [Accessed 24 August 2023]. Available from: https://citeseerx.ist.psu.edu/document?repid=rep1&type=pdf&doi=ffa6a39ac1f1e5604f3f182c02de2cf4932fe7fd

Bhatia, V. 2002. Applied genre analysis: A multi-perspective model. *Ibérica: Revista de la Asociación Europea de Lenguas para fines específicos (AELFE)*, 4, pp. 3–19.

Bruno, M.A. 2023. *Il respeaking intralinguistico – la traduzione diamesica e la valutazione della qualità*. Unpublished MA thesis. University of Bologna – Forlì.

Chesterman, A. 1997. *Memes of Translation*. Netherlands: John Benjamins Publishing Company.

ELAN (Version 6.6) [Computer software]. 2023. Nijmegen: Max Planck institute for psycholinguistics, the language archive. [Online]. [Accessed 24 August 2023]. Available from: https://archive.mpi.nl/tla/elan

Eugeni, C. 2007. Il rispeakeraggio televisivo per sordi. *Per una sottotitolazione mirata del TG, inTRAlinea*, 9. [Online]. [Accessed 24 August 2023]. Available from: https://www.intralinea.org/archive/article/Il_rispeakeraggio_televisivo_per_sordi

Eugeni, C. 2008a. *Le sous-titrage en direct : aspects theoriques, professionels et didactiques*. Macerata: EUM.

Eugeni, C. 2008b. A sociolinguistic approach to real-time subtitling. Respeaking vs. shadowing and simultaneous interpreting. In Kellett Bidoli, C. J. and Ochse, E. eds. *English in International Deaf Communication*. Bern: Peter Lang, pp. 357–382.

Eugeni, C. and Bernabé-Caro, R. 2019. The LTA project: Bridging the gap between training and the profession in real-time intralingual subtitling. *Linguistica Antverpiensia, New Series: Themes in Translation Studies*, 18, 87–100.

Eugeni, C. and Gambier, Y. 2023. *La traduction intralinguistique : les défis de la diamésie*. Timișoara: Editura Politehnica.

Eugeni, C., Gerbecks, W. and Bernabé, R. 2021. Real-time intralingual subtitling through respeaking and Velotype: Cutting-edge theoretical and professional best practices. In *3rd Swiss Conference on Barrier-free Communication (BfC 2020)*, p. 216.

Gambier, Y. 2007. Le sous-tirage: une traduction sélective. *Tradterm*, 13, 51–69.

Gile, D. 2021. The effort models of interpreting as a didactic construct. In Muñoz Martín, R. Sun, S. and Li, D. eds. *Advances in Cognitive Translation Studies*. Singapore: Springer Singapore Pte. Limited (New Frontiers in Translation Studies), pp. 139–160.

Gottlieb, H. 1992. Subtitling-a new university discipline. In Dollerup, C. and Loddegaard, A. eds. *Teaching translation and interpreting*. Amsterdam/Philadelphia: John Benjamins, p. 161.

Groupe_ ICOR. 2007. Convention ICOR. Icar.Cnrs.Fr. [Online]. [Accessed 24 August 2023]. Available from: https://icar.cnrs.fr/ecole_thematique/tranal_i/documents/Mosaic/ICAR_Conventions_ICOR.pdf

Kalina, S. 1992. Discourse processing and interpreting strategies-an approach to the teaching of interpreting. In Dollerup, C. and Loddegaard, A. eds. *Teaching Translation and Interpreting*. Amsterdam/Philadelphia: John Benjamins, p. 251.

Keyes, B. 2007. Real-time by voice: Just what you need to know. In *Intersteno Congress in Prague in July*. [Online]. [Accessed 24 August 2023]. Available from: https://www.intersteno.it/materiale/Praga2007/praga_conferences/BettyeKeyes.htm

Kohn, K. and Kalina, S. 1996. The strategic dimension of interpreting. *Meta*, 41(1), 118–138. [Online]. [Accessed 24 August 2023]. Available from: https://www.erudit.org/en/journals/meta/1996-v41-n1-meta180/003333ar/

Lambert, J. and Delabastita, D. 1996. La traduction de textes audiovisuels: modes et enjeux culturels. In Gambier, Y. ed. *Les transferts linguistiques et l'audiovisuel*. Villeneuve d'Ascq: Presses Universiaires de Septentrion, pp. 33–58.

Live Text Access (LTA). 2018. *IO 1 report: Skills and competences*. [Online]. [Accessed 24 August 2023]. Available from: https://velotype.com/LTA/IO1_LTA_Report_Skills_Competences_SDI.pdf

Ludbrook, G. 2022. From gender-neutral to gender-inclusive English. The search for gender-fair language. In DEP. Deportate, Esule, *Profughe*, *48*, 20–30.

Marsh, A. 2006. Respeaking for the BBC. *Intralinea, Special Issue on Respeaking*. [Online]. [Accessed 24 August 2023]. Available from: https://www.intralinea.org/specials/article/1700

Niemants, N. 2020. Metodi di trascrizione e analisi del parlato interpretato. In A. Ferraresi, R. Pederzoli, S. Cavalcanti, R. Scansani eds. *Metodi e ambiti nella ricerca sulla traduzione, l'interpretazione e l'interculturalità – Research Methods and Themes in Translation, Interpreting and Intercultural Studies, MediAzioni* 29, pp. A52–A82. [Online]. [Accessed 24 August 2023]. Available from: https://cris.unibo.it/retrieve/e1dcb337-3598-7715-e053-1705fe0a6cc9/2020_niemants_martii.pdf

Nord, C. 2000. What do we know about the target-text receiver?. *BENJAMINS TRANSLATION LIBRARY*, *32*, 195–212.

Pagano, A. 2020. Verbatim vs. Edited live parliamentary subtitling. In Dejica, D., Eugeni, C. and Dejica-Cartis, A eds. *Translation Studies and Information Technology – New Pathways for Researchers, Teachers and Professionals*. Timişoara: Editura Politehnica, pp. 32–44.

Remael, A. and Van der Veer, B. 2006. Real-time subtitling in Flanders: Needs and teaching. *Intralinea, Special Issue on Respeaking*. [Online]. [Accessed 24 August 2023]. Available from: https://www.intralinea.org/specials/article/Real-Time_Subtitling_in_Flanders_Needs_and_Teaching

Romero-Fresco, P. 2009. More haste less speed: Edited versus verbatim respoken subtitles. *Vigo International Journal of Applied Linguistics*, 6, pp. 109–133.

Romero-Fresco, P. 2011. *Subtitling Through Speech Recognition: Respeaking*. St Jerome: Routledge.

Romero-Fresco, P. and Pérez, J.M. 2015. Accuracy rate in live subtitling: The NER model. In Díaz-Cintas, J. and Baños Piñero, R. eds. *Audiovisual Translation in a Global Context: Mapping an Ever-Changing Landscape*. London: Palgrave, 28–50.

Russello, C. 2010. April. Teaching respeaking to conference interpreters. In *Intersteno Conference*. [Online]. [Accessed 24 August 2023]. Available from: https://www.intersteno.it/materiale/ComitScientifico/EducationCommittee/Russello2010Teaching%20Respeaking%20to%20Conference%20Interpreters.pdf

Seeber, K.G. 2011. Cognitive load in simultaneous interpreting: Existing theories—new models. *Interpreting*, *13*(2), 176–204.

Szarkowska, A., Krejtz, I., Klyszejko, Z. and Wieczorek, A. 2011. Verbatim, standard, or edited? Reading patterns of different captioning styles among deaf, hard of hearing, and hearing viewers. *American Annals of the Deaf*, *156*(4), 363–378.

van Dijk, T.A. and Kintsch, W. 1983. *Strategies of Discourse Comprehension*. Orlando: Academic Press.

9

REACHING MARS

How to Increase Speed and Accuracy in Formal and Informal Training in Live Subtitling

Carlo Eugeni and Alessio Popoli

Introduction

Since the first systematic studies on live subtitling through respeaking (Eugeni and Mack, 2006; Eugeni, 2008a; Arumí Ribas and Romero-Fresco, 2008; Romero-Fresco, 2011; Eugeni and Zambelli, 2013), live subtitling teaching has always played a pivotal role in research publications. Simultaneously, universities across Europe have started proposing courses mainly within their translation and interpreting programmes – but also modern languages, comparative literature, applied linguistics – each contributing to shaping the didactics of live subtitling through respeaking from multiple perspectives.

After this pioneering phase, live subtitling teaching has moved forward thanks to research in the field as a result of either individual studies on specific topics like quality assessment (e.g. Romero-Fresco and Pöchhacker, 2017), industry (e.g. Robert et al., 2019), challenges (e.g. Remael et al., 2014), perception (e.g. Szarkowska et al., 2016), contexts (e.g. Moores, 2022) etc.; or nationally and internationally funded projects on mainly engineering-related aspects (e.g. SUMAT,[1] SAVAS,[2] EU-BRIDGE,[3] CLAST[4]).

Most recently, live subtitling teaching has received a massive input from teaching-oriented national and international projects (e.g. LTA,[5] ILSA,[6] SMART[7]). These have allowed researchers and teachers to systematise live subtitling teaching, by including stenotyping and market demands (Eugeni and Bernabé, 2019), interlingual live subtitling (Pöchhacker and Remael, 2019; Davitti and Sandrelli, 2020), and quality assessment (Romero-Fresco, 2020). Together, these contributions have managed to identify the skills needed to become a live subtitler, and have tried to provide teaching tools to develop them.

DOI: 10.4324/9781003440994-12

Of all the sets of skills identified, the capacity to deliver rapid and accurate subtitles plays a crucial role. A few contributions have tried to develop taxonomies to account for aspects like accuracy (Eugeni, 2008b, 2009; Romero-Fresco, 2009, 2011; Apone et al., 2010; Ofcom, 2013), delay (EBG, 2014; Mikul 2014; Romero-Fresco, 2015; Eugeni, 2020; Romero-Fresco and Eugeni, 2020), and ways to measure them (Eugeni, 2012; Romero-Fresco and Martínez, 2015; Eugeni, 2017; Romero-Fresco and Pöchhacker, 2017; Eichmeyer, 2021; Moores, 2022). If this manages to usefully describe the final output, live subtitles, in terms of how many words or concepts have been effectively rendered of the original utterance and how much later, there is an evident lack of contributions dealing with how to reach professional standards in terms of accuracy and speed.

To try and bridge this gap, section 2 will provide an overview of what the market demands and what it offers in terms of live subtitling training and services. Then, section 3 will capitalise on the contributions dealing with the skills needed to become a professional live subtitler, with a specific focus on those skills that contribute to producing professional standard live subtitles. Finally, section 4 will illustrate Most Accurate and Rapid Speech-to-text (MARS), an online tool that allows for testing one's capacity to produce accurate and rapid live subtitles, whatever the technology used to produce it. The conclusions will discuss its implications for formal and informal education.

The Live Subtitling Market

In this paragraph, we will illustrate the two main aspects of the market. In particular, we will focus on what the market requires in terms of live subtitling services (paragraph 2.1) and what the market offers in terms of live subtitling training (paragraph 2.2).

Live Subtitling Services

As Eugeni and Bernabé show, the multiple terms for live subtitles (e.g. live captioning, real-time subtitling, speech-to-text interpreting, etc.) are a consequence of the market of live subtitles being often influenced by factors like traditions, technology, target audience, accuracy, time of production, mental activity, and so forth (2019, pp. 88–91). This is reflected by the fragmentation of the market resulting in professionals offering just a type of services like reporting, subtitling, transcription, or only translating specific text types in given contexts (TV programmes, conferences, university classes, parliamentary sessions, live events, trials, etc.). To try and have a clearer view of the market, the Interlingual Live Subtitling for Access (ILSA) and Live Text Access (LTA) projects have tried to survey professionals in the field, and tried to understand its composition.

As a result of the ILSA project, it is known that live subtitlers using respeaking based in Europe and Oceania are mainly "highly educated young women", working in the field of television and live events, not just as live subtitlers but also as subtitlers of pre-recorded programmes, translators, teachers, and/or conference interpreters (Robert et al., 2019: 107–110). In particular, those who also work as interlingual live subtitlers mainly work for broadcasters, with a very limited number of people exclusively working for live events (Robert et al., 2019).

In a similar survey also including court and parliamentary reporters from the United States and using other techniques, like Velotype, stenotype, and QWERTY keyboards, the findings of the LTA project seem to confirm the young age and high education of professionals (Eugeni and Bernabé, 2019). They also confirm their wider portfolio (including audio description and transcripts) and their working contexts, including courts and parliaments (Eugeni and Bernabé, 2019). Interestingly, LTA results show that live subtitling is not a strikingly female-dominated job, as the number of male respondents is higher, though slightly, than that of female participants (Eugeni and Bernabé, 2019).

Live Subtitling Training

According to Lambourne, live subtitling was first introduced on TV. The first professionals offering this service were typists using standard QWERTY keyboards (2006), but they were soon replaced by more speed-efficient stenographers (den Boer, 2001; de Seriis, 2006). Owing to a lack of trained professionals, many broadcasters opted to train their own professionals internally in respeaking (Romero-Fresco, 2018). Simultaneously, Higher Education Institution (HEI) trainers with different backgrounds started approaching it from their angle to make sure that this emerging discipline could fit the different training programmes, the training needs of the prospective students, and the market demand (cf. Eugeni and Bernabé, 2019). This resulted in a fragmentation of formal and informal live subtitling training, that has made it either "too exclusive in terms of time, money or place; or too focused on a particular technique, language, application or context; or too generic" and dependant "on the knowledge and perspective of a single trainer and not on an international reference framework […]" (Eugeni and Bernabé, 2019).

To try and bridge these gaps, the LTA project released a curriculum on live subtitling through respeaking and velotyping, the ILSA project a course on interlingual respeaking, and the SMART project on upskilling language professionals with a combination of skills. These contributions have made it possible to get a thorough picture of the skills needed by professional live subtitlers. These include technique-specific skills, transversal skills, and soft skills. Technique-specific skills include the capacity to listen and speak or type at the same time, the capacity to turn speech into a specific type of written text, the capacity to use the software needed to produce the subtitles via Automatic Speech Recognition (ASR) software or a keyboard, the capacity to monitor and edit the text in case of mistakes. Transversal skills include the capacity to manage all input and output IT tools related to those aspects of the profession that are not specific to the technique, the stamina needed to work under stressful conditions for long shifts, research skills to be prepared for the job, specific linguistic skills to be able to produce an accurate subtitle, interpreting skills, and pre-recorded subtitling skills. Finally, soft skills include an understanding of accessibility in general, in a manner that the services provided are in line with industrial standards, and the capacity to relate with all stakeholders (client, intended and non-intended users, colleagues, technicians, sponsors, editors) so that the services provided meet their expectations.

More generally, these identified skills have been attributed credits to turn them into learning objectives trainees can acquire in formal and informal education, for as many purposes as possible (parliamentary reporting, TV and conference live subtitling, one-to-one access services in education and the workplace, web streams), and in the more personalised way possible. Also, certifications are made available to make these skills and the profession in general as internationally recognised as possible.

The Skills of the Live Subtitler

As shown in the last paragraph, a respeaker is called to do many things at the same time. As a result of the joint efforts in the projects mentioned above, we can establish a set of technique-specific skills that can be tentatively grouped into four main macro-categories: psycho-cognitive skills, diamesic skills, editing skills, and input skills. Before moving to reach MARS, which is the focus of our paper, an overview of the above skills is necessary to understand the place and importance of reaching MARS.

Psycho-cognitive skills are the set of skills that makes live subtitling in general – and respeaking in particular – more similar to simultaneous interpreting (Eugeni, 2008c). In fact, live subtitling involves listening, understanding, and producing live subtitles all at the same time. When it comes to respeaking in particular, producing live subtitles means speaking to an ASR software. This implies that the same channel (i.e. the aural/oral channel of communication) is used to understand what is said by a speaker and to produce an output – the live subtitles – as in simultaneous interpreting, whereby an interpreter listens to a speech in one language and translates it orally on the fly (Baaring, 2006). Similarities appear to be even more substantial when considering interlingual live subtitling, in which case the subtitles are in a different language compared to that of the speaker. Psycho-cognitive skills also include memorising, which is an essential component of the process, as it makes it more bearable in the long run compared to phonemic shadowing, that is, repeating sounds without understanding the meaning of the source text (Norman, 1976). Also essential in any type of live subtitling (verbatim and sensatim, particularly) is the ability to apply exit strategies, meaning to say strategies that allow the live subtitler to deal with challenges like a speaker who speaks too quickly or who is barely understandable; a difficult topic full of acronyms, technical terms, proper nouns, and other culture-specific items; technical issues with the audio system; or a momentary attention flaw. Finally, worth mentioning is the capacity to monitor the output to check that the machine is working and is properly transcribing what the live subtitler intends to produce.

Diamesic skills are those skills that are aimed at turning speech into text. This is not just a transcoding activity (i.e. turning phonemes into graphemes), as it implies that the live subtitler knows how to spell every single word to be written down, as well as its grammatical role and possibly its meaning and its role in the overall text. Furthermore, knowledge of the text type to produce is essential, as some text types may require a different attention to detail than others. For example, political speeches need to be rendered as faithfully as possible, while football match commentaries may be less accurate as many details are visible from action on screen, and in weather forecasts, synchrony is more important than 100% accuracy. Another important aspect is how to deal with features of orality which make a 100% verbatim transcript heavy to read under certain time constraints, especially in the case of an informative text, like breaking news or a conference speech, whose main function is to inform and not entertain through form. Finally, dictating punctuation is very important in live subtitling as it makes understanding more straightforward. Immediately knowing how to turn an utterance into a written sentence with appropriate punctuation may have important consequences in terms of content (Eugeni and Bernabé, 2021). This is again very similar to what interpreters do with intonation in order to be able to provide an acceptable output in difficult situations (Gile, 1985).

Editing skills are also essential because ASR is not impeccable and cannot work alone, despite the huge progress made in the field (Romero-Fresco, 2023). In particular, software used in live subtitling has in-built vocabulary, a list of words that the software is capable of transcribing and that the software matches with utterances in an attempt to reproduce speech as accurately as possible on the basis of syntactical and probability criteria. Being limited, a vocabulary needs to be fed with specific words that a speaker is likely to pronounce. This is called pre-editing (Romero-Fresco and Eugeni, 2020), and is once again very similar to what interpreters do when drafting a glossary in preparation for a conference (Gile, 1995). While live subtitling, a skill similar to an exit strategy used in interpreting is peri-editing, or the capacity to avoid a mistake that the machine is likely to make. Examples of challenges to ASR technology include short words, acronyms, and words the respeaker thinks are not in the software vocabulary or does not know how to pronounce properly. The challenge is to produce sentences that mean the same without using such specific words. An example of that is turning the "EU" – often misrecognised as "the you" or "the ewe" – with "the European Union" or "the Union". A last editing skill is that of post-editing, or editing a mistake the subtitler considers as major once the machine has produced it. This requires the multitasking capacity of monitoring the output and deciding whether the mistake is a minor one, hence not to be corrected, or a standard or major one (Romero-Fresco and Martínez, 2015) which can result in not understanding or misunderstanding a concept.

Finally, input skills – similarly to editing skills above – are the ones that make the difference between live subtitling through respeaking and simultaneous interpreting more evident. While interpreters need to be understandable to their audience, this is not enough in the case of live subtitling through respeaking. In fact, a respeaker must properly breathe to be able and keep producing an output that is easily recognised by the ASR software in the long run. Also, if enunciation is important for interpreters, this is even more important for respeakers as they must keep having the same output (same volume, same clean audio, same pitch) for the whole duration of their shift. Furthermore, a respeaker has to articulate in a manner that the machine does not mistake one word for another (as in "carer" and "career") or other words (as in "unfettered" and "and factored"). Finally, the capacity to produce subtitles as quickly and accurately as possible is something that has been often dealt with, but not as thoroughly as in the LTA project, where the notion of MARS, or the maximum number of accurate words a live subtitler is capable to produce in a minute, was developed. We will see this in the next section.

Reaching MARS

MARS is the acronym for Most Accurate and Rapid Speech-to-text subtitling rate.[8] It is the capacity of a live subtitler to write at a certain speed while guaranteeing a certain accuracy. Knowing one's MARS is essential for every professional as it guarantees they can deal with various types of speeches word for word. For example, somebody with a MARS of 150 words per minute can deal with spontaneous speech (Civera and Orero, 2010) and some sports events (Romero-Fresco, 2009), but not with the news – BBC News average is 180 words per minute (Eugeni, 2008a) – or weather forecasts – BBC's average is 230 words per minute (Eugeni, 2008a) – and would fall far behind the industry standard of 180 words per minute (Santiago-Araujo, 2004; Neves, 2005).

As seen in the introduction to this article, producing subtitles rapidly and accurately has been covered relatively extensively in terms of both accuracy and speed and measured in terms of delay from the source text. These studies were mainly conducted with the aim of trying to find a way to measure quality, which has brought to several methods having words as the minimum unit of analysis – like the WER, short for Word Error Rate (Klakow and Peters, 2002), and its adaptations to live subtitling NER (Romero-Fresco and Martínez, 2015) and NERLE (Moores, 2022) – or idea units as the minimum unit of analysis, like IRA (Eugeni, 2019) and WIRA (Eichmeyer, 2021). The idea behind MARS is not measuring the quality of the product, but improving the quality of the process. In other words, reaching one's MARS allows professionals and trainees not just to measure one's capacity to write at a given speed with professional accuracy, but also to train one's standard and to push it to the next level, and have it certified nationally (e.g. NCRA,[9] Global Alliance[10]) or internationally (e.g. ECQA-Intersteno,[11] LiRICS[12]). In the next paragraphs, the technical aspects of MARS (paragraph 4.1), its application (paragraph 4.2), and one of the certifications using it (paragraph 4.3) will be illustrated.

Technical Aspects

MARS is also the name of the software developed to train one's MARS. It currently offers the possibility to test one's skills in twelve languages, including Czech, Dutch, English, Finnish, French, German, Hungarian, Italian, Polish, Slovenian, Spanish, and Turkish. Upon selecting a language, the user can decide the minimum accuracy (98% by default). After that, a 15-minute audio-only speech on a general topic starts. The speech starts slowly and its speed increases every minute.[13] Users are required to listen to the speech and transcribe it in real time, word for word, for the whole duration of the speech. In case they can no longer deal with the dictation, they can quit the task at any time. Then, the machine grades every single full minute that has been transcribed with an accuracy equal to or above the one set. The final score – that is, one's MARS – is then shown in words-per-minute terms (see picture 1). It is the speed of the last minute that has been transcribed with an accuracy equal or above the set one. This scoring system is based on the one used by the International Federation for Information and Communication Processing (Intersteno)[14] for the Speech Capturing and Real-Time Speech Capturing world competitions.[15]

Technically speaking, MARS was developed using the .NET 5 framework, and has since been upgraded to .NET 6, and is written almost entirely in C#, via the WebAssembly-based Blazor client framework (Himschoot, 2018).[16] The correction engine relies on an adapted version of the edit distance, short for Damerau-Levenshtein distance (Damerau, 1964; Levenshtein, 1966).

128 Carlo Eugeni and Alessio Popoli

TABLE 9.1 Correction Table for "This is my house" Transcribed as "That is your house"

		This	is	my	house
	0	1	2	3	4
That	1	1	2	3	4
is	2	2	1	2	3
your	3	3	2	2	3
house	4	4	3	3	2

The edit distance allows for comparing the transcribed text with the original written text used by the software as a reference, and for counting the transcribed text's accuracy in terms of the number and type of edits needed to match the reference text. The difference between the algorithm used in MARS and the edit distance is that MARS is programmed to also take into account that the transcribed text might be a substring of – that is, it might end before – the dictated one. This means, for example, that several words might be missing at the end of the transcribed text because the trainee can no longer deal with the dictated text's speed. As shown in Table 9.1, MARS manages to consider this aspect and provide a final score, which is one's MARS.

The scoring system relies on two steps. In the first step, a big table is used to understand the number of mistakes. The table contains each word in the original text, listed cell by cell in a single row (This is my house), and each transcribed word listed cell by cell down a single column (That is your house). Every other cell – those at the intersection between the transcribed words and the original words – contains the number of edits required to align the text up to those two words; each contributes to the number contained in the cells under it and in those to its right. In other words, each cell at the intersection between an original word and a transcribed word contains the number of errors that the system would count if the transcribed text and the original text had to be compared up to those two specific words.

Let's take the number 3 at the intersection between "my" in the original text and "That" in the transcribed text as an example. If the transcript only said "That", instead of "This is my", the system would count three wrong words ("That" being replaced by "This" and "is" and "my" being omitted). Similarly, if the transcript only said "That is", the number of counted mistakes would be 2, as the word "is" would no longer be considered as omitted, thus the error count would be one less than the previous case. The bottom-right cell is the one that contains the edit distance, or the final number of differences (or mistakes) between the original text and the related transcript. In the table above, "This is my house", transcribed as "That is your house" has an edit distance value of 2. This means that the transcribed sentence contains two mistakes ("That" being replaced by "This" and "your" being replaced by "my").

Once the edit distance has been calculated, making sure to take into account that the user might not have transcribed the whole original text, an accuracy score is computed in the second step. As mentioned above, Word error rate is the most common way to calculate accuracy scores that resembles the MARS computation. In fact, MARS calculates the opposite, an 'inaccuracy score', and then subtracts it from 100. In other words, the system first computes the number of wrong characters in the transcribed text. Then, a heuristic is used to determine whether a certain mistake is just a wrong character in a word or if all the characters in a word have to be counted as a mistake. For example, if the user wrote "hullo" instead of "hello", only one character would be considered as wrong. On the other hand, if the user wrote "hulki", the whole word would be considered incorrect, and counted as five mistakes and not just the three actually wrong characters. In other words, overall MARS counts the number of errors based on characters, instead of words. This way, a simple typo does not negatively affect the user's accuracy score as much as a whole word would. The rationale behind it is that a typo does not generally affect understandability. However, when the software considers that there are too many typos in a word that make it unintelligible, the software counts as many errors as the number of characters that compose the original word.

The formula behind the computation of wrong characters is $E = S + I + D$; where E is the number of errors, S is the number of substitutions (characters replaced by others), I is the number of insertions (stray characters that did not belong to the original text), and D is the number of deletions (characters that were not transcribed). Once the number of wrong characters is obtained, it is divided by the total number of characters contained in that specific minute to establish the "inaccuracy rate". The accuracy rate is then obtained by subtracting this number from 1 and converting it to a percentage, as per the formula $A = (1-E/T) * 100\%$; where A is accuracy, E is the number of errors and T is the number of characters in the transcribed text. When expanding the value of E into its constituents (i.e., $S + I + D$), the formula becomes $A = [1-(S + I + D) / T] * 100\%$.

Application

A practical example of the application of the MARS correction algorithm can be found by examining the result of a random user, who decided to participate in Dutch and to set the accuracy rate at 98%, as per their company's request. The candidate did not manage to have their MARS calculated because the first minute of their transcript contained too many errors, resulting in an

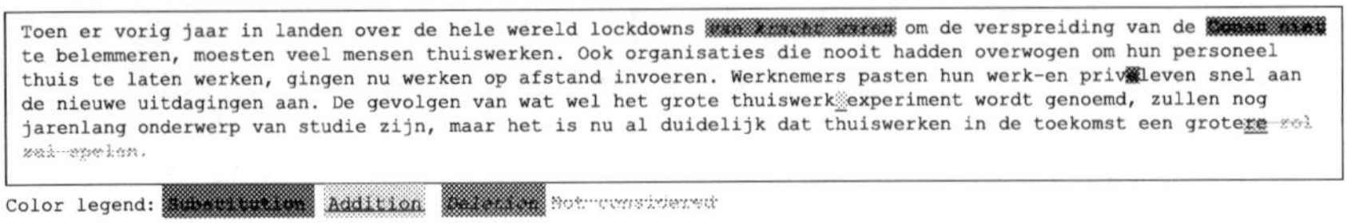

```
Toen er vorig jaar in landen over de hele wereld lockdowns van kracht waren om de verspreiding van de Conan niet
te belemmeren, moesten veel mensen thuiswerken. Ook organisaties die nooit hadden overwogen om hun personeel
thuis te laten werken, gingen nu werken op afstand invoeren. Werknemers pasten hun werk-en privéleven snel aan
de nieuwe uitdagingen aan. De gevolgen van wat wel het grote thuiswerk experiment wordt genoemd, zullen nog
jarenlang onderwerp van studie zijn, maar het is nu al duidelijk dat thuiswerken in de toekomst een grotere rol
zal spelen.

Color legend: Substitution  Addition  Deletion  Not transcribed
```

FIGURE 9.1 MARS correction interface.

accuracy level below the set one. In particular, the user wrote the following text, where mistakes have been highlighted (Figure 9.1):

The user made the following mistakes:

- "van kracht waren" were not transcribed, accounting for 14 deleted characters;
- "Conan niet" was written instead of "coronapandemie", accounting for 9 substituted characters;
- "priveleven" was written instead of "privéleven", accounting for 1 substituted character;
- "thuiswerk experiment" was written instead of "thuiswerkexperiment" accounting for 1 inserted character;
- "grotere" was written instead of "grote", accounting for 2 inserted characters.

This means that the error rate is to be calculated on the basis of the following wrong characters:

$S = 9 + 1 = 10$
$I = 1 + 2 = 3$
$D = 3 + 6 + 5 = 14$

The result of the formula to calculate the error rate ($E = S + I + D$) is then 27. Because the number of characters in the original text (T) in that minute is 565 characters, the accuracy rate is the following:

$A = (1-E/T) * 100\% = (1-27/565) * 100\% = 95{,}22\%$. Because the result is below the 98% accuracy threshold, it is not sufficient to have the first minute calculated and move to the second one. This means that the user's attempt to have their MARS calculated failed. However, after introducing manual correction, which did not include minor mistakes (like the inserted space, the substituted character, and the 2 inserted characters) when calculating the accuracy rate, S was reduced to 9, and I was reduced to 0, resulting in 23 as the number of errors (E). This brings to the following accuracy rate: $A = (1-23/565) * 100\% = 95{,}93\%$. The result is still a fail, but a 0.7% difference could have indeed made the difference between a fail and a pass.

ECQA – Intersteno Certification

In the context of the 53rd Intersteno Congress[17] held in Maastricht in 2022, the first joint European Certification and Qualification Association (ECQA)-Intersteno certification session was held. During this certification session, a job role committee, composed of a certified professional, a representative of Intersteno, and a representative of ECQA [18] assessed the skills of 7 English and Dutch-speaking candidates. To obtain the certification, candidates were asked to pass a quiz about theoretical knowledge in the field, with questions being taken from the course made available by the LTA project; demonstrate their expertise during an interview with the job role committee; and have a MARS of 130 words per minute or above, with an accuracy of the live word-for-word transcript of at least 98%. The candidate's MARS would of course increase with each successfully transcribed minute. The event attracted the interest of candidates, attendees, professionals wishing they could attend the congress to take part in the certification session, and organisers, which meant that ECQA-Intersteno certification sessions will continue being held in the same format in the next Intersteno Congress meetings.[19]

Discussion and Conclusions

In the context of live subtitling teaching, several online and open courses have been produced by professionals and expert educators in the framework of the international projects mentioned above. Training materials can be easily downloaded and substantial guidance is provided to both HEI trainers and self-trainers to make sure that such materials meet the stated theoretical and practical learning objectives. When it comes to the skill of producing text as quickly and accurately as possible, several suggestions are given to let trainees practice their skills. However, a tool that measures this skill is something that has been left to certification stage thus far. Having such a tool before the certification or the assessment session is something that guarantees both trainers and trainees peace of mind when it comes to knowing how rapidly they can subtitle. In particular, trainers can plan formative assessments based on specific speed levels, and trainees can train themselves autonomously without waiting for the certification or the assessment to know exactly how many words per minute they can produce at a given accuracy. Also, it allows professionals and trainees to know how many words per minute they can transcribe in a speech word for word, and when they need to apply exit strategies. Finally, because MARS can be fed with specific texts, companies and HEIs can easily upload one or more speeches to the software that can be used by the trainee to prepare for a specific job. All in all, measuring one's MARS, training to improve one's MARS, and reaching one's ideal MARS are now possible standard activities that can be easily performed online, and for free.

Notes

1. The project website is no longer available. For more information about the project see Georgakopoulou (2013).
2. The project website is no longer available. For more information about the project see Aliprandi (2013).
3. For more information see the project website: https://www.eu-bridge.eu/ (last accessed 29 February 2024).
4. The project website is no longer available. For more information about the project see https://www.pervoice.com/index.php/en/pervoice-en/#Research (last accessed 29 February 2024).
5. For more information see the project website: https://ltaproject.eu/ (last accessed 29 February 2024).
6. For more information see the project website: http://ka2-ilsa.webs.uvigo.es/ (last accessed 29 February 2024).
7. For more information see the project website: https://smartproject.surrey.ac.uk/ (last accessed 29 February 2024).
8. For a demo, see the presentation by Eugeni and Popoli at the 8th International Symposium on Live Subtitling and Accessibility at the Universitat Autònoma de Barcelona, https://webs.uab.cat/livesubtitling/wp-content/uploads/sites/209/2023/08/Demo-MARS.mp4 [last accessed 28/08/2023]. To access the website, visit https://reachmars.eu/ [last accessed 28/08/2023].
9. For more information see https://www.ncra.org/certification/NCRA-Certifications [last accessed 28/08/2023]
10. For more information see https://speechtotextcaptioning.org/NER-Certified-Speech-to-Text-Provider [last accessed 28/08/2023]
11. For more information see https://www.jobcertification.eu/index.php/certification/114-ecqa-certification/327-ecqa-certified-intralingual-real-time-subtitler-respeaker-and-velotypist [last accessed 28/08/2023].
12. For more information see https://galmaobservatory.webs.uvigo.es/services/certification/ [last accessed 28/08/2023].
13. For the English language, the number of words per each of the 15 minutes is the following: 114, 125, 137, 148, 163, 184, 190, 196, 214, 229, 256, 264, 267, 284. For more information see Intersteno regulations at page 6, at https://www.intersteno.org/wp-content/uploads/2022/08/Regulations_Maastricht_2022_ENG.pdf [last accessed 28/08/2023].
14. For more information, see https://www.intersteno.org/ [last accessed 29/08/2023].
15. For a description of competitions see https://www.intersteno.org/competition-types/ [last accessed on 28/08/2023].
16. For more information see https://dotnet.microsoft.com/en-us/apps/aspnet/web-apps/blazor [last accessed on 28/08/2023].
17. For more information see https://www.intersteno2022.org/ [last accessed on 28/08/2023].
18. For more information see https://www.jobcertification.eu/ [last accessed on 28/08/2023].
19. This article was written before the 54th Intersteno Congress took place. The event website confirms an ECQA-Intersteno certification session will be held in the context of the Congress, as per the conference programme available at https://www.intersteno2024.org/program.php [last accessed on 29/02/2024].

References

Aliprandi, C. (2013) Il progetto europeo SAVAS – riconoscimento del parlato per respeaking e sottotitolazione in tempo reale. In Eugeni, C. & Zambelli, L. (eds.)

Respeaking, Specializzazione on-line, Numero monografico n. 1, pp. 117–119. Retrieved from https://accademia-aliprandi.it/public/specializzazione/respeaking.pdf (last accessed 29 February 2024).

Apone, T., Brooks, M. and O'Connell, T. (2010) *Caption Accuracy Metrics Project – Caption Viewer Survey: Error Ranking Of Real-Time Captions In Live Television News Programs.* Boston, MA: WGBH National Center for Accessible Media. Retrieved from https://ncamftp.wgbh.org/ncam-old-site/file_download/CCM_survey_report_final_Dec_17_2010.pdf (last accessed 29 February 2024)

Arumí-Ribas, M. and Romero-Fresco, P. (2008) A practical proposal for the training of respeakers. *The Journal of Specialised Translation*, 10, 106–127. Retrieved from https://jostrans.soap2.ch/issue10/art_arumi.php (last accessed 29 February 2024).

Baaring, I. (2006) Respeaking-based online subtitling in Denmark. In Eugeni, C. & Mack, G. (eds.) *inTRAlinea* Special Issue: Respeaking. Retrieved from https://www.intralinea.org/specials/article/1685 (last accessed 29 February 2024).

Civera, C. and Orero, P. (2010) Introducing icons in subtitles for the deaf and hard of hearing. In Matamala, A. & Orero, P. (eds.) *Listening to Subtitles*. Bern & Berlin: Peter Lang, pp. 59–68.

Damerau, Fred J. (March 1964) A technique for computer detection and correction of spelling errors. *Communications of the ACM*, 7(3), 171–176. Retrieved from https://dl.acm.org/doi/pdf/10.1145/363958.363994 (last accessed 29 February 2024).

Davitti, E. and Sandrelli, A. (2020) Embracing the complexity: A pilot study on interlingual respeaking. *Journal of Audiovisual Translation*, 3(2), 103–139. doi:10.47476/jat.v3i2.2020.135.

de Seriis, L. (2006) Il Servizio Sottotitoli RAI Televideo per i non udenti. In Eugeni, C. & Mack, G. (eds.) *inTRAlinea* Special Issue: Respeaking. Retrieved from https://www.intralinea.org/specials/article/1687 (last accessed 29 February 2024).

den Boer, C. (2001) Live interlingual subtitling. In Gambier, Y. & Gottlieb, H. (eds.) *(Multi)Media Translation. Concepts, Practices and Research*. Amsterdam and Philadelphia: John Benjamins, pp. 167–172.

EBG, The English Language Broadcasters Group. (2014) Report on efforts to improve the quality of closed captioning. Retrieved from https://www.crtc.gc.ca/fra/BCASTING/ann_rep/bmt_cbc_rm_sm.pdf

Eichmeyer-Hell, D. (2021) Speech recognition (Respeaking) vs. the conventional method (Keyboard): A quality-oriented comparison of speech-to-text interpreting techniques and addressee preferences. In Jekat, Susanne J., Puhl, Steffen, Carrer, Luisa & Lintner, Alexa (eds.) *Proceedings of the 3rd Swiss Conference on Barrier-free Communication (BfC 2020)*. ZHAW Winterthur, pp. 209–215. https://digitalcollection.zhaw.ch/server/api/core/bitstreams/993e8530-a1f3-4bab-baa4-0515cf37f4c9/content

Eugeni, C. (2008a) *Le sous-titrage en direct: aspects théoriques, professionnels et didactiques*. Macerata: CEUM.

Eugeni, C. (2008b) *Respeaking the TV for the Deaf For a Real Special Needs-Oriented Subtitling*. Studies in English Language and Literature 21. Retrieved from https://ltaproject.eu/wp-content/uploads/2019/06/Eugeni_C.-2008_Respeaking-the-TV-for-the-Deaf-For-a-Real-Special-Needs-Oriented-Subtitling.pdf (last accessed 29 February 2024).

Eugeni, C. (2008c) A sociolinguistic approach to real-time subtitling: Respeaking vs. shadowing and simultaneous interpreting. In Kellett Bidoli, C. J. & Ochse, E. (eds.)

English in International Deaf Communication, Linguistic Insights Series, 72, Berna: Peter Lang, pp, 357–382.

Eugeni, C. (2009) Respeaking BBC news: A strategic approach. In *SLTI*, vol. 3(1). Manchester: St. Jerome, pp. 29–68.

Eugeni, C. (2012) Measuring audiovisual translation – A model for the analysis of intralingual live subtitles. *US-China Foreign Language*, 10(6), 1276–1286.

Eugeni, C. (2017) La sottotitolazione intralinguistica automatica: Valutare la qualità con IRA. *CoMe*, 2(1), 102–111. Retrieved from https://comejournal.com/wp-content/uploads/2017/12/EUGENI-2017.pdf (last accessed 29 February 2024).

Eugeni, C. (2020) Human-computer interaction in diamesic translation. Multilingual live subtitling. In Dejica, D., Eugeni, C. & Dejica-Cartis, A. (eds.) *Translation Studies and Information Technology - New Pathways for Researchers, Teachers and Professionals*, Timișoara: Editura Politehnica, Translation Studies Series, pp. 19–31.

Eugeni, C. and Bernabé, R. (2021) Written interpretation: When simultaneous interpreting meets real-time subtitling. In Seeber, K. (ed.) *100 Years of Conference Interpreting – A Legacy*. Newcastle upon Tyne: Cambridge Scholars Publishing, pp. 93–109.

Eugeni, C. and Bernabé Caro, R. (2019) The LTA project: Bridging the gap between training and the profession in real-time intralingual subtitling. *Linguistica Antverpiensia, New Series: Themes in Translation Studies*, 18, 87–100. Retrieved from https://lans-tts.uantwerpen.be/index.php/LANS-TTS/article/view/512/453 (last access 29 February 2024).

Eugeni, C. and Mack, G. (2006) Respeaking, inTRAlinea Special Issue. Retrieved from https://www.intralinea.org/specials/respeaking (last accessed 29 February 2024).

Eugeni, C. and Zambelli, L. (2013) Respeaking, specializzazione on-line. *Numero monografico* n. 1. Retrieved from https://accademia-aliprandi.it/public/specializzazione/respeaking.pdf (last accessed 29 February 2024).

Georgakopoulou, P. (2013) Il progetto europeo SUMAT – sottotitolazione assistita dalla traduzione automatica. In Eugeni, C. & Zambelli, L. (eds.) *Respeaking, Specializzazione on-line*, Numero monografico n. 1, pp. 120–122. Retrieved from https://accademia-aliprandi.it/public/specializzazione/respeaking.pdf (last accessed 29 February 2024).

Gile, D. (1985) Le Modèle d'Efforts et l'équilibre d'interprétation en interprétation simultanée. *In Meta* 30(1), 44-48.

Gile, D. (1995) *Regards sur la recherche en interprétation de conférence*. Lille: Presses Universitaires de Lille.

Himschoot, P. (2018) *Microsoft Blazor: Building Web Applications, in.NET 6 and Beyond*. New York: Apress.

Klakow, D. and Peters, J. (2002) Testing the correlation of word error rate and perplexity, *Speech Communication*, 38(1–2), 19–28. Retrieved from https://www.sciencedirect.com/science/article/abs/pii/S0167639301000413?via%3Dihub (last access 29 February 2024).

Lambourne, A. (2006) Subtitle respeaking – A new skill for a new age. In Eugeni, C. & Mack, G. (eds.) *inTRAlinea* Special Issue: Respeaking. Retrieved from https://www.intralinea.org/specials/article/1686 (last accessed 29 February 2024).

Levenshtein, V. I. (1966) Soviet physics-Doklady, binary codes capable of correcting deletions. *Insertions, and Reversals*, 10(8). Retrieved from https://nymity.ch/sybil-hunting/pdf/Levenshtein1966a.pdf (last access 29 February 2024).

Mikul, C. (2014) *Caption Quality: International Approaches to Standards and Measurement*. Sydney: Media Access Australia.

Moores, Z. (2022) Training professional respeakers to subtitle live events in the UK A participative model for access and inclusion. PhD thesis. London: University of Roehampton. Retrieved from https://pure.roehampton.ac.uk/ws/portalfiles/portal/12254477/Moores_Zoe_Final_thesis.pdf (last access 29 February 2024).

Neves, J. (2005) Audiovisual translation: Subtitling for the deaf and hard-of-hearing. Retrieved from https://iconline.ipleiria.pt/bitstream/10400.8/409/1/Thesis%20agosto%202005.pdf (last access 29 February 2024).

Norman, D. (1976) *Memory and Attention*. New York: Wiley.

Ofcom (2013). *The Quality of Live Subtitling*. London: Office of Communications. Retrieved from https://www.ofcom.org.uk/consultations-and-statements/category-1/subtitling (last accessed 29 February 2024).

Pöchhacker, F. and Remael, A. (2019). New efforts?: A competence-oriented task analysis of interlingual live subtitling. *Linguistica Antverpiensia, New Series: Themes in Translation Studies*, 18, 130–143. Retrieved from https://lans-tts.uantwerpen.be/index.php/LANS-TTS/article/view/515/471 (last access 29 February 2024).

Remael, A., Van Waes, L. and Leijtenet, M. (2014) Live subtitling with speech recognition – How to pinpoint the challenges? In Abend-David, D. (ed.) *Media and Translation. An Interdisciplinary Approach*. London: Bloomsbury, pp. 121–147.

Robert, I. S., Schrijver, I. and Diels, E. (2019) Live subtitlers: Who are they? A survey study. *Linguistica Antverpiensia, New Series: Themes in Translation Studies*, 18, 101–129. Retrieved from https://lans-tts.uantwerpen.be/index.php/LANS-TTS/article/view/544/459 (last accessed 29 February 2024).

Romero-Fresco, P. (2009) More haste less speed: Edited vs. verbatim respoken subtitles. *Vigo International Journal of Applied Linguistics*, 6(1), 109–133. Retrieved from https://www.researchgate.net/publication/228502664_More_haste_less_speed_Edited_versus_verbatim_respoken_subtitles (last access 29 February 2024).

Romero-Fresco, P. (2011) *Subtitling Through Speech Recognition: Respeaking*. Abingdon: Routledge.

Romero-Fresco, P. (2015) *The Reception Of Subtitles For The Deaf And Hard Of Hearing In Europe*. 1st edition. Bern, Berlin, Brussels, Frankfurt am Main, New York, Oxford & Wien: Peter Lang.

Romero-Fresco, P. (2018) Respeaking subtitling through speech recognition. In Pérez-González, L. (ed.) *The Routledge Handbook Of Audiovisual Translation*. London: Routledge, pp. 96–113.

Romero-Fresco, P. (2020) *Negotiating Quality Assessment In Media Accessibility: The Case Of Live Subtitling*. Universal Access In The Information Society. doi:10.1007/s10209-020-00735-6.

Romero-Fresco, P. (2023) Interpreting for access – The long road to recognition. In Zwischenberger, Cornelia, Karin Reithofer & Sylvi Rennert (eds.) *Introducing New Hypertexts on Interpreting (Studies) – A tribute to Franz Pöchhacker*. Amsterdam: John Benjamins Publishing Company, pp. 236–253. https://doi.org/10.1075/btl.160.12rom.

Romero-Fresco, P. and Eugeni, C. (2020) Live subtitling through respeaking. In Deckert, M. & Bogucki, Ł. (eds.) *Handbook of Audiovisual Translation and Media Accessibility*. London: Palgrave, pp. 269–297.

Romero-Fresco, P. and Martínez, J. (2015) Accuracy rate in live subtitling: The NER model. In Díaz-Cintas, J. and Baños Piñero, R. (eds.) *Audiovisual Translation in a Global Context. Mapping an Ever-changing Landscape.* London: Palgrave, pp. 28–50.

Romero-Fresco, P. and Pöchhacker, F. (2017) Quality assessment in interlingual live subtitling: The NTR model. *Linguistica Antverpiensia, New Series: Themes in Translation Studies*, 16, 149–167. Retrieved from https://lans-tts.uantwerpen.be/index.php/LANS-TTS/article/view/438/402 (last accessed 29 February 2024).

Santiago-Araújo, V.L. 2004. Closed subtitling in Brazil. In Pilar Orero (ed.) *Topics in Audiovisual Translation.* John Benjamins Publishing. V1, pp. 199–212.

Szarkowska, A., Krejtz, K., Dutka, Ł. and Pilipczuk, O. (2016) Cognitive load in intralingual and interlingual respeaking. *Poznań Studies In Contemporary Linguistics*, 52(2), pp. 209–233. Retrieved from https://discovery.ucl.ac.uk/id/eprint/10038846/1/[Poznan%20Studies%20in%20Contemporary%20Linguistics]%20Cognitive%20load%20in%20intralingual%20and%20interlingual%20respeaking%20%20a%20preliminary%20study.pdf (last accessed 29 February 2024).

10
INTRALINGUAL AND INTERLINGUAL RESPEAKING DIDACTICS

Redefining Human-Machine Interaction Challenges into Opportunities

Alice Pagano

Introduction

This article focuses on Live Subtitling (LS) and Interlingual Live Subtitling (ILS), specifically targeting the technique of respeaking through a didactic perspective. Both LS and ILS provide accessibility to the content of a given Source Text (ST) catering to a written product for audiences who might not access the audio source version. Specifically, ILS does so from one language to another, therefore providing access for the content in L1, in another language, namely a diamesic translation (Eugeni, 2020).

LS and ILS can be produced through different methods, one of which is respeaking, in which an Automatic Speech Recognition (ASR) software is used for the creation of subtitles. Respeaking is what by definition is Human-Machine Interaction (HMI) – sometimes also referred to as Human-Computer Interaction (HCI). In many diverse fields today, we see a rise in technological intervention rather than human agency, which is gradually being replaced. This is the challenge this contribution refers to in its title: the overturn of human participation in tasks that can be solely carried out by machines. In some fields where ASR and Natural Language Understanding (NLU) systems are used, for example, 'technological evolution is reducing the place of humans in this interaction to such an extent, that their profession could hardly be possible without it' (Eugeni, 2019, p. 873). In the same way, respeaking falls into a computer-aided category of services, as it is achieved via human dictation on one hand, but it also requires the assistance of a machine for the transcript, without which other methods such as keyboard typing would have to be used. In the wake of awes concerning AI and technology gradually replacing many human tasks in the field of translation, the

DOI: 10.4324/9781003440994-13

author wants to stress which opportunities instead can be detected in HMI in respeaking, identifying room for human improvement in better cooperation with the machines.

It was sought to do so spotting the strengths and weaknesses of both ASR systems and human performances in two respeaking academic training courses given by the author as a trainer. The courses were integrated as modules in an interpreters and translators' curriculum, exploiting the same cognitive activations and skills required for respeaking that the trainees are already taught in Simultaneous Interpreting (SI) (Pagano, forthcoming).

On completion of the first course two main issues were detected in students' performances, concerning specifically their interaction with the ASR software: the trainees' dictation was not clear enough for the machine to recognize the utterances correctly, therefore resulting in many misrecognitions, and the dictated sentences were too long and syntactically complex, leading to a long delay in subtitles production.

These shortcomings in the final outcome could lead one to think that the human participation in the respeaking process undermined the subtitles' quality, and that the ASR or automatic translation alone could have guaranteed a more accurate transcription and translation with shorter delay.

The goal of this paper is to try to suggest that, through the remodulation of the course, the human interaction with the software can be improved and could ultimately lead to a better final outcome (more accurate subtitles), transforming a challenge, therefore, into an all-round, more comprehensive training opportunity. The following pages present the structure, the methodology and the teaching materials of the second training course.

Speech Recognition-Based Live Subtitling: Respeaking

LS refers to the production of subtitles in real-time for live programs – sports matches, TV shows, the news, weather forecasts – or live events such as conferences, meetings, court sessions or parliamentary procedures. Due to the live creation of captions, LS can be considered the most demanding form of subtitle creation, as their real-time production allows for minimum review before they are broadcast (Eugeni, 2007), features that do not pertain to pre-recorded subtitle production. As said, LS and ILS can be broadcasted through different methods and with different approaches, one of which is through ASR-based systems, namely, respeaking. To carry out a respeaking task, the respeakers are involved in the repetition and reformulation of audio content, interacting with a machine to produce as a final output, a written text (subtitles), always bearing in mind that '[...] the respeaker, far from being a mere parrot, has to perform a process of message comprehension and reformulation that often requires a certain distancing from word-for-word formulation' (Romero-Fresco, 2011). As pointed out by Díaz Cintas and Remael in an overview of different LS methods, '[t]raditionally professionals used stenotype or shorthand techniques or different keyboards to transcribe or translate the original dialogue, but these days respeaking, or speech-based live subtitling, is gaining ground in the industry' (Díaz Cintas & Remael, 2021, p. 10). As a relatively new technique, intralingual respeaking is currently more widely known and employed than interlingual respeaking, although research is thriving in the latter as well (Moores, 2020; Romero-Fresco, 2019; Romero-Fresco & Eugeni, 2020; Wallinheimo et al., 2023).

Respeaking would not be possible without ASR, which allows the human to interact with the machine using voice commands, either resulting in an automatic transcription of the audio input or carrying out the command that has been given, with the machine responding in a meaningful way thanks to a proper voice information processing and recognition. When listening to voice and audio inputs, ASR engines break down words for analysis, as they are normally made up of different models that are activated at different stages of the recognition process: an acoustic model, a vocabulary or a lexicon model, and a language model. An acoustic model consists of speech and audio data properly pronounced and spelt, together with their digital sound representation (i.e., how it is read and decoded by the engine). ASR these days not only extracts the recognized text that was spoken, but also interprets its semantic meanings through Deep Learning (DL). At a basic level, when a sentence is dictated, the acoustic model digitizes it and breaks it down into phonemes, the basic building block sounds of words, but to do so, the soundtrack needs to be prepared and represented digitally. At this stage, the lexicon model is activated: it checks the recognized sound waveforms against the vocabulary, obtaining different possible words that can be recognized, due to the assonance of the same/similar pronunciation. Finally, to pick one word against another, the language model comes in. To do that, a language model consists of a corpus of texts that the speech engine can go through to analyze occurrences, collocations and word position, statistically analyzing the probability of words being pronounced before or after the previous and next word, for example, and finally deducing the whole sentence as a meaningful unit. As pointed out by many professional respeakers, since the engine draws from text corpora, normally the longer the dictation, the better the recognition having provided more context to the algorithm to cater for the language model. With good ASR software and capable professionals carrying out the task, this is often the case. Nonetheless, when first introducing respeaking to SI trainees, it is advisable to teach them how to segment – that is, divide long and more complex sentences into smaller idea units to let the software process less information (i.e., fewer words) and minimize delay in the production of the transcript. Shorter sentences to respeak, intra- and even more interlingually, also support short-term memory activation in retrieving the information from the source.

A Research-Informed Training Model for Respeaking

A research-informed training model for interlingual respeaking was first proposed by Dawson (2020) through doctoral research that intertwined with the Erasmus+ Interlingual Live Subtitling for Access (ILSA) project.[1] The research outcomes – Dawson's research and the ILSA project – proposed two training courses for interlingual respeaking training. Despite bearing a common purpose, they differed in structure and modules: the ILSA course was conceived to be integrated into Higher Education courses, providing open-access learning resources and materials to be selected and used by trainers and trainees. The training model 'can be used as a guide to develop future interlingual respeaking training' (Dawson, 2020, p. 231), designing a tutoring to be integrated as part of a master's program, or adapted to other needs such as shorter modules only. The two training proposals introduced the speech-recognition software use to trainees in two different sections: in the ILSA course, it was introduced inside the intralingual respeaking module at a later learning and practising stage, while in the research-informed training course proposal it was brought up as an independent 'Dictation and software management' module from the very first stage of training to help students familiarize with it from the beginning. For more on research-informed training model for interlingual respeaking in particular, also see Dawson and Romero-Fresco (2021).

The intralingual and interlingual respeaking courses outlined in this paper drew from both proposals: for the first edition, the ILSA course structure was emulated only partially, hence introducing the SR software use and management only within the intralingual respeaking module; for the second edition, the research-informed model was implemented in order to introduce the SR software before and independently in one module, way before the intralingual respeaking practice. This change was implemented to face the major issues emerging in students' performances, as mentioned, namely dictation and sentence segmentation as skills directly deriving from the students' interaction with and management of the SR engine.

Through an Action Research (AR) methodological framework as presented by Reason and Bradbury (2006), the first training course was closely observed and, bringing together action and reflection in search for solutions to the main issues discovered, room for improvement was sought for future trainings. Later on, some changes in training modules were implemented in a second course specifically referring to the main HMI-related issues. On its completion, performance results were observed to monitor if the changes implemented throughout the training had been effective or not.

The idea behind an AR process is, indeed, that any activity can be analyzed in cycles that entail 'planning a change, acting and observing the process and consequences of the change, reflecting on these processes and consequences, and then replanning, acting and observing, reflecting, and so on' (Kemmis &

McTaggart, 2000, p. 595). On this note, having observed struggles in SR management, dedicating an independent module to it created the opportunity to spend more time on both dictation and segmentation in order to observe an improvement in such skills by subsequent students. For more on AR methodology and its application to some Translation and Interpreting Studies, refer to Dawson (2020, pp. 48–53).

Intralingual and Interlingual Respeaking Training Proposals

On respeaking training, research has flourished in the past two decades (Arumí Ribas & Romero-Fresco, 2008; Romero-Fresco, 2012; Robert et al., 2019; Russello, 2013). In light of the labelling identified by Gile in his interpreting Effort Model (2015), Pöchhacker & Remael (2019) identify different competencies required in respeaking. Even though their proposal focuses specifically on ILS, some are shared by intralingual respeaking, such as listening comprehension, strategic reformulation, dictation and monitoring. Therefore, it is a multitasking process involving different skills, sometimes applied at the same time, requiring great coordination and control. Other recent research (Dawson, 2020) identified five task-specific skills for interlingual respeaking thanks to an experiment involving different participants and trainees: multitasking, dictation, live translation, language and comprehension, reduced to the first three as proposed by Dawson and Romero-Fresco (2021). Similar skills were identified also by Russello (2010) as multitasking skills, live skills and delivery skills. Either comprised of multitasking or live skills for some scholars, dictation is conceived by many as a separate, individual skill in the whole respeaking process. For training students at University who are not professional interpreters quite yet, a respeaking task involving all these skills and competencies can be challenging, indeed. One of the aspects that emerged in the first training was precisely how to properly dictate to the software when interacting with it. Dictation depends on both the human capacity and speed of articulation, and the software accuracy in transcribing the audio input, which can greatly depend on which ASR software is used. During training, Dragon Naturally Speaking version 15 was mainly used, with individual professional licenses for each student to guarantee customized voice profiles and higher accuracy when trained, in addition to the chance of adding and training some terms beforehand. Nevertheless, many other free and open-access ASR platforms online that build on Google's SR were also explored so students could get acquainted with diverse interfaces, commands and functionalities. Among these were Web Captioner,[2] Speechlogger,[3] Talk-Typer,[4] Speechnotes,[5] with no need to install any program. Web Captioner and Speechnotes, as it is the case for the Google Chrome integrated speech Application Programming Interface (API),[6] allow for different language recognition, not for automatic punctuation addition, that needs to be dictated. None of these three lets respeakers edit the transcript while it is being written, or interact directly on the text window. TalkTyper interface allows for checking and editing the output on an upper window and ultimately approve it to a lower window as with LS software, but it has no automatic punctuation. Speechlogger does add punctuation automatically, although not always very accurately, and also allows for live machine translation of the written text in several languages, on purchase of credit for bigger chunks of translation.

Action Research-Based Remodulation of the Course

The first-ever training in respeaking at Università di Genova, Italy, was offered in 2020/2021 in the Department of Modern Languages and Cultures for doctoral research on different ILS workflows (Pagano, 2022a). Two respeaking courses, both entailing theoretical framework as well as intralingual and interlingual respeaking practice, were given: English to Italian in the first edition, and Spanish to Italian in the second. In compliance with the competence-oriented model (Pöchhacker & Remael, 2019) the participants were students and practitioners enrolled in the master's degree in Translation and Interpreting at the University of Genoa, who had previous experience in translation and in either SI or pre-recorded subtitling. For the second course, there were five students whose mother tongue was Italian – four females and one male aged between 21 and 23 years old – with a strong level of Spanish (approximately C1 proficiency level according to the CEFR, slightly varying from student to student). Four had also studied Russian as a C language, while one studied French. Three students were in their first year and the remaining two were in their second year. All of them had some previous experience, albeit introductory, in subtitling, but three of them only had a basic competence in SI since they had only just begun their first year of the master's program. Nevertheless, they had experience from their bachelor's degree in other types of interpretation, dialogue or consecutive for approximately 60 hours. Those in their second year could count on approximately 150 hours of Spanish to Italian SI, and the same amount for their other language combination. In addition, they had all previously obtained bachelor's degrees in either 'Language Mediation' or 'Modern Languages and Cultures'.

Trainings were delivered remotely via the Microsoft Teams platform and lasted approximately 70 hours including synchronous, at-distance learning and individual practical exercises as well (approx. 20 hours), requiring students to attend two-hour lessons twice a week over three months. All students subscribed voluntarily as it was an optional 3 ECTS workshop and it was not integrated into the master's course lessons plan. The resources varied from reading tasks to video lessons and tutorials or exercises.

The first EN-IT course (see Figure 10.1, left side) was made up of four modules including an introduction to Media and live events accessibility:

Intralingual and Interlingual Respeaking Didactics **143**

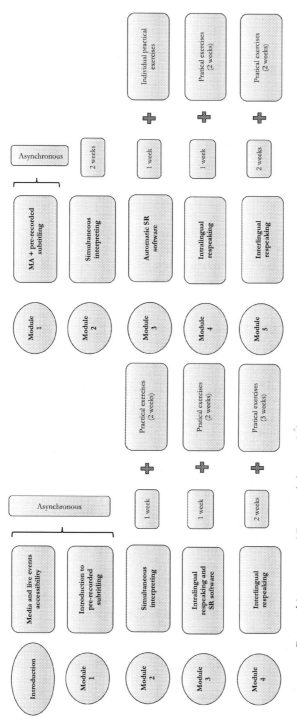

FIGURE 10.1 Respeaking course AR remodulation (left to right).

(i) Introduction to pre-recorded subtitling; (ii) Simultaneous Interpreting; (iii) Intralingual respeaking and SR software; iv) Interlingual respeaking. The second ES-IT respeaking course (see Figure 10.1, right side) condensed the theoretical framework with subtitling, running through five modules in total: (i): Media Accessibility (MA) and pre-recorded subtitling'; (ii) 'Simultaneous interpreting'; 'Automatic SR software'; 'Intralingual respeaking'; 'Interlingual respeaking'.

As mentioned, a close observation of students' performances at the end of the first teaching experience highlighted some crucial areas that required further training. Therefore, the use of SR software through dictation and segmentation practice was introduced earlier in the second training, and as a part of a dedicated module (Module 3). This way, it was hoped that students' SR competencies could be strengthened, as they had the chance to train their voice profiles more robustly and practice more.

In addition, dictation of punctuation was deemed a problem during the first training; as they were more familiar with interpreting rather than respeaking, they tended not to make any frequent pauses or segment their output to let the speech-recognition software process the information. The result was that some very long sentences were processed together and with too many seconds of delay.

Table 10.1 shows the summary of the independent Module 3, which was the object of the AR-remodulation of the training. Module 1 introduced MA, Audio-Visual Translation (AVT), access services and live events accessibility theoretically, with an overview on pre-recorded subtitling (fundamentals and guidelines, text condensation and line breaks, SDH). This module was covered asynchronously by students and later discussed together in class. Synchronous lessons started with Module 2, which focused on reviewing and strengthening SI, while Module 3 introduced the use of the software beforehand. Three units were prepared: the first aimed at framing the technique of respeaking in Italy and clarifying the main guidelines for the task; the second focused on how SR engines work and how to dictate, and several online ASR platforms (ibid., Intralingual and Interlingual Respeaking Training Proposals) were shown to first approach the task. Furthermore, students worked on how to handle live error corrections, pronounce clearly and use word stress, that is, working on intonation. Unit 3 was entirely dedicated to Dragon Naturally Speaking: creation and training of voice profile, creation and addition of word lists, customizations and preferences as well as exercises. The preliminary exercises using Dragon consisted of shadowing exercises with enunciation of punctuation marks, to get used to what would have been required of them while respeaking. Last, Modules 4 and 5 covered intralingual and interlingual respeaking training and practice.

The processes and practices of intralingual respeaking were introduced by asking students to work with Dragon, first on some ad-lib speeches by

TABLE 10.1 Units Structure of Newly Created Module 3 on ASR Software

MODULE 3 – ASR software
Unit 1: Live subtitling and respeaking
1.1 Live subtitling and respeaking
1.2 Respeaking in Italy
Unit 2: Speech recognition and dictation
2.1 Speech recognition and dictation
2.2 Speech recognition engines + online tools
2.3 Misrecognitions and live error editing
2.4 General dictation: punctuation
2.5 General dictation: word stress
Unit 3: Dragon Naturally Speaking and other SR engines
3.1 Dragon Professional Individual – Administrator + User Guide
3.2 Dragon Instructions and tutorials
3.3 Customizing the SR software
3.4 Exercises and practice with Dragon v. 15

the tutor and then with some self-paced videos. At the beginning, the speech rate was low and gradually increased throughout. Intralingual and interlingual final practice was moderated through different degrees of difficulty. For detailed feedback collected on the course's materials and delivery and overall satisfaction, also see Pagano, 2022b.

As a preliminary result, on completion of the second AR-adapted course, improvements in dictation and segmentation were actually detected, possibly thanks to the dedicated module. In addition, students themselves felt more at ease when performing with and managing the ASR.

Intralingual and Interlingual Respeaking Training Materials

Materials used in the training courses for intralingual and interlingual respeaking are displayed in Table 10.2: the first lines are dedicated to IT-IT materials, followed by EN-IT and ES-IT videos.

Before moving to the proper intralingual respeaking practice, preliminary exercises consisted of counting, intralingual shadowing exercises, paraphrasing and summarizing and sight translation with the enunciation of punctuation out loud. The generic subject matter was used that did not require any extra preparation on any specific terminology by the students. In SI, the speech rate variable considered comfortable in order to keep up with the ST is between 100 and 130 words per minute (wpm), while 150–170 wpm is set as the threshold beyond which SI cannot be performed (Riccardi, 2015). Supposing that the same can be applied to respeaking, exercises were calibrated

TABLE 10.2 Some of the IT-IT + EN/ES-IT Intra and Interlingual Respeaking Training Materials

Title	Duration	N. of words	Wpm
Excerpt from *I dieci comandamenti* by Roberto Benigni	00:04:52	573	118
Part of *Meditazione 3.0*, TEDx Talk	until 00:05:11	628	124
Part of *Chi è Salvatore Aranzulla*, TEDx Talk	until 00:05:04	703	140
Speech by Senator Liliana Segre at the EU Parliament	until 00:12:07	986	82
Unusual art performances 'In orbit' description	00:07:46	952	123
'The future of work', Speech Repository	00:06:22	765	120
'The Lord of the Rings Trilogy overview'	00:09:50	1,167	118
'Friday 13th', Speech Repository	00:07:14	943	130
'The food app revolution', Speech Repository	00:05:49	656	129
'The origins of language', Speech Repository	00:09:11	1,294	141
'Mobile phones', Speech Repository	00:09:26	1,556	166
'The secret of becoming mentally strong', TEDx Talk	00:15:00	2,374	158
Speech by King Felipe VI	00:13:05	960	74
Speech by Antonio Banderas, Premios Goyas	00:04:25	443	96
Speech by José Mujica, Río +20	00:07:40	936	128
Speech by Isabel Allende, 2006 Olympic Games	00:12:00	1,556	130
Stanford University's commencement speech by Steve Jobs (ES)	00:17:15	2,059	119
'Los peligros del teléfono móvil', Speech Repository	00:04:53	591	122
'El reciclaje de medicamentos', Speech Repository	00:05:40	748	140
'Lo positivo de fracasar en el amor', TEDx Talk	00:08:03	1,338	167

on gradually increasing speech rates (however, the added capacity required by respeakers to carry out additional tasks such as dictation to software, and even more so when shifting from one language to another, cannot be understated). First, some off-the-cuff speeches with a fairly slow speech rate (85–95 wpm) were given by the trainer to allow students to properly adjust to the task: listening while speaking into the software and trying to summarize subject matter when possible, dictating punctuation marks and monitoring the transcribed output in search of any misrecognition. At a later stage, some faster pre-recorded speech (100–120 wpm) was introduced, and ultimately up to 140 wpm speeches also entailed the additional complexity of slides being shown by the speaker on video, thus requiring as little delay as possible to synchronize the subtitles with what was displayed on the screen. These last practices were deemed to be particularly fit by the trainer for reformulation and condensation in order to keep up with the pace of the ST. The speech material used also varied in terms of duration: first students worked with shorter videos, and then videos of up to 10–12 minutes were respoken. Some of these pre-recorded real-life videos used as training material are detailed below.

The same approach of gradually increasing the speech rate during intralingual respeaking was also applied to the interlingual respeaking modules. First, pre-recorded speeches in English with a lower speech rate were given (approximately 85–100 wpm: former US President Obama's 'back to school' speech, Albert Einstein's Nobel dinner remarks and former US President Trump's speech on the Mexican wall). Then, students worked on pedagogical material videos mainly retrieved from the Speech Repository[7] at basic and beginner levels at first, then intermediate, and last on some TED Talks with a faster speech rate (between 130 and 160 wpm). For the faster speeches, students were allowed to listen to the videoclips once before respeaking them, to adjust to the speed and note down any unfamiliar terms and expressions and better understand the context and topic. This was deemed important to reduce anxiety (Davitti & Sandrelli, 2020), since respeaking is feasible, as demonstrated (Dawson, 2019), yet it is also challenging, especially for students who were not professionals in SI and were attempting it the very first time. Some of the training materials detailed below were pre-recorded videos, and some others were recordings and ad-lib (or almost ad-lib) comments and reviews of movies or art performances, for example, given by the trainer.

For the Spanish-to-Italian respeaking training, the rationale behind progressive exercises from beginner/basic to intermediate level was consistent with the previously proposed trainings. Pre-prepared speeches were first delivered by the tutor at a slow speech rate and at the beginning, recorded or live-delivered speeches were given at a much slower pace than the originals. This was the case for pre-recorded speeches by King Felipe VI, actor Antonio Banderas, former Uruguay President José Mujica and novelist Isabel Allende. All speakers also had varying Spanish accents, which would have made it more complex for students to comprehend. After the completion of the speech by the tutor, they also attempted to respeak the originals anyway. For longer videos, these were split and respoken in two parts, and for particularly fast speech rates (TEDx Talks 'Lo positivo de fracasar en el amor') students were allowed to watch them once before respeaking, and then play them with a slightly reduced playback speed (0.75x), thereby lowering the speech rate to one more feasible for their level.

Discussion and Conclusions

On completion of both training courses, two final experiments were carried out. The results obtained in these tests and their quantitative and qualitative analyses are discussed in depth in the doctoral thesis of reference (Pagano, 2022a). The experiments sought to calculate the overall quality of the produced subtitles in both language combinations the NTR model for linguistic accuracy calculation on one hand, and calculating the subtitles' latency on the other. For more on the NTR evaluation system and the calculation of the scores, please refer to Romero-Fresco and Pöchhacker (2017). The analyses of the two experiments were carried out on all chunks of text and to minimize subjectivity in the assessment, three evaluators completed them. When their opinion differed on some errors' severity, they would discuss it and eventually agree on the same grading for the three assessments.

The NTR final results combined with delay calculation for the subtitles, together with a comprehensive evaluation of the respeaking performances highlighted that misrecognitions by the SR software after the second training were less frequent and the recognized sentences were indeed shorter (Pagano, 2022a). Overall, the results of the second experiment after the second training course achieved better scores. Since the same starting conditions were guaranteed for both experiments (Dragon was used as the ASR software on both occasions, and ST speeches had the same complexity level) the first preliminary conclusion that can be drawn is that the AR-based remodulation was effective. In some way, what represented a challenge for students in their interaction with the machine, was turned into an opportunity. Opportunity to better interact with the software thanks to closer training on how to do so and, ultimately, the opportunity to demonstrate that the human and machine combination can deliver high-quality ILS under the right conditions.

Moreover, students' feedback on their performance did underline a stronger self-confidence in performing the respeaking tasks when dictating to the software, deriving from more comprehensive training on how to interact with it. Globally, all students showed a good level of satisfaction with the training, and they declared that it contributed to strengthening and improving some SI skills as well. On this matter, the dictation skill in the interaction with the software played a major role since their output needed to be clear of hesitations, false starts and self-corrections as much as possible (Pagano, 2022b), something that is also useful for a neater interpreting task. Last but not least, the courses highlighted the importance of training SI students for MA (Greco, 2019; Greco & Jankowska, 2020) to combine both techniques (Romero-Fresco, 2015; Sandrelli, 2020), and prepare much-needed professionals in this field (Eugeni & Bernabé, 2019).

To conclude, the AR-based reformulation of the respeaking course led to higher accuracy in the final subtitles. This could suggest that the reason behind this was that students had the chance to familiarize and train with the software thanks to the dedicated SR module introduced in the second training, namely, improve their HMI with positive results. In addition, they could better practice sentence segmentation and condensation strategies.

A limitation to this assumption is that the better results can also derive from the easier language combination of Spanish to Italian of the second course and experiment since they are two syntactically similar languages. This is why this contribution is far from approaching an exhaustive result and it is only hoped that it can spark interest in how to increase an effective HMI in this field. Since respeaking is impossible to perform without the assistance of a machine, it is all the more important to redefine the HMI in this process and to be aware of the risks and opportunities.

One of the challenges for future training and for the future of respeaking as a profession is that the process will be fully automated and led only by the ASR systems. If this is the case, then the human component in the process could be confined to a post-editing task. If a combination of humans and machines in the process is maintained instead, a better overall quality in ILS can be provided.

Notes

1 For more on the project see: http://ka2-ilsa.webs.uvigo.es/project/.
2 https://webcaptioner.com/captioner
3 https://speechlogger.appspot.com/it/
4 https://talktyper.com/it/index.html
5 https://speechnotes.co/it/#content
6 https://www.google.com/intl/it/chrome/demos/speech.html
7 European Commission Speech Repository: https://webgate.ec.europa.eu/sr/.

References

Arumí Ribas, M. and Romero-Fresco, P. 2008. A practical proposal for the training of respeakers. *The Journal of Specialised Translation*, 10, pp. 106–127. Available from: https://www.jostrans.org/archive.php?display=10
Davitti, E. and Sandrelli, A. 2020. Embracing the complexity: A pilot study on interlingual respeaking. *Journal of Audiovisual Translation*, 3(2), pp. 103–139. Available from: https://jatjournal.org/index.php/jat/article/view/135/40
Dawson, H. 2019. Feasibility, quality and assessment of interlingual live subtitling: A pilot study. *Journal of Audiovisual Translation*, 2(2), pp. 36–56. Available from: https://www.jatjournal.org/index.php/jat/article/view/72
Dawson, H. 2020. *Interlingual live subtitling – A research-informed training model for interlingual respeakers to improve access for a wide audience*. Ph.D. dissertation, University of Roehampton, London.
Dawson, H. and Romero-Fresco, P. 2021. Towards research-informed training in interlingual respeaking: An empirical approach. *The Interpreter and Translator Trainer*, 15(1), pp. 66–84. Available from: https://www.tandfonline.com/doi/full/10.1080/1750399X.2021.1880261
Díaz-Cintas, J. And Remael, A. 2021. *Subtitling: Concepts and Practices*. Routledge, London & New York.

Eugeni, C. 2007. Il rispeakeraggio televisivo per sordi: per una sottotitolazione mirata del TG. *InTRAlinea* 8. Available from: http://www.intralinea.org/archive/article/Il_rispeakeraggio_televisivo_per_sordi

Eugeni, C. 2019. Technology in court reporting – Capitalising on human-computer interaction. *International Justice Congress Proceedings, Uluslararası Adalet Kongresi (UAK)*, 2–4 May 2019, pp. 873–881.

Eugeni, C. 2020. Human-computer interaction in diamesic translation. Multilingual live subtitling. In: Dejica, D., Eugeni, C. and Dejica-Cartiş, A. *Translation Studies and Information Technology – New Pathways for Researchers, Teachers and Professionals*. Translation Studies Series Editura Politehnica, Timişoara, Politehnica University Timişoara, pp. 19–31.

Eugeni, C. and Bernabé, R. 2019. LTA project – Bridging the gap between training and the profession in real-time intralingual subtitling. *Linguistica Antverpiensia New Series: Themes in Translation Studies*, 18. Available from: https://lans-tts.uantwerpen.be/index.php/LANS-TTS/issue/view/20

Gile, D. 2015. Effort models. In: Pöchhacker, F. *Routledge Encyclopedia of Interpreting Studies*. London: Routledge, pp. 135–137.

Greco, G.M. 2019. Towards a pedagogy of accessibility: The need for critical learning spaces in media accessibility education and training. *Linguistica Antverpiensia, New Series: Themes in Translation Studies*, 18, pp. 23–46.

Greco, G.M. and Jankowska, A. 2020. Media accessibility within and beyond audiovisual translation. In: Bogucki, Ł. and Deckert, M. *The Palgrave Handbook of Audiovisual Translation and Media Accessibility*. Palgrave Studies in Translating and Interpreting, pp. 57–81. Available from: https://doi.org/10.1007/978-3-030-42105-2_4

Kemmis, S. and McTaggart, R. 2000. Participatory action research: Communicative action and the public sphere. In: Denzin, N. and Lincoln, Y. S. *Handbook of Qualitative Research*. Thousand Oaks, CA: SAGE, pp. 271–330.

Moores, Z. 2020. Fostering access for all through respeaking at live events. *JoSTrans, Journal of Specialised Translation*, 33. Available from: https://jostrans.org/issue33/art_moores.php

Pagano, A. 2022a. *Testing quality in interlingual respeaking and other methods of interlingual live subtitling*, Ph.D. dissertation, Università degli Studi di Genova, IT.

Pagano, A. 2022b. Interlingual respeaking training for simultaneous interpreting trainees: New opportunities in media accessibility. *CoMe, Studi di Comunicazione e Mediazione linguistica e culturale*, VI(1). Available from: https://comejournal.com/wp-content/uploads/2022/11/2.-Pagano.pdf

Pagano, A. [Forthcoming]. Formación de intérpretes simultáneos para la accesibilidad: relato de una experiencia didáctica. In: Varela Salinas, M. J. and Plaza L. C. *Aproximaciones teóricas y prácticas a la accesibilidad desde la traducción y la interpretación*. Editorial Comares, Granada.

Pöchhacker, F. and Remael, A. 2019. New efforts? A competence-oriented task analysis of interlingual live subtitling. *Linguistica Antverpiensia, New Series: Themes in Translation Studies*, 18, pp. 130–143.

Reason, P. and Bradbury, H. 2006. *The SAGE handbook of Action Research: Participative Inquiry and Practice*. 2nd ed. London: SAGE.

Riccardi, A. 2015. Speech rate. In: Pochhacker, F. *Routledge Encyclopedia of Interpreting Studies*. London: Routledge, pp. 397–399.

Robert, I., Schrijver, I. and Diels, E. 2019. Trainers' and employers' perception of training in intralingual and interlingual live subtitling: A survey study. *Journal of Audiovisual Translation*, 2(1), pp. 1–25. Available from: https://www.jatjournal.org/index.php/jat/article/view/61

Romero-Fresco, P. 2011. *Subtitling Through Speech Recognition: Respeaking.* Manchester: St. Jerome Publishing.

Romero-Fresco, P. 2012. Respeaking in translator training curricula. Present and future prospects. *The Interpreter and Translator Trainer*, 6(1), pp. 91–112. Available from: https://www.tandfonline.com/doi/abs/10.1080/13556509.2012.10798831?journalCode=ritt20

Romero-Fresco, P. 2015. Respeaking as a bridge between subtitling and interpreting. In: Pöchhacker, F. *Routledge Encyclopaedia of Interpreting Studies.* New York & London: Routledge, pp. 349–351.

Romero-Fresco, P. 2019. Respeaking: Subtitling through speech recognition. In: Perez-González, L. *The Routledge Handbook of Audiovisual Translation.* Oxon & New York: Routledge, pp. 96–113.

Romero-Fresco, P. and Eugeni, C. 2020. Live subtitling through respeaking. In: Bogucki, Ł. and Deckert, M. *Handbook of Audiovisual Translation and Media Accessibility.* Palgrave MacMillan, Cham, Switzerland, pp. 269–295.

Romero-Fresco, P. and Pöchhacker, F. 2017. Quality assessment in interlingual live subtitling: The NTR model. *Linguistics Antverpiensia, New Series: Themes in Translation Studies*, 16, pp. 149-167. Available from: https://lans-tts.uantwerpen.be/index.php/LANS-TTS/article/view/438

Russello, C. 2010. Teaching respeaking to conference interpreters. In: *Intersteno, Education Committee Archive.* Available from: https://www.intersteno.it/materiale/ComitScientifico/EducationCommittee/Russello2010Teaching Respeaking to Conference Interpreters.pdf

Russello, C. 2013. Aspetti didattici. In Eugeni, C. and Zambelli, L. Respeaking. *Specializzazione Online*, pp. 44–53. Available from: https://www.accademia-aliprandi.it/public/specializzazione/respeaking.pdf

Sandrelli, A. 2020. Interlingual respeaking and simultaneous interpreting in a conference setting: A comparison. In: Spinolo, N. and Amato, A. *Technology in Interpreter Education and Practice.* inTRAlinea, Special issue. Available from: https://www.intralinea.org/specials/article/2518

Szarkowska, A., Krejtz, K., Dutka, Ł. and Pilipczuk, O. 2018. Are interpreters better respeakers? *The Interpreter and Translator Trainer*, 12(2), pp. 207–226. Available from: https://www.tandfonline.com/doi/full/10.1080/1750399X.2018.1465679

Wallinheimo, A., Evans, S. and Davitti, E. 2023. Training in new forms of human-AI interaction improves complex working memory and switching skills of language professionals. In: *Frontiers in Artificial Intelligence*, 6, Frontiers Media. Available from: https://www.frontiersin.org/articles/10.3389/frai.2023.1253940/full

11
TEACHING LIVE SUBTITLING THROUGH MOCK CONFERENCES

Faruk Mardan

Introduction

Live Subtitling Through Respeaking

Live subtitling is 'the real-time transcription of spoken words, sound effects, relevant musical cues and other relevant audio information in live or pre-recorded events' (International Telecommunications Union, 2018). Live subtitling is usually performed through respeaking, a technique where the practitioner (usually referred to as a 'respeaker') respeaks the utterance from a live performance by dictating both the speech and punctuation into a piece of speech recognition software. The dictated sound is then converted into text and broadcast on the screen as subtitles almost simultaneously (Romero-Fresco, 2020). According to Romero-Fresco and Eugeni (2020), respeaking is performed predominantly through speech recognition software and is gradually taking over other modes of live subtitling, including stenography and Velotype. Although respeaking is by no means a perfect solution to the challenges faced in the live subtitling front, it has been gaining momentum as the predominant mode of producing live subtitles. Demand for respeaking talents is on the rise (Romero-Fresco, 2020), and such a demand has translated into a demand for respeaker training. As respeaker training is a relatively young discipline, only a handful of higher education institutions provide such training (Romero-Fresco, 2012). The University of Leeds is one such institution (University of Leeds, 2023).

Respeaking is a highly practical skill and situated learning is one of the most effective approaches to honing practical skills, as it provides content and context and creates a community of practice through meaningful

DOI: 10.4324/9781003440994-14

participation (Stein, 1998). The benefits of situated learning in translation and interpreting training have already been well documented in numerous sources, and González-Davies and Enríquez-Raído (2016) are but one of them. At the Centre for Translation and Interpreting Studies of the University of Leeds (henceforth Leeds CTIS), respeaking was launched as an optional module across all its MA programmes in the 2021–2022 academic year and is currently in its third year of teaching. Mock projects have long been a vital part of translation, interpreting and subtitling training at Leeds CTIS, which set up the stage for respeaking as a new addition to the complex.

Situated Learning in Simultaneous Interpreter Training

Simultaneous interpreter training has evolved from its original form of apprenticeship to a more systematic and research-led form of training, mainly provided by higher education institutions and international organisations (Moser-Mercer, 2015). Professionalisation and diversification of interpreting practices mean that interpreter training is increasingly in demand. Requirements of professional competence are rising and emphasis in training has shifted from memory training to a contextualised approach, in which students engage with authentic materials and use role play to simulate a professional setting (Wadensjö, 2014). Earlier accounts of situated interpreter training models include Ardito (1999), who argues that impromptu speeches delivered in multilingual contexts are an effective approach to training interpreters.

Mock conferences are an important approach to training interpreters. There have been numerous reports on using mock conferences as an effective means of interpreter training. The following are but a few examples. Conde and Chouc (2019) highlight the effectiveness of mock conferences in boosting their key skills in conference interpreting by placing them in a realistic setting. Fomina (2018) concludes that mock conferences boost not only the students' interpreting skills, but also other essential non-linguistic competencies, such as psychological, strategic and problem-solving abilities. Li (2015), among others, provides guidelines for designing and organising mock conferences in interpreter training. Mock conferences can be implemented in various formats, but normally consist of several roles to facilitate the setup, including conference coordinators, interpreters, speakers from different linguistic backgrounds and IT technicians, just to name a few (Conde and Chouc, 2019; Li, 2015). A typical mock conference consists of a topic, prepared speeches by speakers of different languages and student interpreters. Students are normally informed of the topic so that they can prepare for the conference (Li, 2015). This situated approach provides more context and renders the conference more authentic, by applying some real but healthy pressure as well as responsibilities on the interpreters (Li, 2015).

Simultaneous Interpreting and Respeaking

Interpreting and respeaking bear many similarities, as both require listening to the speech and speaking at the same time. Both demand a high cognitive load, excellent communication skills and the ability to paraphrase and summarise. Both skills require nearly simultaneous output and split attention (Ribas and Fresco, 2008). Respeaking and simultaneous interpreting are also used in similar situations, including conferences and television (Eugeni and Bernabé, 2021). Both practices involve a speaker, whose utterance is transmitted to the interpreter or the respeaker through audio signals, who then processes the information and dictates the output into a microphone (Eugeni and Bernabé, 2021). Both interpreting and respeaking output are typically produced with a 2–10-second delay (Eugeni and Bernabé, 2021). However, respeaking, contrary to what one may expect, is not necessarily a verbatim of the utterance, but rather a paraphrased version of the original message (Romero-Fresco, 2009). Similarly, paraphrasing has been well documented as one of the important skills for interpreters (Ballester and Jimenez Hurtado, 1992).

The most noteworthy difference between respeaking and interpreting is that in the former, punctuation and some other cues are also dictated through speech recognition software, to facilitate understanding for the deaf and hard of hearing (Diaz-Cintas, 2020). In interpreting, punctuations are not uttered and are hardly a concern for interpreters. Another difference is that in respeaking, the dictation is processed by an Automatic Speech Recognition (ASR) tool, and the final output is presented in the form of text.

It is precisely because of these similarities that many lessons can be learnt from interpreter training when we train respeakers. It is then natural to envisage that mock conferences could also be an effective mode of respeaker training.

Teaching Live Subtitling Through Mock Conferences

Sandrelli (2020) compared the performances of English-to-Italian interpreters and respeakers in real conference settings and showed promising results in terms of similar error frequency and distortion of meaning. By providing authentic content and context to the trainees, an environment in which many critical skills in respeaking can be practised and improved is provided. These include audience dependence, stress management, teamwork, technical setup and troubleshooting. However, till the time of writing, no literature has been documented, to the best of the author's knowledge, on the teaching of respeaking through mock conferences. This chapter addresses this gap in research, and reports on the use of mock conferences as an approach to teaching live subtitling through respeaking at the Centre for Translation and Interpreting Studies (CTIS) Symposium at Leeds.

Leeds CTIS Symposium

Leeds CTIS Symposium (henceforth, 'the Symposium') is a cross-disciplinary and multilingual team project organised by Leeds CTIS. Scholars and practitioners in translation studies and the language service industry are invited to present on a topic related to their work as well as to the theme of the Symposium in their native languages. They are required to provide relevant literature, their biographies and other written information related to their presentations in their native languages, which typically include English, French, Italian, Spanish, Portuguese, German, Chinese and Arabic. These documents are subsequently translated into English, Chinese and Arabic, wherever applicable and possible, by students of MA Applied Translation Studies. A glossary is provided in each language pair and all documents are supplied to the rest of the CTIS cohort in advance. On the day of the Symposium, speakers are invited to speak at the Interpreting Training Facility of Leeds CTIS or online, where interpreting trainees provide simultaneous interpreting into various languages. The Symposium is held in a hybrid mode, both in person and online, to ensure all staff and students can tune into the Symposium in the language with which they are familiar. The hybrid mode also caters to the recent trends that shift towards Remote Simultaneous Interpreting (RSI) in the industry (Przepiórkowska, 2021). In addition to simultaneous interpreting, students enrolled in the respeaking module are allocated exclusive booths to provide live subtitles in English through respeaking.

Since 2022, three Symposiums have been organised. All Leeds CTIS students participated in the projects in various capacities. The Symposiums were entirely organised by the students. The teaching staff act as 'ignorant clients' who outsource the entire project to the 'Language Service Provider (LSP)', that is, students who take on the role of project managers. All other students act as the vendors of this project, who would review the job requests sent by the project managers and supply individual quotations for their services. Negotiations and onboarding processes then take place. The LSP is responsible for liaising between the vendors and the clients while ensuring the whole project runs smoothly. All aspects of the project, including vendor recruitment, translation, terminology management, revision, machine translation post-editing, interpreter coordination, interpreting, respeaking, subtitling for the deaf and hard of hearing (SDH), project quotation, invoice and management are carried out entirely by the students.

This chapter focuses on the provision of live subtitling through respeaking during the second Symposium in 2023. A total of six languages were spoken by six speakers during the Symposium, including Chinese, Spanish, French, English, Portuguese and Italian. Live subtitling was provided only in English through respeaking as a pilot project. Where the speaker spoke English, the respeakers produced live subtitles by directly engaging the speaker output;

where a language other than English was spoken on the floor, the respeaker produced live subtitling by relaying from the English interpreting. The reason why interlingual respeaking was not directly adopted is that the Symposium was the first time the respeakers practised what they had learnt in real situations, and intralingual respeaking was already sufficiently challenging without the added stress of interpreting in another language.

The online aspect of the Symposium was held on BoostEvents, which is 'a virtual event platform that offers virtual simultaneous interpretation services to assist (users) in reaching their target audience in any language (Boostlingo, n.d.)'. Dragon Naturally Speaking and StreamText were deployed for dictation and streaming the live subtitles, respectively, during the Symposium.

Number, edition error and recognition error (NER) and Number, Translation error and Recognition error (NTR) Models

Since the beginning of live subtitling as a professional practice, there have been different approaches to assessing the quality of live subtitles (Romero-Fresco and Pöchhacker, 2018). In addition, countries around the world have opted for various approaches to live subtitling, with some countries such as the UK adopting the verbatim approach, while others choosing to edit the subtitles to different extents (Romero-Fresco and Pérez, 2015). Therefore, a focus on the accuracy of meaning was emphasised in the assessment of the quality of live subtitling. Over the years, the main approach to assessing accuracy has evolved from a generic word error rate (WER) model to a more targeted NER model (Romero-Fresco and Pérez, 2015) for intralingual live subtitling and NTR model (Romero-Fresco and Pöchhacker, 2018) for interlingual subtitling.

Both NER and NTR models are more detailed manifestations of the WER model (11.1):

$$\text{Accuracy rate} = \frac{N - \text{Errors}}{N} \times 100\% \qquad (11.1)$$

where N represents the number of words recognised.

However, the difference between these models and the WER model is that the former acknowledges that there are different degrees of errors that affect accuracy to varying extents. Another distinct feature of the NER and NTR models is that the errors are further categorised into editing error (in NER)/ translation error (in NTR) and recognition error, with three levels of severity within each category, including serious error (equivalent to one error), standard error (0.5-point error) and minor error (0.25-point error). Editing/ translation errors mainly occur as a result of the subtitler's misjudgement due to many factors such as high speech rate, high cognitive load, omission and so forth. On the other hand, recognition errors are those deriving from the misrecognised, mispronounced output by either the respeaker or the speech recognition technology (Romero-Fresco and Pöchhacker, 2018).

Formulae (11.2) and (11.3) below reflect the NER and NTR models, respectively. In both models, N stands for the word count of the subtitles and R represents recognition errors. The difference between the two models lies in the 'E' and the 'T'. E stands for editing errors in intralingual live subtitling, whereas T represents translation errors in interlingual live subtitling. As a rule of thumb, 'E' and 'T' errors represent those made by the respeaker, especially the errors made in the decision-making process; 'R' errors are normally errors caused by the speech recognition software (Romero-Fresco and Pöchhacker, 2018).

$$\text{Accuracy rate} = \frac{N - E - R}{N} \times 100\% \qquad (11.2)$$

$$\text{Accuracy} = \frac{N - T - R}{N} \times 100\% \qquad (11.3)$$

Methodology

Two presentations from the 2nd CTIS Symposium were chosen as samples for quality assessment, one in English and the other in Chinese. English-English respeaking was performed on the English speech to produce intralingual live subtitles. The Chinese speech was first interpreted into English by a student interpreter, and the English interpreting output was respoken to produce interlingual English live subtitles. The English speech lasted 10 minutes 37 seconds, generating a total of 1,147 respoken words and the Chinese speech lasted 17 minutes and 20 seconds, generating a total of 1,178 words. The significant discrepancy in the number of words was mainly due to the style of speaking of the two speakers and the fact that the Chinese speaker deliberately slowed down to allow more time for the interpreter. Another reason is that Chinese is a character-based language, and a word is usually formed of more than one character.

To assess the quality of output, the NER model (Romero-Fresco and Pöchhacker, 2018) was applied to evaluate both intralingual and interlingual live subtitles. The interlingual live subtitles in this case were compared against the English interpreting. Subsequently, the NTR model was applied to assess the quality of interlingual live subtitles by comparing them against the Chinese speech. These comparisons focus on the accuracy rate of intralingual live subtitles produced directly from the original speech and interlingual live subtitles relaying from interpreting.

The chapter then looks into the distribution of errors through the duration of output, to explore whether the performance is consistent across different phases or if there is a particular section of the production that presents a peak performance.

Here, a distinction must be made between interlingual live subtitling and interlingual respeaking. The term 'interlingual respeaking' was avoided in this chapter because no interlingual respeaking was performed. The term 'interlingual live subtitling' was used because, in essence, the respeaker supplied live subtitling in English for the Chinese speech, regardless of the intermediary channel or the fact that the respeaker did not know Chinese. Interlingual respeaking is the process of delivery, while interlingual live subtitling is the rendition between languages and refers to the final product.

Results

Respeaking Accuracy Rate

Table 11.1 is a breakdown of the numbers and types of errors as well as the NER score of English-English intralingual live subtitling. Table 11.2 shows the accuracy rate of interlingual live subtitling for the Chinese speech, compared against the English interpreting output. Table 11.3 illustrates the NTR score for Chinese-English interlingual live subtitling.

TABLE 11.1 Numbers and Types of Errors and NER Score of English-English Intralingual Live Subtitling

Source Language	Word count	Editing Errors			Recognition Errors			Score
		Severe	Standard	Minor	Severe	Standard	Minor	
English	1,138	4	2	3	1	4	8	99.1%

TABLE 11.2 Numbers and Types of Errors and NER Score of Chinese-English Interlingual Live Subtitling for the Chinese Speech, Compared against the English Interpreting Output

Source Language	Word count	Editing Errors			Recognition Errors			Score
		Severe	Standard	Minor	Severe	Standard	Minor	
English (interpreting)	1,489	12	7	5	5	5	18	98.3%

TABLE 11.3 Numbers and Types of Errors and NTR Score of Chinese-English Interlingual Live Subtitling for the Chinese Speech

Source Language	Word count	Editing Errors			Recognition Errors			Score
		Severe	Standard	Minor	Severe	Standard	Minor	
Chinese	1,489	39	7	5	5	5	18	96.5%

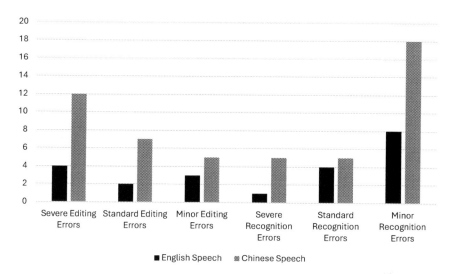

FIGURE 11.1   Intralingual respeaking performances of the English and Chinese speeches.

NER Analysis of Respeaking Performance

Respeaking for English speech and English interpreting achieved accuracy rates of 99.1% and 98.3%, respectively. Overall, the quality of subtitles for the English speech was better than that of the Chinese speech. This is reflected in the smaller number of errors across all categories (see Figure 11.1). The starkest contrast between the two performances lies in the number of minor recognition errors (8 versus 18) and severe editing errors (4 versus 12). The smallest difference is seen in the number of standard recognition errors, where four errors were made for the English speech, while five were made for the Chinese speech.

Intralingual versus Interlingual Live Subtitling

The accuracy rates for the intralingual and interlingual live subtitling stood at 99.1% and 96.5%, respectively (see Figure 11.2). The discrepancies between NER and NTR figures for the Chinese speech is that the 27 omissions by the Chinese-English interpreter were factored in. Here, omissions refer to the failure to deliver a complete unit of sense. In this case, if we disregard the numerous omissions made by the Chinese-English interpreter, the interpreting output was highly accurate. In addition, the performance of the interpreter was out of the scope of discussion in this chapter. Only four severe editing errors were made in the intralingual live subtitling, while

160 Faruk Mardan

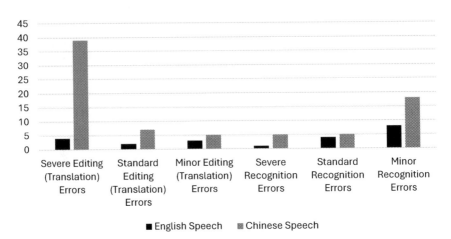

FIGURE 11.2 Intralingual live subtitling versus Interlingual live subtitling.

TABLE 11.4 Error Distribution of Intralingual Subtitling during Performance

Language	First third		Middle third		Final third	
	No. of Errors	% of total	No. of Errors	% of total	No. of Errors	% of total
English	4	18.18	10	45.46	8	36.36
Chinese	20	38.46	17	32.69	15	28.85

39 severe translation errors were made in the interlingual live subtitling, including the 27 omissions.

Error Distribution of Intralingual Respeaking in Different phases

To examine how performance changed over time, the English speech was divided into three roughly equal sections of 3 minutes and 32 seconds. Similarly, the Chinese speech was divided into three portions of 5 minutes and 40 seconds. Table 11.4 indicates the number of errors and their relevant percentages of total in intralingual respeaking in the third portion of each of the speeches.

As indicated in Figure 11.3, there is little consistency between the two speeches in terms of error distribution in different phases. For the English-English respeaking, the errors peaked at 45.46% in the middle-third portion, with the best performance displayed in the first-third portion. In comparison, the Chinese-English respeaking showed a steady downward trend, with nearly 40% of the errors occurring in the first-third portion but was more evenly distributed than the English speech.

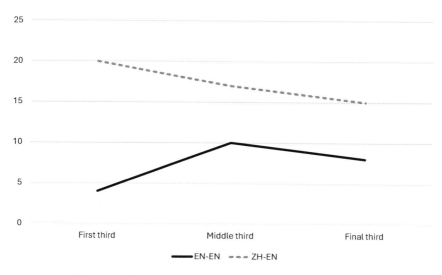

FIGURE 11.3 Number of errors by time section for the English and Chinese speeches.

Discussion

Correct Editing in English-English Intralingual Respeaking

The intralingual respeaking for the English speech boasted a high accuracy rate of 99.1%. One factor that explains such a high accuracy rate was the ability of the speaker, who was a native speaker of English, to articulate in a clear and concise manner, which reduces the stress and cognitive load of the respeaker. On the other hand, the Chinese-English interpreting was provided by a Chinese native speaker, increasing the challenges for the respeaker to convey the message in English under stress. However, it should be noted that such a high accuracy can never be achieved if the model of measurement is based on a verbatim approach. The respeaker made a series of excellent editing decisions to paraphrase the speaker, and such an approach is welcomed by academics and practitioners alike. In fact, studies (such as Luyckx et al., 2013) argue that it is nearly impossible to produce a full verbatim output of the audio input. The ability to paraphrase, condense and summarise the speaker's message is critical for respeakers to produce effective live subtitling. Table 11.5 lists a few examples of correct editing in English-English intralingual respeaking.

Spoken language is often redundant by nature. The examples above exhibited an effective strategy whereby the 'fillers' and redundant utterances were removed and the text was shortened to different extents, ranging from 2–11 fewer words than the original sentences. It can be observed that the respeaker was actively looking for shortcuts in their rendition, even if it is

162 Faruk Mardan

TABLE 11.5 Examples of Correct Editing in Intralingual Live Subtitling for the English Speech

Examples	Audio	Respeaker
1	So, you can see on the fronts here of the slides, there is a photograph of Chrissie Maher.	You can see on the front of the slides, there is an image of Chrissie Maher.
2	Chrissie Maher is the woman who founded the Plain English campaign.	She's the one who founded the Plain English Campaign.
3	So, the campaign not only has a very serious and important mission, it also has a good sense of humour.	As well as having a serious and important mission, the campaign also has a good sense of humour.
4	In the same set of awards, they also gave Greta Thunberg an award, it was an international award for her inspiring message that she gets across by simply and clearly stating the facts.	Greta Thunberg was also honoured with the international award for her inspiring message that she gets across by simply and clearly stating facts.
5	These are all documents that are intended for everybody to read, no matter what their level of education is.	These are all documents intended for everyone to read, no matter the level of education.
6	So they advise you to use words such as 'you' and 'we', and to use words that are appropriate for the reader.	Use 'you' and 'we', as well as words that are appropriate for the reader.

a synonym with fewer syllables that was readily available. Examples of this include 'image' instead of 'photograph' (Example 1), and 'everyone' instead of 'everybody' (Example 5). These strategies effectively reduce the respeakers' cognitive load, save critical seconds and allow them to focus on the subsequent message, without losing any sense or meaning.

Effective Editing in Chinese-English Interlingual Live Subtitling

Compared with the English-English intralingual live subtitling, interlingual live subtitling between Chinese and English presented extra layers of challenges. To begin with, the respeaker had no real-time access to the Chinese speech, as they did not know Chinese. In other words, they were completely reliant on the English interpreting output, which was 'second-hand' information. This challenge was exacerbated by the fact that the interpreter was still a trainee at the university, so errors and miscommunication were almost inevitable. However, despite these challenges, a high accuracy rate of

98.3% was achieved by the respeaker, when we disregard the 27 omissions made by the interpreter. In Table 11.6, some examples of effective editing in interlingual live subtitling are presented.

As the live subtitles were a product of relay from the interpreter, effective editing is a joint effort by the interpreter and the respeaker, who were both novice trainees and who were placed in a highly demanding and stressful

TABLE 11.6 Some Examples of Effective Editing in Interlingual Live Subtitling

Example	Audio	Back translation	Interpreter	Respeaker
1	我希望大家能清楚地看到我的PPT	I hope everyone can see my slides clearly.	I hope that everyone can see clearly my slides.	I hope my slides are clear to everyone.
2	我叫XXX，我毕业于利兹大学。	My name is XXX, and I graduated from the University of Leeds	My name is XXX and I graduated from the University of Leeds.	My name is XXX. I'm a graduate of Leeds University.
3	香港在殖民地时期口述影像滞后于西方国家主要是因为香港经济。	Due to economy, Hong Kong lagged behind the West in Audio Description during the colonisation period.	Hong Kong was lagging behind Western countries in terms of Audio Description. The reason is Hong Kong's overall economy.	Hong Kong was lagging behind Western countries in terms of A.D. because of its economy.
4	这个协会致力于提供、推广口述影像以及多样化服务，口述影像工作者培训、公众教育和顾问服务。这个协会在香港和澳门提供服务。	The association aims to provide and promote Audio Description and diverse services, training of audio describers, public education and consultancy services. The association operates in Hong Kong and Macau.	The association aims to promote A.D. services and provide diverse services, including education, public education as well as consultancy services. They provided services in Hong Kong and Macau.	The association aims to promote A.D. services and other diverse services, including education, public education and consultancy services in Hong Kong and Macau.

situated learning environment, arguably for the first time. The continuous effort to condense and summarise the message has led to some effective editing outcomes as indicated above. In Example 1 (see Table 11.6), the word count is not necessarily smaller, but the delivery is more coherent and natural. In Example 2, the respeaker decomposed the sentence into two more digestible and simpler syntactic units. Examples 3 and 4 were illustrative of the respeaker's (and the interpreter's to some extent) ability to summarise the message and render it succinctly.

In both intralingual and interlingual live subtitling, two main factors have contributed to the high quality of delivery. First, the situated nature of the setup was a highly effective motivation for the students to take the task seriously and strive to showcase their ability to the highest standards. The fact that there are viewers who rely on their subtitles and the fact that the Symposium was an authentic academic forum meant that they had to shoulder responsibility for delivering high-quality live subtitles. Second, the respeakers were supplied with reference materials, and translation thereof, by the translators and glossaries by terminologists. They were also given sufficient time to conduct subject-related research. This means that they took part in the Symposium with great familiarity with the subject matter and terminology.

Preparation is paramount to high-quality interpreting and respeaking services. These factors have positively contributed to the impressive performance of the respeakers, even though this was the first time they put their knowledge into practice. This is a promising outcome that indicates the effectiveness of situated learning in skills training.

Analysis of Error Distribution in Different Phases

The two modes of live subtitling did not exhibit a similar distribution of errors in different phases when we split the speeches into three sections. While it is impossible to reach a convincing conclusion by comparing merely two sets of results, one can still venture an educated guess as to why this was the case. The initial upward trajectory indicated by the English-English respeaking output can probably be attributed to fatigue and accumulation of delay. This is also exemplified by a few missing sentences towards the middle of the transcript. Once the respeaker caught up with the speaker, the number of errors began to drop.

In comparison, the English interpreting was off to a rocky start and its quality suffered as a consequence. In addition, the respeaker also needed some time to adjust to the style of speaking and the condensed messages supplied by the interpreter at the beginning. It was probably for this reason that errors were most frequent in the first third of the delivery. After some time of adjustment, the distribution of errors showed a steady decrease towards the end.

Analysis of Results Across Different Modes of Live Subtitling

When comparing the errors in intralingual respeaking of the two speeches, the English-English rendition demonstrated a higher accuracy than the Chinese-English output, as indicated by Figures 11.1 and 11.2. If we factor in the omissions made by the interpreter, the contrast is even greater. The challenges of relay led to decreased quality and change of strategy compared to direct rendition. This phenomenon is reported in studies on interpreting, such as Song and Cheung (2019) and Aguirre Fernández Bravo (2022). The finding of this report may also serve to extend the same conclusion to live subtitling, whereby direct respeaking is usually met with fewer stumbling blocks than respeaking from interpreting output.

For the English speech, the respeaker had more freedom to adopt a literal approach, as they understood the source language. However, the respeaker for the Chinese speech did not have any knowledge of Chinese to capitalise on this advantage. There were omissions in the English interpreting, and the respeaker had to work with whatever was provided to them. The English interpreter had to also produce interpreting under a considerable amount of stress while paraphrasing and multitasking. Therefore, the two respeakers did not perform their tasks on equal footing. This can account for much of the discrepancies in quality between the two outputs. Despite this, good preparation and extensive subject matter research meant that both respeakers could still provide high-quality respeaking.

Conclusion

Mock conferences have already proven to be an effective mode of learning in interpreter training, thanks to their contextualised setting, authentic content, audience expectations and sense of community learning. Skills cannot be taught independently of the situation in which they are applied, making situated learning an essential means to enhance skills training. Just as interpreting, respeaking is a practical skill that requires constant practice and sufficient context, and the desired learning outcome can hardly be achieved by solitary learning. Trainee respeakers should be placed in a situated learning environment as should their interpreting counterparts and learn to address different challenges in real time. Therefore, mock conferences can potentially be the key to effective respeaking training.

By testing their knowledge in an authentic environment with real speakers and a designated theme, respeakers were able to accelerate their learning curve by making a thorough preparation for the event and taking advantage of the resources put together by their colleagues in the same cohort. They have demonstrated professionalism, expertise and most importantly, high-quality rendition of live subtitles. Although the quality of live subtitles differed between intralingual and interlingual live subtitling, the differences can be accounted for when the backdrop of the exercise that had led to the discrepancies was analysed.

Respeaking can be easily added to an interpreting mock conference. Alternatively, mock conferences can be set up solely for respeaking and the production of live subtitling where applicable. This chapter has shown that mock conferences are an effective approach to training respeakers. Where appropriate, direct, intralingual subtitling should be the preferred mode of delivery for trainee respeakers. However, respeaking can also be performed to a reasonably high level by relaying from an interpreting output, through which interlingual live subtitling can be supplied for the conference.

The limitations of this study were threefold. First, the sample size was small, which contained respeaking for only two speeches, one in English and one in Chinese. While the effect of situated learning and group effort could still be illustrated to some degree, one may argue that two examples are not sufficient to provide a comprehensive perspective. Second, due to limitations in the author's understanding of other languages spoken at the two Symposiums, the full set of data have not yet been harnessed. More data in French, Spanish, Italian and Portuguese were available, which will be analysed in the near future with the help of other colleagues with relevant linguistic backgrounds and expertise. In addition to the respeaker, an editor should be in place to provide real-time editing of the respoken text. Nevertheless, the study has still proven that mock conferences are an excellent way to train respeakers and should be incorporated into the curriculum wherever possible.

References

Aguirre Fernández Bravo, E. 2022. Indirect interpreting: Stumbling block or stepping stone? *Target. International Journal of Translation Studies* 34(3), pp. 512–536.

Ardito, G. 1999. The systematic use of impromptu speech in training interpreting students. *The Interpreters' Newsletter* 9, Trieste, EUT Edizioni Università di Trieste, pp. 177–189.

Ballester, A. & Jimenez Hurtado, C. 1992. Approaches to the teaching of interpreting. In: Dollerup, C., & Loddegaard, A. (Eds.). (1992). *Teaching Translation and Interpreting.* John Benjamins Publishing Company. https://doi.org/10.1075/z.56, pp. 237

Boostlingo n.d. BoostEvents – Real-Time Event Interpreting from Boostlingo. [Accessed 15 October 2023]. Available from: https://boostlingo.com/boostevents/

Conde, J. M. & Chouc, F. 2019. Multilingual mock conferences: A valuable tool in the training of conference interpreters. *The Interpreters' Newsletter* 24, pp. 1–17.

Luyckx, B., Delbeke, T., van Waes, L., Leijten, M. & Remael, A. (2013). Live subtitling with speech recognition causes and consequences of text reduction. *Across Languages and Cultures* 14, pp. 15–46. Available from: https://api.semanticscholar.org/CorpusID:61086480

Díaz-Cintas, J. (2020). The Name and Nature of Subtitling. In: Bogucki, Ł., Deckert, M. (eds) *The Palgrave Handbook of Audiovisual Translation and Media Accessibility*. Palgrave Studies in Translating and Interpreting. Palgrave Macmillan, Cham. https://doi.org/10.1007/978-3-030-42105-2_8.

Eugeni, C. & Bernabé, R. 2021. "Written interpretation: When simultaneous interpreting meets real-time subtitling. In Seeber, K. (ed.) *100 Years of Conference Interpreting – A Legacy*. Newcastle upon Tyne: Cambridge Scholars Publishing, pp. 93–109.

Fomina, M. 2018. The mock conference as a teaching tool to promote communication and interpreting skills. *iceri2018 Proceedings*, pp. 4312–4318.

González-Davies, M. & Enríquez-Raído, V. 2016. Situated learning in translator and interpreter training: Bridging research and good practice. *The Interpreter and Translator Trainer* 10(1), pp. 1–11.

International Telecommunications Union. 2018. F.791: Accessibility terms and definitions. [Accessed 15 October 2023]. Available from: https://www.itu.int/rec/T-REC-F.791-201808-I

Li, X. 2015. Mock conference as a situated learning activity in interpreter training: A case study of its design and effect as perceived by trainee interpreters. *The Interpreter and Translator Trainer* 9(3), pp. 323–341.

Moser-Mercer, B. (2015). Pedagogy, in *Routledge Encyclopedia of Interpreting Studies* (F. Pochhacker, Ed.). Routledge, pp. 303–307. https://doi.org/10.4324/9781315678467

Przepiórkowska, D. 2021. Adapt or Perish: How forced transition to remote simultaneous interpreting during the COVID-19 pandemic affected interpreters' professional practices. *Między Oryginałem a Przekładem* 27(4/54), pp. 137–159. https://doi.org/10.12797/MOaP.27.2021.54.08

Ribas, M., & Fresco, P. R. (2008). *A practical proposal for the training of respeakers*. https://api.semanticscholar.org/CorpusID:62651614

Romero-Fresco, P. 2009. More haste less speed: Edited versus verbatim respoken subtitles. *Vigo International Journal of Applied Linguistics* 6, pp. 109–133.

Romero-Fresco, P. 2012. Respeaking in translator training curricula. *The Interpreter and Translator Trainer* 6(1), pp. 91–112.

Romero-Fresco, P. 2020. *Subtitling Through Speech Recognition* (1st ed.). Taylor and Francis. Available from: https://www.perlego.com/book/1899876/subtitling-through-speech-recognition-respeaking-pdf

Romero-Fresco, P. & Eugeni, C. 2020. Live subtitling through respeaking. In: Bogucki, Ł., Deckert, M. (eds.) *The Palgrave Handbook of Audiovisual Translation and Media Accessibility*. Palgrave Studies in Translating and Interpreting. Cham: Palgrave Macmillan. https://doi.org/10.1007/978-3-030-42105-2_14

Romero-Fresco, P. & Pérez, J.M. 2015. Accuracy rate in live subtitling: The NER model. In: Piñero, R. B. & Cintas, J. D. (eds.) *Audiovisual Translation in a Global Context*. Palgrave Studies in Translating and Interpreting. London: Palgrave Macmillan. https://doi.org/10.1057/9781137552891_3

Romero-Fresco, P. & Pöchhacker, F. 2018. Quality assessment in interlingual live subtitling: The NTR Model. *Linguistica Antverpiensia, New Series – Themes in Translation Studies* 16. https://doi.org/10.52034/lanstts.v16i0.438

Sandrelli, A. 2020. Interlingual respeaking and simultaneous interpreting in a conference setting: A comparison. inTRAlinea Special Issue: Technology in Interpreter

Education and Practice. Stable. Available from: https://www.intralinea.org/specials/article/2518

Song, S. and Cheung, A.K.F. 2019. Disfluency in relay and non-relay simultaneous interpreting. *FORUM. Revue internationale d'interprétation et de traduction / International Journal of Interpretation and Translation* 17(1), pp. 1–19.

Stein, D.S. 1998. Situated learning in adult education. ERIC Digest No. 195. Available from: https://api.semanticscholar.org/CorpusID:141318533

University of Leeds 2023. Module and programme catalogue. *leeds.ac.uk*. [Online]. [Accessed 1 April 2024]. Available from: https://webprod3.leeds.ac.uk/catalogue/dynmodules.asp?Y=202324&M=MODL-5250M

Wadensjö, C. 2014. Perspectives on role play: Analysis, training and assessments. *The Interpreter and Translator Trainer* 8(3), pp. 437–451.

12
PROFESSIONAL TRAINING IN VALENCIAN LIVE SUBTITLING

Navigating Diglossia and Language Variation

Luz Belenguer Cortés

Introduction

Subtitling for the deaf and hard of hearing (SDH) is a mode within Audiovisual Translation (AVT) that seeks to guarantee accessibility for users with any type of hearing impairment. In terms of audience, the target for SDH could be extended beyond deaf and hard-of-hearing users, thus including language learners and users with no access to the sound of the audiovisual product. This has led to the term "inclusive subtitling" (Martínez-Lorenzo, 2021) being introduced to include any user who might use SDH, irrespective of their purpose, needs, or condition (Romero-Fresco, 2018). Live subtitling, which involves generating instant captions for live broadcasts or events, is still a developing area – despite being practised and investigated for more than two decades now (Eugeni, 2006) – and requires language and technology expertise. Nevertheless, live subtitling in terms of diglossia, code-switching, and code-mixing can be subject to geographical, historical, political, sociological, and linguistic variations (Belenguer Cortés, 2023) that lead to difficulties in professional training. Hence, the present chapter reviews the teaching methods, difficulties, and progress in live subtitling training by combining information from different studies and reports to present a thorough summary of the current status of live subtitling education. The chapter then shifts its focus to the case of the Valencian TV station À Punt, and the techniques and strategies used by professionals to subtitle their programmes live. Conclusions address how educators and researchers can further explore and enhance the effectiveness of live subtitling training by introducing students to language variation.

DOI: 10.4324/9781003440994-15

Live Subtitling Training

Effective live subtitling courses combine theoretical understanding with practical application for a comprehensive learning experience. Although translator training has shifted from a teacher-centred tradition to a student-centred approach to knowledge construction (Kelly, 2005), research highlights the importance of providing students with a foundation in linguistic theory, such as syntax, semantics, and pragmatics, prior to engaging in practical subtitling tasks (Romero-Fresco, 2012). In addition, training in the most up-to-date subtitling software and hardware is also frequent (Eugeni et al., 2021).

Before considering the competencies expected of live subtitlers, we will first explore the techniques involved in live subtitling. According to Lambourne (2006), three main methods have been used for generating real-time captions: standard QWERTY keyboards used by one or more typists together, stenograph keyboards that allow for typing syllables or sounds instead of characters, and automatic speech recognition (ASR) used by professionals called respeakers who dictate the subtitles to the machine. Workflows can also include live editors who correct mistakes in real time. ASR can also be used, as of today, without human intervention as in the case of the subtitles automatically generated by videotelephony or video-sharing platforms. Consequently, respeaking distinguishes itself from other subtitle production techniques through its unique process. Because operators do not transcribe the source text directly but create an intermediate version of the text – which is then converted into the final target text by speech recognition technology (Romero-Fresco, 2012) – Fresno and Romero-Fresco (2022) agree that professional respeakers are expected to master linguistic skills to guarantee not just the understanding of the message, but also a proper delivery. Hence, respeakers usually find themselves editing the original message so that the meaning is not lost while also verbalising punctuation commands and editing possible mistakes produced by the software.

In terms of educational strategies, simulation-based training involves creating fictitious live situations that give students a realistic practice setting. Through professional training, students can use these simulations to practice managing the stress and uncertainty of real-time subtitling (Eugeni, 2006), which goes hand-in-hand with the task-based approach (Hurtado-Albir, 1999; González-Davies, 2004). Concerning professional training, it is also worth noting that there is a clear connection between the skills required for simultaneous interpreters and respeakers (Baaring, 2006, Marsh, 2006; Orero, 2006; Remael and van der Veer, 2006; Russello, 2009; Chmiel et al., 2018, Sandrelli, 2020), as both practices share the nature of the production: listening and speaking at the same time (Belenguer Cortés, 2024).

In the case of those areas in the world where regional and minority languages are spoken and officially recognised, unique challenges impact the accuracy and reliability of live subtitles produced through respeaking, due to diglossia and the related ASR systems. Clear pronunciation, well-articulated speech, and a deep familiarity with vocabulary and subject matter are essential for successful recognition by any ASR software. Nevertheless, variations in regional languages may pose distinct challenges compared to more standardised languages. These differences require nuanced adaptations in respeaking techniques and technologies, which will be further explored in subsequent sections from the perspective of the Valencian language.

The Valencian Language

To explore the challenges of live subtitling training in diglossic areas, the case of Valencian looks particularly interesting. Before discussing the specifics of live subtitling training involving Valencian, it is important to understand its background context. In 1985, Casanova (pp. 25–33) explores the linguistic landscape of the Valencian region and identifies distinct language varieties within this area, notably Spanish (Castilian), Valencian, *Xurro*, and Murcian. While Valencian and Catalan are often used to mean the same language, Casanova distinguishes between Eastern Catalan (Valencian) and Western Catalan (Catalan), by identifying several phonetic and orthographic characteristics of Valencian (1985, p. 25). In terms of written Eastern Catalan, inchoatives end in -isc [isk], while in Western Catalan, they end in -esc [esk], as seen in examples like 'servisc' [sərˈvisk] or 'servesc' [sərˈvesk]. Subjunctive endings differ, with -a, -e [e], -o [ɒ] in the Eastern variant and -i [ɪ] in the Western variant, as illustrated by 'vinga' [ˈβiŋɡə] or 'vingui' [ˈβiŋɡi]. The first person present simple singular ending varies, with -e [e] or -o [ɒ] in the Eastern variant and ø, i [ɪ], or u [ʊ] in the Western variant. In terms of pronunciation, there is no neutralisation of palatal and velar atonic vowels in the Eastern variant, unlike in the Western one. Additionally, there is a phonetic conservation of the vowel i [ɪ] in the iš [ɪʃ] group in Eastern Catalan, unlike in the Western variant.

Together with the Valencian language, there are issues of language identity and politics. There is a long-standing debate over whether Valencian is a distinct language or a dialect of Catalan, which often has political and cultural implications, affecting language policy and educational practices (Hoffmann, 1995). Political parties and regional governments may have differing views on the status and promotion of Valencian, leading to inconsistent support and varying degrees of language protection. Ensuring consistent and high-quality Valencian language education across the region is challenging, especially given the variations in political support and resources (Archilés and Martí, 2001).

Despite the existence of well-trained teachers proficient in Valencian, capable of delivering education in the language across various subjects (Bolitho and Rossner, 2020), developing and distributing educational materials in Valencian that meet standardised linguistic and pedagogical criteria can be difficult given its limited presence in mainstream media compared to Spanish. This affects the language's visibility and everyday use. Ensuring that local media, including television, radio, and online platforms, provide adequate content in Valencian is therefore crucial (Vázquez-Calvo, 2021), as well as promoting the use of Valencian on digital platforms, social media, and new technologies despite the dominance of Spanish and English. In addition, in many areas, Spanish is preferred for practical reasons, leading to a decline in the day-to-day use of Valencian (Lado, 2011). To increase the prestige and perceived utility of Valencian, official institutions – with adequate funding and political backing – should be dedicated to promoting and preserving the Valencian language (Morelló, 2002). In the media, the main TV station that broadcasts programmes in Valencian is À Punt (Belenguer Cortés, 2022), which follows the conventions of the style guide from Corporació Valenciana de Mitjans de Comunicació (CVMC, 2017). Nevertheless, there are no criteria concerning how to deal with the widespread diglossia, code-switching, code-mixing and other phenomena related to language variation present in the region when live subtitling. Hence, getting close to professionals should be considered to understand the collaborative methodologies and technologies followed by live subtitlers who work in À Punt.

López Rubio and Sansaloni (2021) carried out a comprehensive analysis of À Punt's processes, tools, and professional methods used to create accessible content. In terms of live subtitling, respeaking and keyboard typing are used to produce live subtitles (Belenguer Cortés, 2022). The choice of technique depends on the number of professionals available. If two professionals are available, respeaking is used (one professional respeaking and the other one editing live), whereas if only one professional is available, keyboard typing is used (Belenguer Cortés, 2022).

Regardless of the technique, subtitlers must be familiar with linguistic variations in terms of grammar, but also in terms of vocabulary. For instance, there are different ways of saying 'pimentó' (in English, 'pepper') in the Valencian region: 'pebrera', 'pibrera', 'pebrera', 'bajoca', or 'pebre', among others'(Beltrán Calvo and Segura-Llopes, 2022, p. 386).

In this particular case, in respeaking, the ASR software might not understand every linguistic variant of this term, unless it is added to the software vocabulary. Given that the vocabulary cannot be fed with too many words for accuracy and speed reasons, professionals may be asked to spot the mistake and amend the misspelt word before broadcasting the subtitle featuring the appropriate variant. So, improving the technology behind ASR should be considered to obtain optimal results in terms of diglossia and linguistic varieties, but specific strategies should also be considered through specialised training, assistance from technology, and collaborative methodologies.

Language Variation

In many of the programmes broadcast on À Punt, language variation is present in pre-recorded audiovisual products, but also in live programmes. In pre-recorded programmes, the linguistic variety serves the purpose of characterising the characters and positioning them within the social hierarchy. In other words, textual-linguistic elements, analysed as a code based on prior knowledge, are associated with a subcode of extratextual elements to reveal the function of enhancing characterisation (Ramos Pinto, 2017).

In live programmes, language variation in spontaneous speech is influenced by a multitude of interrelated factors: social determinants such as age, gender, socioeconomic status, education, and social networks significantly impact linguistic adaptation to various contexts and audiences (Maekawa, 2009).

As Ramos Pinto (2009, p. 392) points out, such variation leads to linguistic, pragmatic, and semiotic difficulties since they add meaning beyond the linguistic level. Therefore, diglossia in Valencia, where both Spanish and Valencian coexist and are spoken by the same speech community, poses unique challenges for live subtitling. Typically, live subtitlers must navigate the dynamic interplay between these varieties in real time. Next, the specific problems live subtitlers at À Punt face when dealing with both Valencian and Spanish, will be explored and the strategies employed to overcome these issues illustrated.

Understanding Diglossia: The Current Challenges

Diglossia often involves code-switching – intended here as the switching from one variety to the other within the same speech – or code-mixing – intended here as the use of a word or group of words belonging to a variety in a speech in the other variety. This implies a multiplication of vocabulary, grammar, pronunciation, and spelling. This also means that live subtitlers must face constant linguistic changes that could be (or could not be) reflected in the subtitles, independently of the technique used to create them.

In À Punt, professionals must deal with switching between Spanish and Valencian within the same speech or sentence. This implies subtitlers must recognise and adapt subtitles to these switches so accuracy and coherence are maintained (Alshamrani, 2012). Furthermore, professionals are required to also be familiar with all regional sub-varieties, which could lead to potential misunderstandings and inaccuracies, due to the semantic and syntactic discrepancies involved. For example, words with the same meaning in both varieties might have different connotations or usage contexts (Hudson, 2002). This also applies to cultural and contextual nuances, context sensitivity, formality, and register, as misinterpreting nuances could lead to subtitles that are culturally insensitive or incorrect (Kaye, 2001).

FIGURE 12.1   Diglossic conversation between two speakers, © Larrauri (2023).

At the Valencian TV station À Punt, code-switching between Spanish and Valencian requires the live subtitling team to activate a specific function of the subtitling machine used that enables seamless transitions between the two languages during live broadcasts or events. This ensures that respeakers can switch between ASR in Spanish and ASR in Valencian fluidly, thus accommodating the linguistic preferences of the speakers and audience comprehension needs effectively. Nevertheless, the ASR system is thought to perform in one language at a time, not in a diglossic context. Hence, changing from one language to another can be ineffective since the ASR systems might not switch from one language to another immediately, as it needs a few seconds to start working in a new language. This can be problematic when speakers speak two different languages to communicate with each other, as seen in Figure 12.1.

In Figure 12.1, in the television programme *La Vida al Màxim.* the guest (subtitled in white) says in Spanish "Mucha curiosidad por el programa" (in English, "I am very curious about the show"), whilst Màxim (subtitled in yellow) says, in Valencian, "Benvingut a la festa" (in English, "Welcome to the party"). This scenario illustrates a common occurrence in spontaneous discourse where speakers, despite using different languages, understand each other. However, it underscores the professional imperative for concentration and mastery of respeaking skills to navigate dialogue fluidly without confusion, while adhering to linguistic choices – whether Valencian or Spanish – consistent with À Punt's practice of subtitling according to the speaker's language.

Occasionally, speakers mix Spanish and Valencian within the same sentence, normally adding a Valencian word into a Spanish sentence or vice versa.

FIGURE 12.2 Example of code-mixing in Valencian, © Martínez and Llorens (2017).

However, both the respeaker and the ASR software may struggle to accurately identify these cases of code-mixing. As a result, live editors play a crucial role in real-time subtitling, manually correcting and adjusting the subtitles to ensure accuracy and clarity for the audience. This can be found in Figure 12.2, featuring the term "uelo", a commonly used but non-standard word for grandfather in Valencian (Belenguer Cortés, 2023).

In this context, we can see a speaker user saying in Valencian "Jo penso que 'ma uelo' Ramón" (in English "I think 'my grandpa' Ramón"). The term 'ma uelo' has quotation marks because the correct word should be "iaio", or "avi", and not "uelo" (which comes from "abuelo" the Spanish term from which "uelo" originates). According to the Valencian television guidelines (CVMC, 2017, 2021), professionals are advised to minimise the use of unnecessary foreign words. However, the guidelines recognise that spontaneity and expressiveness may sometimes obscure distinctions between formal and informal contexts. As a result, these foreign words can evolve into what are considered acceptable forms, despite still being recommended for avoidance. For example, from "uelo" to "abuelo", "iaio" or "avi" in Valencian (Belenguer Cortés, 2023). Despite this, guidelines recognise that live subtitlers – be they respeakers or keyboard typists – may find it problematic to go for this option, given the lack of flexibility the workflow implies.

A further issue related to code-mixing pertains to the ASR system used at À Punt, which was originally trained to recognise Catalan words, not Valencian ones. This limitation becomes particularly evident in situations where the spelling and pronunciation of words differ between standard Catalan and Valencian. An example of this can also be found in Figure 12.2, where the speaker says [pense], spelt "pense" in Valencian) and not [pensʊ], spelt "penso" in Catalan), as the subtitle in the Figure reads. Consequently, respeakers need to navigate these differences skilfully to ensure that the spoken content is accurately transcribed into subtitles, maintaining linguistic fidelity and comprehensibility across regional variations. This shows the urgent need to reflect on specialised training supported by technology and collaborative approaches.

Strategies for Overcoming Linguistic Varieties

In order to surmount the numerous challenges inherent in live subtitling, practitioners must demonstrate proficiency across various domains. Eugeni (2008) and Arumí Ribas and Romero Fresco (2008, pp. 119–121) enumerate the skills required for professional live subtitlers. In a nutshell, professionals are expected to know how to train the software for optimum performance, learn to analyse the source text by detecting the sense units and reducing them for segmentation, and identify key elements of the source text to apply reformulation and editing strategies. They must also learn to speak while listening, overcome the stress caused by a live situation, express thoughts lively and concisely, dictate in short stretches of text at a higher-than-average speed, and dictate with a flat and clear pronunciation.

In terms of training in strategies to overcome challenges and difficulties related to linguistic variation, a proposal could focus on the following aspects. First of all, training and familiarisation have to be combined with dialect exposure and cultural education. Future professionals should receive training that includes extensive exposure to all varieties and subvarieties spoken in a community. Immersive practice sessions with a variety of dialects can enhance their adaptability and accuracy. In addition, in-depth cultural education helps subtitlers understand the context in which different varieties are used, improving their ability to capture the speaker's message accurately.

Second, professionals should also undergo continuous training and practice with continuously updated ASR systems. The latter should also be able to recognise and process regional dialects, with AI-driven tools that could also be explored, so as to provide contextual suggestions based on the speaker's language variety and context. This would allow respeakers to make quick, accurate decisions (Wassink et al., 2022; Iranzo-Sánchez et al. 2022).

Finally, team collaboration is key to success. Collaboration with native speakers of different dialects can improve the accuracy of ASR systems and colleagues can provide real-time feedback and corrections to each other (Romaine, 2000). Furthermore, implementing a peer review and continuous feedback system helps subtitlers refine their skills and adapt to the nuances of diglossia more effectively.

In the context where À Punt works, respeakers collaborate in pairs, offering one another encouragement and aid as necessary. While exceeding the limited pace of traditional typing – this reduces the gap between video and subtitle presentation, which increases viewer engagement – there are some issues to consider. Because speaker-independent software is used at À Punt, only standard words in either Spanish or Valencian are captured through respeaking at a time. This means that there is a need to think of strategies when dealing with both code-switching and, in particular, code-mixing. Because the software is equipped with a function that allows switching between Spanish and Valencian ASR, the respeaker can use this function to react to cases of code-switching, though with the issues related to delay mentioned above. When it comes to code-mixing, though, the whole workflow becomes less easy, because the respeaking team must:

- Realise that a Valencian word is used in Spanish instead of a Spanish word, or vice versa;
- Decide whether it is a case of code-switching or code-mixing;
- Decide whether to switch to the ASR system in the other language or not;
- Decide whether to dictate the word in a variety or the other;
- Correct the misrecognised word to adapt to the spelling of the target variety.

What is more, the same issue occurs with a word in Valencian that is spelt differently from a word in standard Valencian. Because the software is speaker-independent – which means that words cannot be added to the vocabulary – only shortcuts to the typing method can be introduced. However, the number of variants is enormous and this would entail an excessively high number of shortcuts, which would be hard to remember.

When the respeaking team realises that code-mixing is recurrent in the same speech, they may decide to turn to keyboard typing. This makes it possible to preserve Valencian's unique characteristics and ensure accessibility for deaf or hard-of-hearing users. This approach ensures accuracy, resulting in well-structured and understandable subtitles that convey the original idea. Undoubtedly, typing what is being said introduces a further delay in delivering the message, leading to reduced immediacy. Moreover, they may make orthographic errors, paradoxically, as the typist may make mistakes or the software could be confused about which spelling conventions the text of the subtitles should follow and then turn correctly spelt words into misspelt words.

To face the above-mentioned challenges, specific skills and strategies are required by professional live subtitlers. As said, an ad hoc training approach should, in particular, incorporate advanced technology, cultural and dialectal exposure, and robust team collaboration. This professional training should also include developing protocols for real-time error detection and correction, so as to minimise the impact of mistakes on the viewer's experience, while training in error management helps subtitlers remain efficient under pressure (Romero-Fresco and Martínez, 2015). Establishing a structured feedback system, where subtitlers receive constructive criticism and suggestions for improvement, while encouraging self-assessment and peer reviews could also benefit training. Waiting for customisable ASR systems to be trained to recognise specific varieties and regional variants, thus improving overall accuracy, regular updates in terms of shortcuts could ensure the machine remains responsive to linguistic changes and new inputs.

In practice, considerations should include exploring hybrid approaches that combine respeaking and keyboarding more smoothly, to leverage the strengths of both methods: respeaking could be used for its speed and immediacy, while transcription to provide accuracy and clarity. Providing specialised training programs tailored to different broadcasting contexts, such as news, sports, and entertainment, where the demands on subtitlers can vary significantly, is also essential, by incorporating scenario-based training, which prepares subtitlers for unexpected challenges, such as rapid topic shifts and technical difficulties.

Conclusions

Live subtitling in diglossic contexts presents unique challenges due to the linguistic, semantic, and cultural differences between the two language varieties. Hence, overcoming these challenges requires specialised training, technological support, and collaborative approaches. As subtitling technologies and pedagogical methods continue to evolve, the ability to effectively navigate diglossia in live subtitling will improve, enhancing accessibility and understanding for diverse audiences. Therefore, even if language variations are context-dependent, future live subtitlers must acquire the required abilities and learn how to adapt to diglossia, code-switching and code-mixing in particular, to excel at delivering the original message without omitting linguistic diversity. These recommendations could also be applied to any diglossic region, even though they have come out of the specific context of Valencian, where such a nuanced approach is all the more required. By integrating advanced ASR systems, fostering continuous professional development, and adopting flexible practices, live subtitling quality can then be enhanced, catering for both accuracy and speed. This ensures accessibility and inclusivity for all viewers, particularly those who are deaf or hard of hearing, while preserving the unique linguistic characteristics of regional varieties. Only further research and empirical data can provide a path to deepen future studies related to diglossia in live subtitling.

References

Alshamrani, H. 2012. Diglossia in Arabic TV stations. *Journal of King Saud University-Languages and Translation* 24(1), pp. 57–69. https://doi.org/10.1016/j.jksult.2011.04.002

Archilés, F. and Martí, M. 2001. Ethnicity, region and nation: Valencian identity and the Spanish nation-state. *Ethnic and Racial Studies* 24(5), pp. 779–797. https://doi.org/10.1080/01419870120063972

Arumí Ribas, M. and Romero Fresco, P. 2008. A practical proposal for the training of respeakers. *Journal of Specialised Translation* 10, pp. 381–392. https://jostrans.soap2.ch/issue10/art_arumi.php

Baaring, I. 2006. Respeaking-based online subtitling in Denmark. In: Eugeni, C. and Mack, G. *Intralinea, Special Issue on Respeaking*. Available from: https://www.intralinea.org/specials/article/1683

Belenguer Cortés, L. 2022. La subtitulación en vivo y la audiodescripción en lenguas minoritarias: El caso de la televisión autonómica valenciana À Punt Mèdia. In: Castillo Bernal, C. and Estévez Grossi, M. Translation, *Mediation and Accessibility for Linguistic Minorities*. Berlin: Frank & Timme, pp. 85–100.

Belenguer Cortés, L. 2023. Challenges of code-switching and code-mixing in live subtitling at the Valencian tv station. *TIRO. The Journal of Professional Reporting and Transcription* 23(7). Available from: https://tiro.intersteno.org/2023/07/challenges-of-code-switching-and-code-mixing-in-live-subtitling-at-the-valencian-tv-station/

Belenguer Cortés, L. 2024. The role of accessibility in language teaching: Respeaking in the foreign language classroom. *Paralèlles* 36(1), pp. 147–163. https://dx.doi.org/10.17462/para.2024.01.09

Beltrán Calvo, V. and Segura-Llopes, C. 2022. *Els parlars valencians*. Valencia: Publicacions de la Universitat de València.

Bolitho, R. and Rossner, R. 2020. *Language Education in a Changing World: Challenges and Opportunities*. Bristol: Multilingual Matters.

Casanova, E. 1985. El valenciano dentro del diasistema lingüístico catalán. *Revista de Filología Románica III*, Madrid, pp. 25–34.

Chmiel, A., Lijewska, A., Szarkowska, A. and Dutka, Ł. 2018. Paraphrasing in respeaking–comparing linguistic competence of interpreters, translators and bilinguals. *Perspectives* 26(5), 725–744. https://doi.org/10.1080/0907676X.2017.1394331

Corporació Valenciana de Mitjans de Comunicació, CVMC. 2017. *Llibre d'Estil de la Corporació Valenciana de Mitjans de Comunicació*. Available from: https://static.apuntmedia.es/apunt/public/content/file/original/2021/0227/19/llibre-d-estil-86bdcdb.pdf

Eugeni, C. 2006. "Introduzione al rispeakeraggio televisivo". In: Eugeni, C. and Mack, G. *Intralinea, Special Issue on Respeaking*. Available from: https://www.intralinea.org/specials/article/1683

Eugeni, C. 2008. *Le sous-titrage en direct: Aspects théoriques, professionnels et didactiques*. Macerata: CEUM.

Eugeni, C., Gerbecks, W. and Bernabé, R. 2021. Real-time intralingual subtitling through respeaking and Velotype: Cutting-edge theoretical and professional best practices. In: Jekat, S. J., Puhl, S., Carrer, L. and Lintner, A., *Proceedings of* the 3rd Swiss Conference on Barrier-free Communication (BfC 2020). Winterthur, June 29–July 4, 2020. Winterthur: ZHAW Zurich University of Applied Sciences.

Fresno, N. and Romero-Fresco, P. 2022. Strengthening respeakers' training in Spain: The research-practice connection. *The Interpreter and Translator Trainer* 16(1), pp. 96–114. https://doi.org/10.1080/175039 9X.2021.1884442

González-Davies, M. 2004. Undergraduate and postgraduate translation degrees: Aims and expectations. In Malmkjaer, K. *Translation as an Undergraduate Degree*. Amsterdam: John Benjamins, pp. 67–81.

Hoffmann, C. 1995. Monolingualism, bilingualism, cultural pluralism and national identity: Twenty years of language planning in contemporary Spain. *Current Issues in Language & Society* 2(1), pp. 59–90.

Hudson, A. 2002. Outline of a theory of diglossia. *International Journal of the Sociology of Language 157*, pp. 1–48. https://doi.org/10.1515/ijsl.2002.039

Hurtado-Albir, A. 1999. *Enseñar a traducir. Metodología en la formación de traductores e intérpretes*. Madrid: Edelsa.

Iranzo-Sánchez, J., Jorge-Cano, J., Pérez-González De Martos, A., Giménez, A., Garcés Díaz-Munío, G., Baquero-Arnal, P., Silvestre Cerdà, J. A., Civera, J. and Juan A. 2022. MLLP-VRAIN UPV systems for the IWSLT 2022 Simultaneous Speech Translation and Speech-to-Speech Translation tasks. *Association for Computational Linguistics (ACL)*, pp. 255–264. https://doi.org/10.18653/v1/2022.iwslt-1.22

Kaye, S. A. 2001. Diglossia: The state of the art. *International Journal of the Sociology of Language 152*, pp. 117–129. https://doi.org/10.1515/ijsl.2001.051

Kelly, D. 2005. *A Handbook for Translator Trainers*. Manchester: St. Jerome.

Lado, B. 2011. Linguistic landscape as a reflection of the linguistic and ideological conflict in the Valencian community. *International Journal of Multilingualism* 8(2), pp. 135–150. https://dx.doi.org/10.1080/14790718.2010.550296

Lambourne, A. 2006. Subtitle respeaking. In: Eugeni, C. and Mack, G. *Intralinea, Special Issue on Respeaking*. Available from: https://www.intralinea.org/specials/article/Subtitle_respeaking

Larrauri, J. L. 2023. *La vida al Màxim*. À Punt Mèdia. València Imagina Televisió (VITV).

López Rubio, M. and Martín Sansaloni, V. 2021. Media accessibility services at the Valencian regional TV station À Punt. A professional overview. In: Mejías Climent L. i and Carrero Martín J. F. *New Perspectives in Audiovisual Translation. Towards Future Research Trends*. Valencia: Universitat de València, pp. 167–184.

Maekawa, K. 2009. Analysis of language variation using a large-scale corpus of spontaneous speech. In S.-C. Tseng (Ed.) *Linguistic Patterns in Spontaneous Speech*. Taipei.: Academia Sinica, pp. 27–50.

Marsh, A. 2006. "Respeaking for the BBC". In: Eugeni, C. and Mack, G. *Intralinea, Special Issue on Respeaking*. Available from: https://www.intralinea.org/specials/article/1700

Martínez, P. and Llorens, M. 2017. *Ciutats desaparegudes*. À Punt Mèdia. The Fly Hunter, contenidos audiovisuales.

Martínez-Lorenzo, M. 2021. *Media Accessibility in Galicia(n): Guidelines for Inclusive Subtitling*. Universidade de Vigo: Investigo. Repositorio Institucional de la Universidade de Vigo (Doctoral dissertation). Available from: https://hdl.handle.net/11093/2548

Morelló, E. 2002. Actituds de la població migrant davant l'ús del valencià: una altra perspectiva al voltant de la situació social del valencià. *Treballs de sociolingüística catalana*, 6, pp. 241–254.

Orero, P. 2006. "Real-time subtitling in Spain: an overview". In: Eugeni, C. and Mack, G. *Intralinea, Special Issue on Respeaking*. Available from: https://www.intralinea.org/specials/article/1689

Ramos Pinto, S. 2009. How important is the way you say it?: A discussion on the translation of linguistic varieties. *Target. International Journal of Translation Studies* 21(2), pp. 289–307. https://dx.doi.org/10.1075/target.21.2.04pin

Ramos Pinto, S. 2017. Film, dialects and subtitles: An analytical framework for the study of non-standard varieties in subtitling. *The Translator* 24(1), pp. 17–34. https://doi.org/10.1080/13556509.2017.1338551

Remael, A. and van der Veer, B. 2006. Real-time subtitling in Flanders: Needs and Teaching. In: Eugeni, C. and Mack, G. *Intralinea, Special Issue on Respeaking*. Available from: https://www.intralinea.org/specials/article/1702

Romaine, S. 2000. *Language in Society: An Introduction to Sociolinguistics*. New York: Oxford University Press.

Romero-Fresco, P. 2012. Respeaking in translator training curricula: Present and future prospects. *The Interpreter and Translator Trainer* 6(1), pp. 91–112.

Romero-Fresco, P. 2018. In support of a wide notion of media accessibility: Access to content and access to creation. *Journal of Audiovisual Translation*, 1(1), pp. 187–204. https://www.jatjournal.org/index.php/jat/article/view/53/12

Romero-Fresco, P. and Martínez, J. 2015. Accuracy rate in live subtitling: The NER model. In: Díaz Cintas J. and Baños, R. *Audiovisual Translation in a Global Context: Mapping an Ever-changing Landscape*. Basingstoke/New York: Palgrave Macmillan, pp. 28–50.

Russello, C. 2009. Respeaking e Interpretazione simultanea: un'analisi comparata e un contributo sperimentale Roma: Libera Università degli Studi San Pio V di Roma (Doctoral thesis).

Sandrelli, A. 2020. Interlingual respeaking and simultaneous interpreting in a conference setting: A comparison. Technology in Interpreter Education and Practice, *inTRAlinea, Special issue*. Available from: https://www.intralinea.org/specials/article/2518

Vázquez-Calvo, B. 2021. Guerrilla fan translation, language learning, and metalinguistic discussion in a Catalan-speaking community of gamers. *ReCALL* 33(3), pp. 296–313. https://doi.org/10.1017/S095834402000021X

Wassink, A. B., Gansen, C. and Bartholomew, I. 2022. Uneven success: automatic speech recognition and ethnicity-related dialects. *Speech Communication*, 140, pp. 50–70. https://dx.doi.org/10.1016/j.specom.2022.03.009

INDEX

Note: **Bold** page numbers refer to tables; *italic* page numbers refer to figures and page numbers followed by "n" denote endnotes.

2030 Agenda 46

accessibility skills 112, 113
accredited training 76
acoustic model 139
action research (AR) methodological framework 140, 148
adaptation strategies 111
Aguirre Fernández Bravo, E. 165
Ahrens, B. 80
Allende, I. 147
alternating serial reaction time (ASRT) task 42, 43
Amato, A. 93, 95
Anderson, J. R. 65
anthropological drive 56
application programming interface (API) 141
À Punt 169, 172–174, 177
Ardito, G. 153
Article 3(1), United Nations Convention on the Rights of the Child 69
artificial intelligence (AI) 2, 3, 20, 137
Arumí Ribas, M. 176
Association of Programmes in Translation and Interpreting Studies (APTIS) 2022 Conference 3
associative stage 65
"attitudes toward language learning" *see* L2 learning experience

audio-mediated interpreting service 56
audio-visual translation (AVT) 105, 106, 144, 169
automatic speech recognition (ASR) software 103, 105, 108, 111, 112, 118, 124–126, 137–139, 141, 144, 145, 148, 149, 154, 170–172, 174–178
autonomous stage 65

Bancroft, M. A. 73, 77
Banderas, A. 147
BBC News 126
Biggs, J. 32
body language 71, 80, 88, 94
Bologna Process (1998) 11
BoostEvents 156
bootstrapping analysis 44, 45
Bradbury, H. 140
brain plasticity 63
Braun, S. 56, 71
Brill, K. 43, 47
British education system 87
British school system 90
Bruno, M. A. 5, 106, 107, 112, 117
Buján, M. 9, 61

Campus Rutli 96
Carpenter, H. S. 47
Casadei, S. 90, 92

Casanova, E. 171
Catalan 171, 175
Cattaneo, Z. 27
Centre for Translation and Interpreting Studies (CTIS), University of Leeds 12, 153
Chesterman, A. 106
Cheung, A. K. F. 165
Children Act (2002) 69
China Accreditation Test for Translators and Interpreters 42
Chinese-English interlingual live subtitling **158**; effective editing in 162–164, **163**; error distribution analysis in different phases 164; results analysis 165
Chinese-English respeaking 160, 165
Chinese speech 157, 158, 165
Chiofalo, T. A. 90, 91
Chouc, F. 4, 153
CI test speech materials 43
civil society organisations 9
code-mixing 169, 173, 175, *175*, 177, 178
code of conduct 87, 88, 98
code-switching 169, 173, 174, 177, 178
cognitive flexibility theory 39
cognitive load 76, 154, 156, 162
cognitive processes 9, 11
cognitive stage 65
Collard, C. 9, 61
CO-Minor-IN/QUEST project 76
communication: autonomy 73, 76, 77, 79; skills 154; technology 56, 70, 76–78
computer-aided interpreting 2
Conde, J. M. 153
conference interpreting 10–13, 15, 16, 19, 22, 153
confidentiality 78
consecutive interpreting (CI) 39, 40, 42, 66; errors 43, 44; skills 43–45; tests 43
continuous professional development (CPD) 19–20, 22
Corporacio Valenciana de Mitjans de Comunicacio (CVMC) 172
corrective feedback (CF) 40–43, 47
COVID-19 pandemic 2–4, 22, 34, 56, 70, 74, 81, 86, 94, 118
Criminal Evidence Act (1992) 69
cultural differences 71, 90, 111, 178

Damerau-Levenshtein distance 127
Dawson, H. 140, 141
d/Deaf audience 117

deep learning (DL) 139
Degree Programme in Public Service Interpreting 92
Delabastita, D. 106
delivery skills 141
Department of Modern Languages and Cultures 142
Diaconia University of Applied Sciences 92
dialogue interpreting 66
diamesic skills 112, 124, 125
diamesic translation (DT) 106–110, 112, 113, 117
Díaz Cintas, J. 138
diglossia 169, 171–176, *174*, 178
Directive 2010/64/EU 70
distance education 86
Dornyei, Z. 27–29
Dragon Naturally Speaking version 15 141, 144, 156
Duchin, F. 1
dummy-booth practice 11

economic drive 56
ECTS workshop 142
editing skills 124–126
effort model 141
Einstein, Albert 147
elaborative inferencing strategies 111
ELAN 107
Ellis, R. 40, 41, 71
employability 11, 22, 22n1, 97
English-English intralingual live subtitling **158**, 165
English-English intralingual respeaking 157, 160; correct editing in 161–162, **162**; error distribution analysis in different phases 164; results analysis 165
English proficiency 76
English-to-Mandarin CI tests 42
EN-IT course 142, 144, 145
Enríquez-Raído, V. 153
entrepreneurship education (EE) 11
enunciation skills 105, 112
Erasmus+ 140
Erdilmen, M. 92
ethical approval 60
ethnographic approach 40
Eugeni, C. 104, 106, 107, 111, 117, 122, 152, 176
European Certification and Qualification Association (ECQA)-Intersteno certification session 127, 131

European Commission 21; Website 92
European education policies 11
EU speech repository 14, 20
Evans, J. R. 71
evasion strategies 107, 111, 114
exit strategies 110, 114–117
experiential learning 11, 33
explicit learning environment 38–42, 44–48
exposure approach 41

face masks 57
face-to-face interpreting 70, 72, 78
factor analysis 30–32
Faculty Research Ethics Committee, University of Leeds 60
Fantinuoli, C. 2, 56, 61, 66
Felipe VI (king) 147
Fomina, M. 153
foreign language learning 26
Franceschetti, M. 90, 92
freelance professionals 9, 10
Fresno, N. 170

GALA conference (2024) 2
Gambier, Y. 106, 107, 117
Garcia-Beyaert, S. 73
Garwood, C. 93, 95
garwood strategy 115
General comment No. 24 (2019) 69, 70, 75
generalisation strategy 115
genre skills 113
Gigliobianco, S. 57
Gile, D. 141
globalisation 9
González-Davies, M. 153
Google Chrome 141
Google's SR 141
gordian knot strategy 114, 116, 117
Gottlieb, H. 106
Greek identity 90
Groupe ICOR 115

Hale, S. 72
Harvey, L. 22
hearings 71, 75
Heidegger, Martin 72, 73
Heideggerian phenomenology 73
hermeneutics 73
higher education institution (HEI) 22, 123, 131, 152, 153
human-computer interaction (HCI) *see* human-machine interaction (HMI)

human-machine interaction (HMI) 3, 108, 137, 138, 140, 149
Husserl, Edmund 72
Husserlian phenomenology 73

illegal immigration 78
ILSed accessibility conference 106
implicit learning environment 38–42, 44–48
inclusive subtitling 169
Industrial Revolution 1, 2
input skills 124, 126
Inquisit platform 42, 43
integration process 91, 93
intercultural education 90
"Intercultural Mediator Profile and Related Learning Outcomes" 93
intercultural mediators/mediation in schools 86–98;
interlingual live subtitles/subtitling (ILS) 3, 109, 124, 137, 138, 141, 142, 149, 157, 158
interlingual live subtitling for access (ILSA) 122, 123, 140
interlingual respeaking 123, 156; research-informed training model for 140–141
International Association of Conference Interpreters 60
International Federation for Information and Communication Processing 127
International Organisation for Migration 92
international protection 74
interpreting studies (IS) 2, 22, 39, 108
interpreting theory 14, 20
interpretivism 73
intralingual and interlingual respeaking didactics 137–149
intralingual and interlingual respeaking training proposals 141–142, 144–147; action research-based remodulation 142, *143*, 144–145, **145**; training materials 145–147, **146**
intralingual live subtitles/subtitling (ILS) 105, 107, 108, 156, 157; error distribution of 160, **160**, *161*; *vs.* interlingual live subtitling 159, *160*, 166
intralingual respeaking 156; of English and Chinese speeches *159*; error distribution in different phases 160
IRA 127

Kalina, S. 110, 111, 117
Kendall's tau-b partial test 47
Keynes, John Maynard 1
Kintsch, W. 110
Kohn, K. 110, 111, 117

L2 ideal self 28, 29
L2 learning experience 28, 29
L2 Motivational Self System (L2MSS) 28–30; adaptation 29–30; L2 ideal self 28; L2 learning experience 29; L2 ought-to self 29
L2 ought-to self 29
Lambert, J. 106
Lambourne, A. 123, 169, 170
language selection 95
Language Service Provider (LSP) 87, 155
La Vida al Maxim (TV programme) 174
learning environment types 38–48; data analysis 43–44; effects on interpreting skills 45; implicit *vs.* explicit learning environments 38–42, 46–47; participants 42; procedural learning abilities effects 45–47; procedure 42–43; research type and approaches 40
Leeds CTIS Symposium 154–157; presentations as samples for quality assessment 157–158
legal encounters with minors in Ireland during COVID-19 pandemic 69–81; briefings 76–78; conceptual framework 73; methodological approach 72–73; non-verbal communication 80–81; participants 73–75, **74**; rapport building 78–79; remote interpreting 70–72; semi-structured interviews 73; training 75–76
Le Messageur 106, 107, 110, 112, 113, 117, 118
Leontief, W. 1
Les Assises Regionales de l'Accessibilite ('The Regional Accessibility Conference') 106, 113
lexicon model 139
Li, X. 153
Li, Z. 62
Likert scale questions 12, 30
linguistic accuracy calculation 148
linguistic barriers, removal of 94
linguistic skills 87, 124, 170
LinkedIn 12
litteratim 106–108
Littlewood, W. 32

live performance 152
live skills 141
live subtitling (LS) 3, 103–106, 114, 116, 117, 121–131, 137, 169; formal and informal training 123–124; and live subtitler skills 124–126; market 122–124; Most Accurate and Rapid Speech-to-text subtitling rate *see* Most Accurate and Rapid Speech-to-text subtitling rate (MARS); services 122–123; speech recognition-based 138–139; teaching through mock conferences 154, 165–166; through respeaking 152–153
live television link 69, 70
live text access (LTA) 122, 123, 126, 131
local coherence strategies 110
López Rubio, M. 172
Luddites 1

macrostrategies 110
MARS *see* Most Accurate and Rapid Speech-to-text subtitling rate (MARS)
Martín Sansaloni, V. 172
Máster en Migraciones, Mediación, y Grupos Vulnerables 92
Master in Intercultural Mediation and Social Intervention 92
Máster Oficial en Traducción y Mediación Intercultural 92
media accessibility (MA) 5, 144
memorising strategies 41, 46, 111
memory skills 43–47
Microsoft Teams 76, 142
minors 4, 30, 69, 70, 72–81, 109, 126, 130
mixed learning environment 38
mock conferences 153–154, 165, 166
monitoring strategies 111
Moser-Mercer, B. 58, 63, 65
Most Accurate and Rapid Speech-to-text subtitling rate (MARS) 5, 122, 124, 126–131; application of correction algorithm 129–130, *130*; European Certification and Qualification Association-Intersteno certification 131; technical aspects 127–129, **128**
Motivational Self System Questionnaire 29
Mujica, J. 147
multiculturalism 90
multiple-choice questions 12
multitasking skills 112, 141

natural language understanding (NLU) systems 137
NER *see* number, edition error and recognition error (NER) model
NERLE 127
.NET 5 framework 127
neutralisation 107, 111, 114, 171
Nimdzi Interpreting Index 20
non-native language skills 47
non-verbal communication 71, 80–81, 90
non-verbal cues 57
NTR *see* number, translation error and recognition error (NTR) model
number, edition error and recognition error (NER) model 127, 156–157, **158**; analysis of respeaking performance 159
number, translation error and recognition error (NTR) model 148, 156–157, **158**, 159

Obama, B. 147
one-way ANCOVA 45, 47
online education 86
online remote interpreting platforms (ORI) 9, 14, 15, 17–22
open-ended questions 12
oralism 105

Paley, J. 73
paraphrasing 111, 145, 154
Pearson partial correlation 45, 47
pedagogical model 10, 87, 91, 93, 97, 98
peer-to-peer approach 90, 96, 97
phenomenology 72, 73
Pöchhacker, F. 141, 148
post-CI-test interviews 42, 44
post-editing machine translation 2
Powell, M. B. 76
practisearchers 10
pre-editing 125
pre-prepared speeches 106, 147, 153
pre-recorded subtitling 124, 142, 144
procedural learning abilities (PLA) effects on skills interpretation 39, 40, 42–48; *see also* learning environment types
procedural memory 47
processing strategies 111–114
production strategies 5, 107, 111–114, 117

professional freelance conference interpreters 11, 21
professionalisation 86, 153
propositional strategies 110
Provincial Centres for Adult Education (CPIA) 88
psycho-cognitive skills 105, 112
psychological drive 56

Quade test 47
qualitative approach 40, 72
quality assurance 61
Qualtrics 12
QWERTY keyboards 123, 170

Ramos Pinto, S. 173
Reason, P. 140
Remael, A. 138, 141
remote interpreting 70–72, 78, 80; definition 56, 57
remote simultaneous interpreting (RSI) 4, 55–66, 155; development, challenges, and advantages 56–58; empowerment 64; familiarising with 63; implications for post-pandemic practice 61–62; methodology 59–60; participants and their perspectives on 60–61; for research purposes 58–59; stress management and feedback 63–64; training ideas 64–66
research-informed training model 140–141
respeakers and respeaking 103–118; diamesic translation analysis 107–110; exit strategies 114–117; ILSed accessibility conference 106; processing and production strategies 111–114; simultaneous interpreting and 104–105; skills 105–106; subtitling for the deaf and hard of hearing 104–105; transcription and alignment method 106–107; understanding strategies 110–111, 117
respeaking accuracy rate 158
Robinson, D. 32
Roma Health Mediators 96
Romero-Fresco, P. 105, 141, 148, 152, 170, 176
Russello, C. 141

Saina, F. 63
Sandrelli, A. 154

Sani, S. 90
schematic strategies 110
Schwab, K. 1
Seeber, K. G. 104
self-evaluation 33
self-models 33
sensatim 106–108, 110, 116–118
Separated Children Seeking International Protection (SCSIP) 74
SFT 11, 12, 21
Shaffer, S. A. 71
signatim 106, 107, 110
sign language (SL) 15, 16, 105
Silvanto, J. 27
simultaneous interpreter training: situated learning in 153
simultaneous interpreting (SI) 3, 63, 66, 103–105, 108, 110, 117, 118, 124, 138, 144, 145; and respeaking 154
simultaneous interpreting delivery platforms (SIDPs) 15, 20, 57, 58, 61, 62, 65
situated learning 153, 164
SMART project 123
social distancing 57
social inclusion 87, 90, 91, 96, 97
socially integrated migrants 96
soft skills 123, 124
Song, S. 165
sound quality 61, 64
source text (ST) 104, 105, 108–117, 137, 145, 147
Spanish-to-Italian respeaking training 147
Speech Capturing and Real-Time Speech Capturing world competitions 127
speech comprehension 47
Speechlogger 141, 142
Speechnotes 141
speech recognition-based live subtitling 138–139
speech repository 14, 20, 147
Spiro, R. J. 39
stamina 19, 20, 124
statistical analysis 30, 40, 43, 44
Statistical Package for the Social Sciences (SPSS) software version 29 30
statistical testing 40, 47
stenography 152
stenotype 123, 139
strategic discourse processing 110
strategic model of discourse comprehension 110

StreamText 156
stress management 15, 19, 63–64, 77
student-centred environment *see* implicit learning environment
subtitles/subtitling for the d/Deaf and the hard-of-hearing (SDH) 103–105, 155, 169
Susskind, D. 2; *World Without Work, A* 2
sustainable development 46

tactics 39, 44–46, 104, 107, 108, 110, 111, 117
TalkTyper 141, 142
target text (TT) 104–105, 108–111, 113–118
teacher-practitioners 11
technique-specific skills 123–124
technological competence 62
technological turn 56, 66
TED Talks 147
telephone interpreting 70–72, 80, 81
Tikhonova, E. V. 47
Train Intercultural Mediators for a Multicultural Europe (TIME) Project 92, 93
transcription and alignment method 106–107
translation and interpreting (T&I): programmes 94, 95, 97; training 10
transversal skills 123, 124
traumatic content interpretation 77
trial-and-error learning 65
Trump, D. 147
Tusla 74, 82n9

UN Committee on the Rights of the Child 69, 75
Universidad de Almeria 92
Universita di Genova, Italy 142
University of Birmingham (UoB) 28, 29
University of Leeds 3, 152
University of Salamanca 92
University Paris Diderot 93
US-Mexico border 78
US National Academy of Sciences 1

vague rules 41–42
Valencian language 171–176; diglossia 173–176, *174*; variation 173
Valencian live subtitling 160–178; strategies for overcoming linguistic

varieties 176–178; training courses 170–171; Valencian language 171–176
van Dijk, T. A. 110
Velotype 123, 152
verbatim 106–108, 110, 115, 116, 118, 161
videoconference interpreting 70–72, 80, 81
video court appearances 69
video-mediated interpreting 56
video-sharing platforms 170
videotelephony 170
vision/mental imagery in interpreter training 26–34; auditory style 33; cross-cultural implications 33–34; definition 27; effort allocation 33; factor analysis 30–32, **31**; individualised learning 32–33; L2 Motivational Self System 28–30; motivation enhancement 32; overview 27–28; vivid imagery as successful interpreters 33
visual cues 71, 80
visual input 57, 60, 64, 65
voice management 16, 17, 20
VooV Meeting 42

Wang, H. 62
weather prediction task (WPT) 42, 43
WebAssembly-based Blazor client framework 127
Web Captioner 141
WIRA 127
word error rate (WER) 127, 129, 156
working memory (WM) 104, 108, 118
World Economic Forum 1–2
World Without Work, A (Susskind) 2

Yerevan Communique 11

zero tolerance policy 78
Zhao, Y. 40, 41
Ziegler, K. 57
Zoom 15, 20, 42, 58, 59

Printed in the United States
by Baker & Taylor Publisher Services